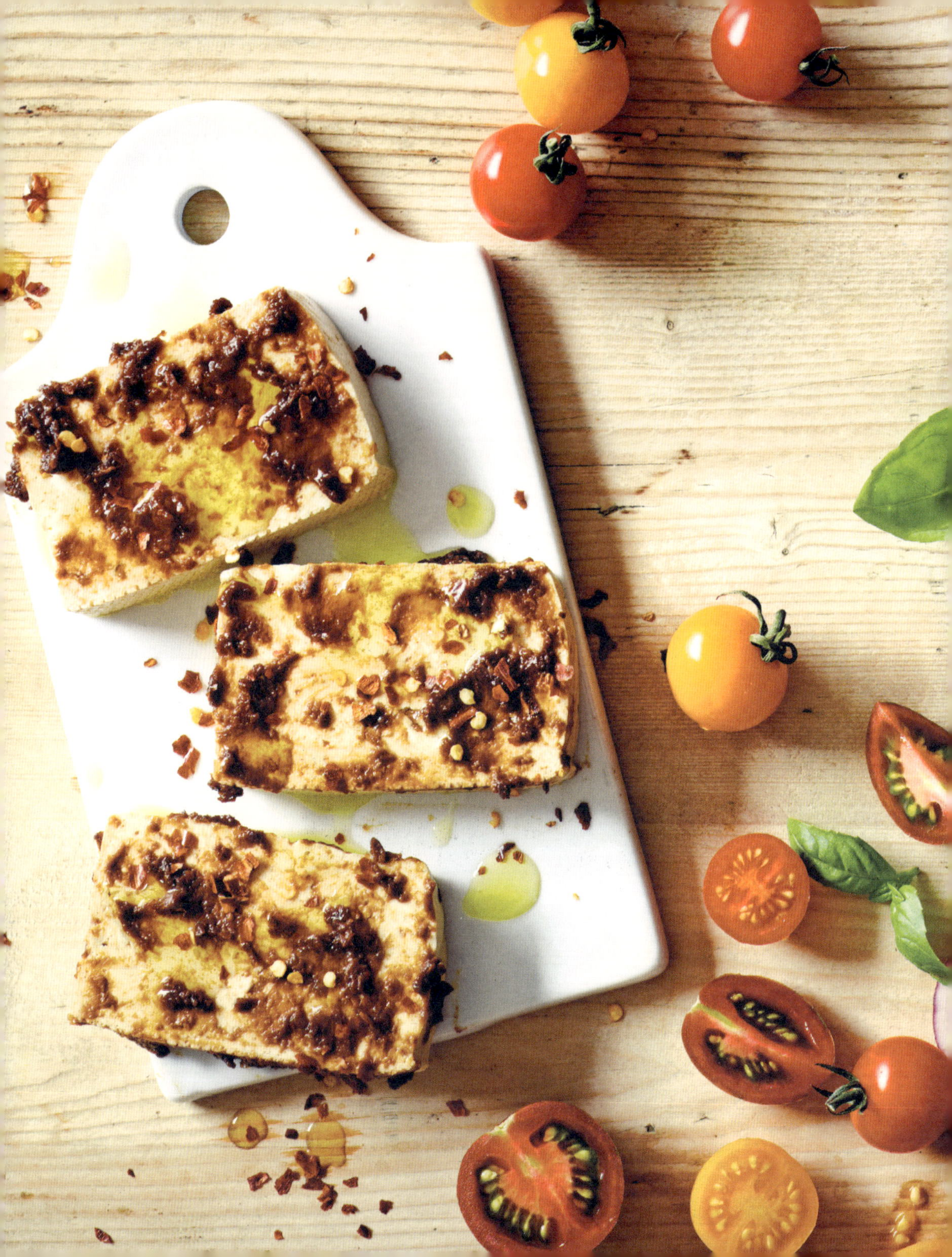

Totally TOFU

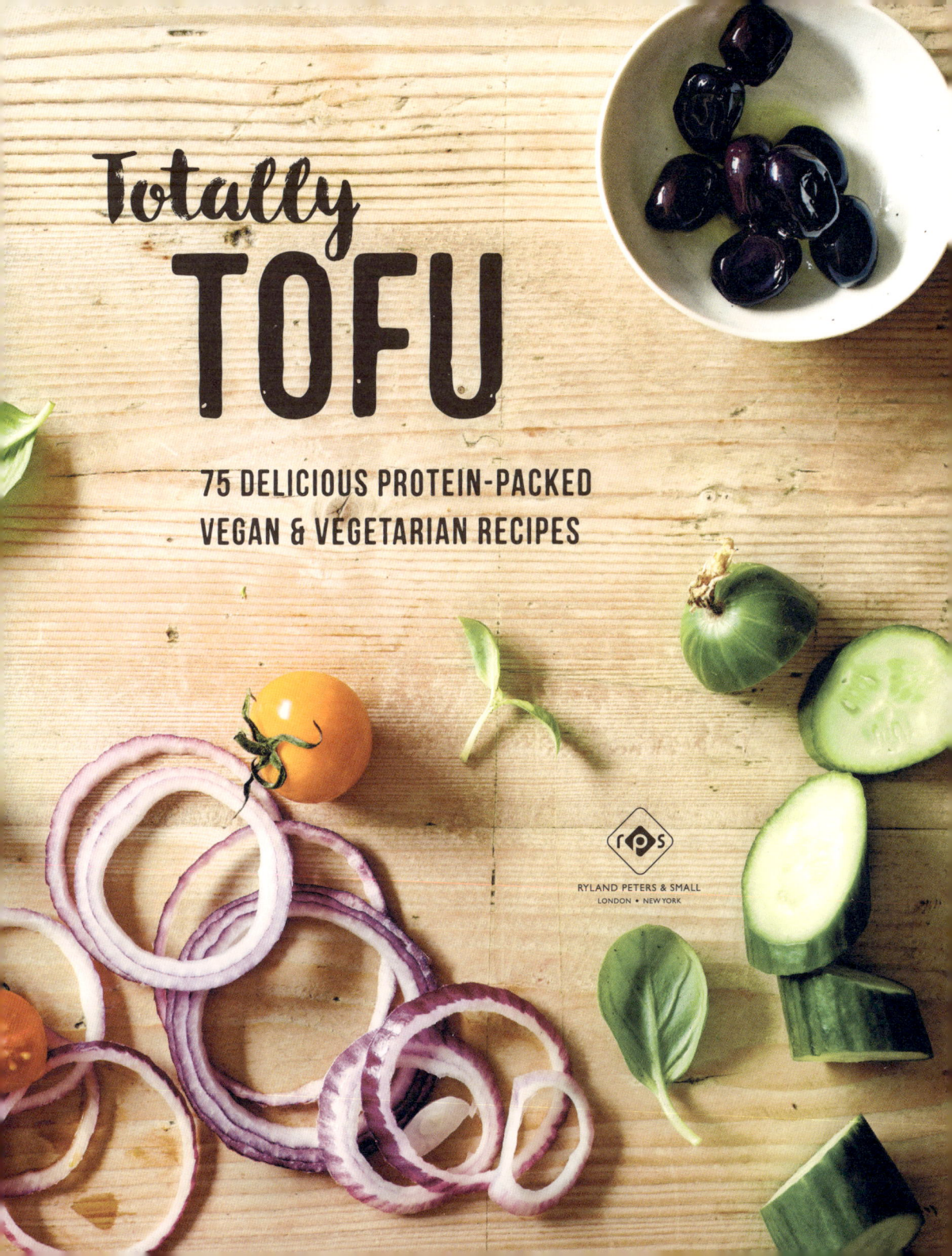

75 DELICIOUS PROTEIN-PACKED VEGAN & VEGETARIAN RECIPES

RYLAND PETERS & SMALL
LONDON • NEW YORK

Senior Designer Megan Smith
Editor Sarah Vaughan
Production Gordana Simakovic
Art Director Leslie Harrington
Editorial Director Julia Charles
Publisher Cindy Richards
Indexer Vanessa Bird

First published in 2021
by Ryland Peters & Small,
20-21 Jockey's Fields,
London WC1R 4BW
and
341 E 116th St,
New York NY 10029

www.rylandpeters.com

10 9 8 7 6 5 4 3 2 1

Text © Valerie Aikman-Smith, Caroline Artiss, Ghillie Basan, Jordan Bourke, Julia Charles, Chloe Coker, Amy Ruth Finegold, Mat Follas, Ben Fordham, Felipe Fuentes Cruz, Nicola Graimes, Dunja Gulin, Carole Hilker, Atsuko Ikeda, Jenny Linford, Loretta Liu, Jane Montgomery, Louise Pickford, Milli Taylor, Laura Washburn Hutton, Sarah Wilkinson and Ryland Peters & Small 2021. Design and photographs © Ryland Peters & Small 2021. This recipe collection compiled by Julia Charles.

ISBN: 978-1-78879-347-6

The authors' moral rights have been asserted. All rights reserved. No part of this publication may be reproduced, stored in a retrieval system or transmitted in any form or by any means, electronic, mechanical, photocopying or otherwise, without the prior permission of the publisher.

A CIP record for this book is available from the British Library.

US Library of Congress cataloging-in-publication data has been applied for.

Printed and bound in China.

Notes
• Both British (Metric) and American (Imperial plus US cup) measurements are included in these recipes for your convenience – however it is important to work with one set of measurements and not alternate between the two within a recipe.
• All spoon measurements are level unless specified.
• All eggs are medium (UK) or large (US), unless specified as large, in which case US extra-large should be used. Uncooked or partially cooked eggs should not be served to the elderly or frail, young children, pregnant women or those with compromised immune systems.
• Ovens should be preheated to the specified temperatures. We recommend using an oven thermometer. If using a fan-assisted oven, adjust temperatures according to the manufacturer's instructions.
• When a recipe calls for the grated zest of citrus fruit, buy unwaxed fruit and wash well before using. If you can only find treated fruit, scrub well in warm soapy water before using.
• Always check the product packaging to ensure the particular brand of ingredient you are buying is vegan.

CONTENTS

Introduction 6

Small Bites & Snacks 12

Salads 40

Soups, Noodle Bowls & Stews 64

Main Plates 84

Sweet Things & Drinks 118

Index 142

Credits 144

INTRODUCTION

Tofu is a wonderfully versatile superfood, packed with protein, iron and calcium, as well as plenty of other essential vitamins and minerals. Not only is it nutrient-dense, it also comes in many different textures and flavours, making it an easy-to-use, multi-purpose ingredient that can slot right in to your current cooking habits. From the extra-soft to the extra-firm, the marinated and the smoked, tofu is a trendy, one-stop ingredient ideal for most vegan and vegetarian cooking needs. So, whether you're in the mood for a speedy stir-fry or want to whip up a creamy cheesecake, there's a tofu out there for you!

Made from condensed soy milk using a process similar to cheesemaking, tofu has been enjoyed in Asian cuisine for centuries as a meat substitute. It is at the heart of many well-known Chinese and Japanese recipes – absorbing all the delicious flavours, whilst also adding extra nourishment, substance and texture. And, though you will come across many Asian-inspired dishes in this book, there are also plenty of fun, tasty recipes that take a modern tofu spin on classics from all around the world. Rustle up a Greek Salad with Tofu Feta, Tex-Mex Tofu 'Cheese' Nachos and Tofu Tacos, and even a Delicious Tofu Curry. The foodie possibilities for tofu are endless… and may even convince any committed tofu-haters out there to give it another go!

Totally Tofu brings you over 60 inventive recipes for snacks and light bites, salads, main meals and even sweet treats and drinks, that will make this wonder ingredient the star of your plant-based kitchen! You may want to begin your day with a nourishing plate of Tofu Scramble, perfect for former egg-lovers and delicious when pimped with whatever herbs and spices take your fancy. Or for those who are always on the go, grab some Strawberry Tofu 'Yogurt' or a Blackberry Crumble Smoothie. When hunger strikes and you want a satisfying lunch, choose Crunchy Tofu Faux-lafel or Bean & Tofu Dip, or for a lighter option try an Asian Tofu & Raw Kale Salad or a Rice Noodle & Smoked Tofu Salad. For something more substantial, or to feed a crowd, make Versatile Tofu Pizzas, Asparagus, Tofu & Paprika Tart or a warming pot of Tofu & Mushroom Goulash. And let's not ignore that sweet tooth – discover delightful tofu-based desserts, from Baked Lemon-scented Pancakes to a decadent Dark Chocolate & Tofu Tart.

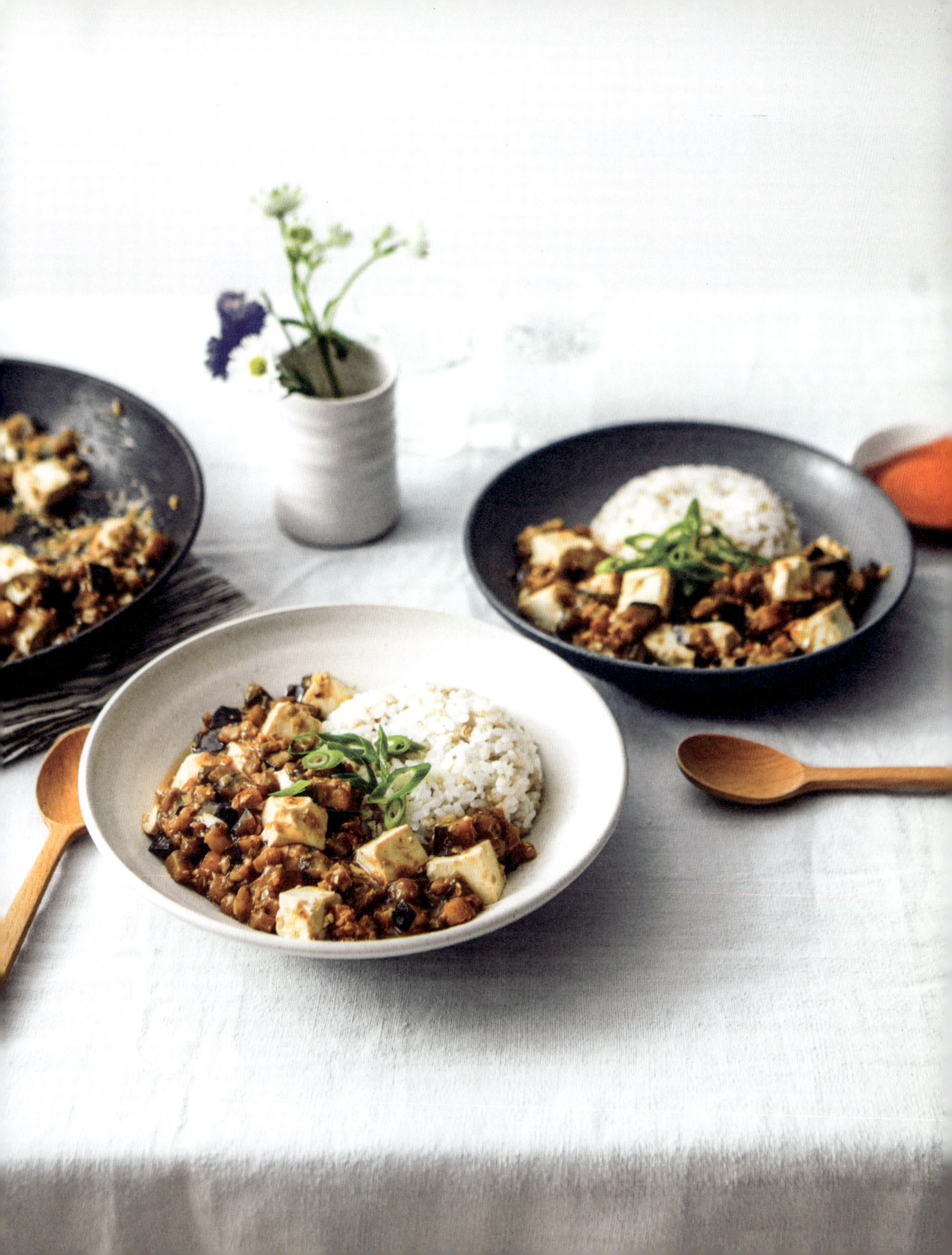

MARINATING & FRYING TOFU

To make your stews, ragouts, sauces, curries and other lovely dishes extra yummy, it is very important to marinate and fry the tofu properly in advance. This way, each piece soaks up the flavours from the oils and spices, and forms a nice crunchy crust. As such, these bite-sized pieces of tofu also make a delicious plant-based snack just as they are, and can be made a few days ahead and kept in the fridge. You can adjust spices, herbs and oils to your liking.

290 g/10 oz. tofu cut into 2 x 2-cm/¾ x ¾-in. cubes

FOR THE MARINADE
4 teaspoons tamari
1 teaspoon oil of your choice (aromatic oils like olive or dark sesame work best)
2 teaspoons water
2 teaspoons Dijon mustard (optional)
2 teaspoons dried herbs or ground spices of your choice
2 garlic cloves, crushed
handful of plain/all-purpose flour or millet flour, for frying
200 g/1 cup sunflower oil, for deep-frying

Place the tofu cubes in a deep plate. Put all ingredients for the marinade in a small jar, close and shake. Pour this mixture over the cubes and mix well so that all the pieces are covered in the marinade. If the marinade turns out overly thick, add 1–2 teaspoons of extra water, just to make it runny enough to cover all the cubes. Cover with clingfilm/plastic wrap and let it sit at room temperature for at least 30 minutes. You can also do this a day in advance and let it sit in the fridge.

Put a little flour in a bowl and roll each cube separately in it. Be sure to coat the sides of each the cube with flour, but be careful not to wipe the marinade off. It's also important that the layer of flour is thin, so remove any excess by shaking each cube between the palms of your hands.

Layer a tray or a big plate with paper towels, which you'll use to drain the tofu after frying it. You may want to use a small pot and deep-fry the prepared cubes in a few batches, but if you want you can fry them all at once in a big pan – just make sure you don't overcrowd it! The oil is ready for frying when it starts bubbling once you drop a piece of tofu in it.

Fry the cubes for 1–2 minutes, until golden brown, then drain on the paper towels before using in other recipes. However, you could snack on these cubes as they are, add them to a salad instead of croutons or make quick skewers, adding pieces of raw or cooked vegetables alongside.

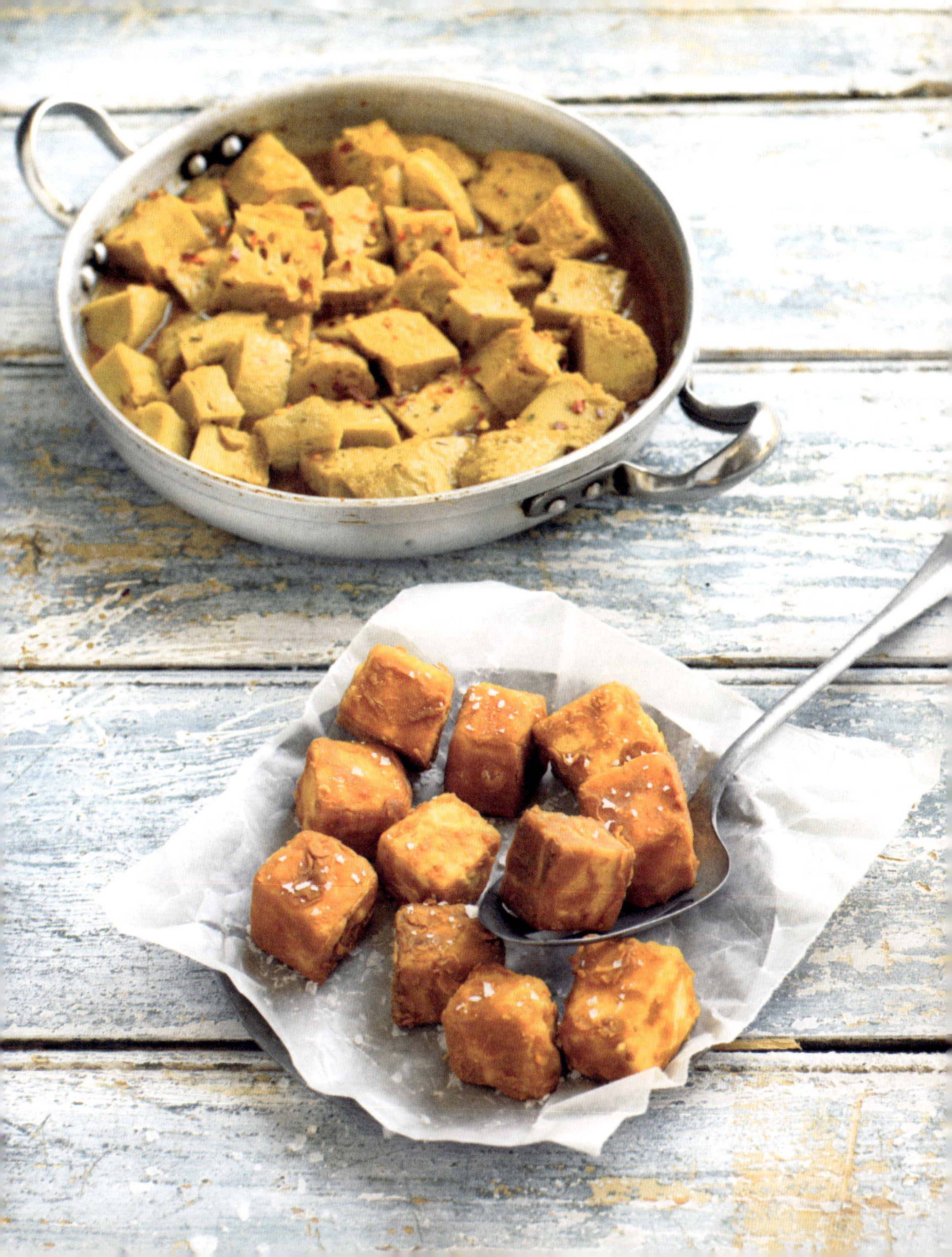

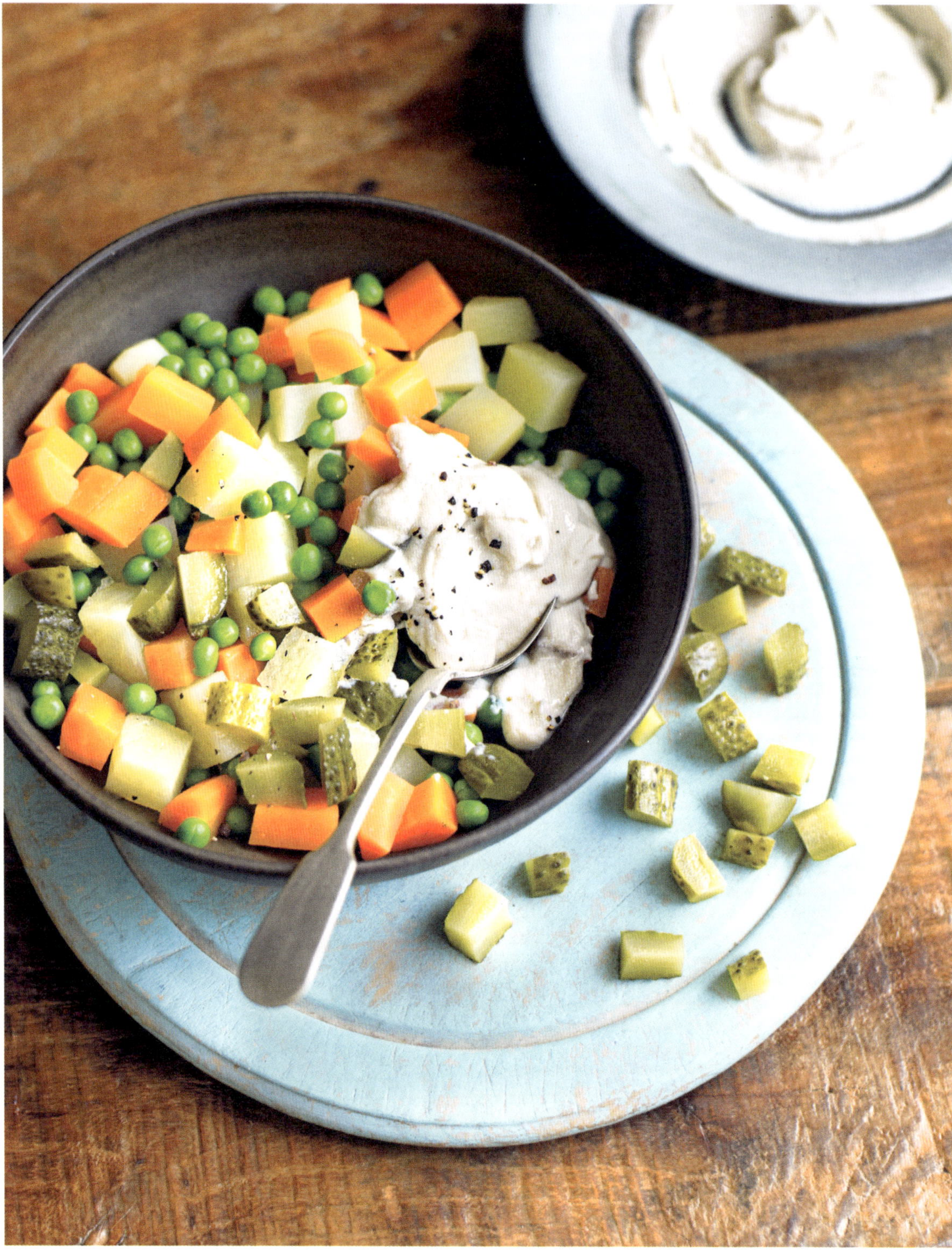

TOFU MAYONNAISE

A vegan version of popular mayonnaise that is much lighter and much less oily than regular mayo or even store-bought vegan mayo. This pairs up very well with the faux-lafel (see pages 16–19).

300 g/2 cups tofu
60 ml/¼ cup olive or sunflower oil
3 tablespoons freshly squeezed lemon juice or apple cider vinegar, to taste
1 soft date
½ teaspoon salt

MAKES ABOUT 240 ML/1 CUP

Blend all the ingredients together with 6 tablespoons water until completely smooth. Taste and adjust the seasonings. If you prefer it tangier, you can add a little more lemon juice or vinegar.

Also, pay attention to what you will serve it with; if used as a salad dressing, it needs to be more sour, and if used with salty foods like falafel, make it less salty.

RICH MISO-TOFU DRESSING

This dressing stays fresh in the fridge for days and adds some extra protein from tofu into your salad or snack. Use any leftovers as a dip for raw vegetables and crackers, or as a bread spread.

200 g/1 cup tofu
2 teaspoons barley or rice miso
4 teaspoons freshly squeezed lemon juice
2 teaspoons Dijon mustard
3 teaspoons dark sesame oil
½ teaspoon salt
2 tablespoons finely chopped onion
60 ml/¼ cup water

MAKES 360 G/1½ CUPS

Blend all the ingredients well until the mixture reaches a velvety consistency.

Serve immediately or let sit in the fridge overnight before using. Add more water if you prefer a less dense dressing.

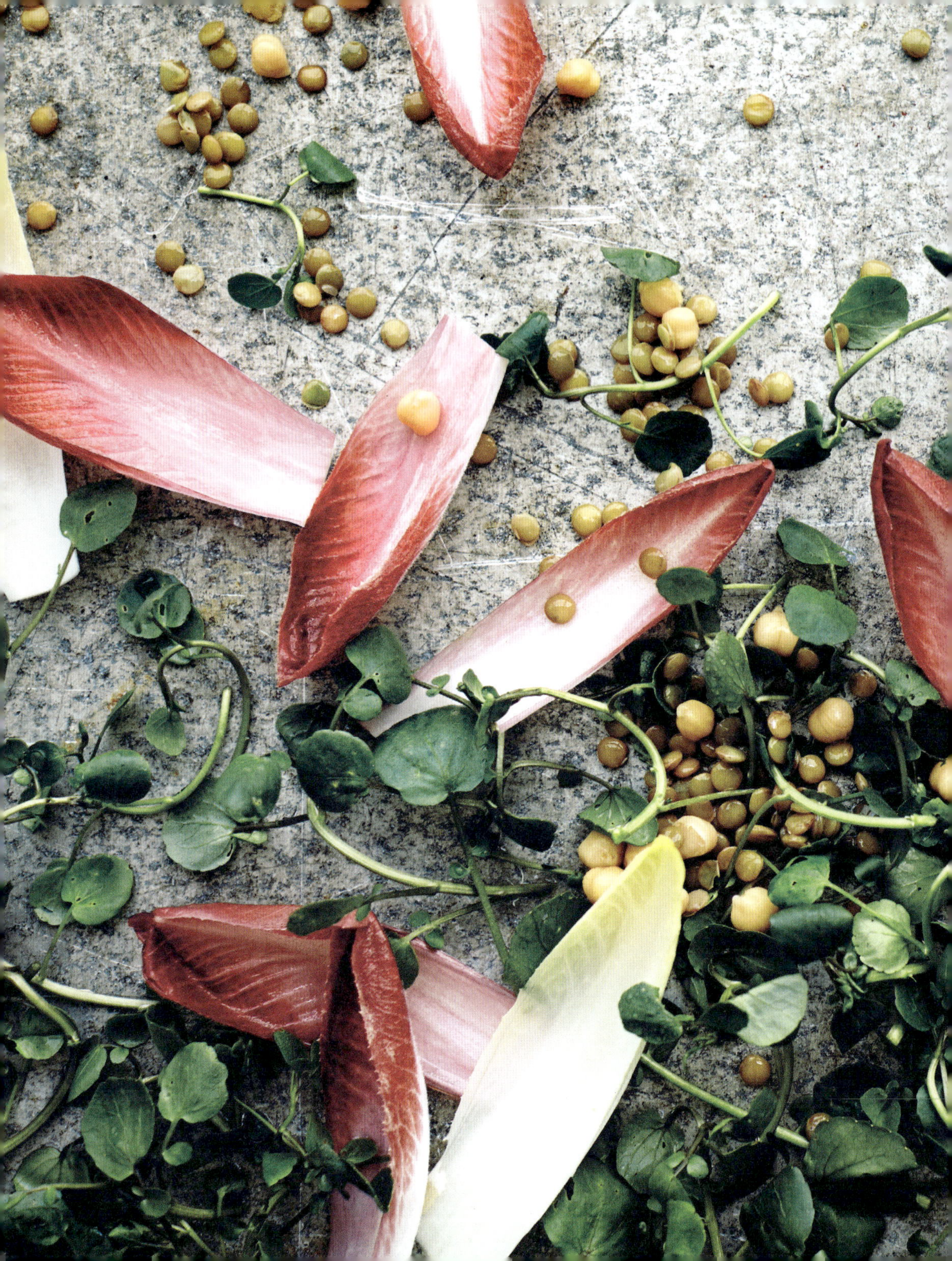

SMALL BITES & Snacks

JAPANESE TOFU DIP WITH VEGETABLES

This is a Japanese salad dressing or dip recipe, and one of the most traditional 'aemono'. This literally means 'white mixture' because of the creamy texture of the mashed tofu. Even now, it is still a staple of Japanese home cooking.

300 g/10½ oz. soft tofu
130 g/4¾ oz. mixture of spinach and watercress
2 teaspoons light soy sauce
2 teaspoons agave syrup
1 tablespoons Japanese white sesame paste (or light tahini)
pinch of salt
dried goji berries, soaked and drained, to garnish

MAKES 4 SERVINGS

Wrap the tofu in plenty of paper towels and compress under a heavy kitchen utensil for 30 minutes to remove excess water.

Bring some water to the boil in another saucepan. Add the spinach and watercress and boil for 1 minute, then drain. Immediately rinse under cold water, then drain. Sprinkle with 1 teaspoon of the light soy sauce, then squeeze out water from the leaves. Use your hands to form the leaves into a cylinder shape and then chop into 3-cm/1¼-inch lengths. Set aside.

Combine the tofu, agave, sesame paste, remaining 1 teaspoon light soy sauce and salt in a food processor. Blend until smooth.

Mix the watercress and spinach with the tofu paste to combine well. Garnish with the goji berries and serve cold.

EASY BEAN & TOFU DIP

When you want to serve up a hummus-alternative at a gathering with friends, this quick and easy dip won't disappoint. Double or triple the quantities if you're feeding a crowd.

410-g/14-oz. can mixed beans, drained
4–7 tablespoons soft tofu
1 tablespoon balsamic vinegar
salt and freshly ground black pepper, to season

MAKES ABOUT 500 ML/2 CUPS

Put the beans and 4 tablespoons tofu in the bowl of a food processor and process until smooth. Add more tofu as desired for a thinner texture. Transfer to a bowl, stir in the vinegar and season to taste. Serve with crudités.

The dip will keep for 2–3 days if stored in an airtight container in the fridge.

WHIPPED TOFU, AVOCADO & HERB DIP

This fresh and bright vegan dip is delicious served with any vegetable crudités, breadsticks or crackers for dipping, or use it as a tasty spread on toast or in sandwiches.

455 g/1 lb. soft tofu
1 ripe avocado, stoned/pitted
20 g/1 cup fresh basil leaves
10 g/½ cup fresh coriander/cilantro leaves
5 g/¼ cup fresh flat-leaf parsley
1 small garlic clove, peeled
1 teaspoon finely grated lime or lemon zest
freshly squeezed juice of 1 lime or 1 small lemon
salt and freshly ground black pepper, to season

MAKES 8 SERVINGS

Add all the ingredients to a food processor. Blend until smooth, scraping down the sides of the blender cup as necessary.

Season to taste with salt and pepper, transfer to a serving bowl and garnish with any leftover herbs. Serve with breadsticks or crackers for dipping. Best served as soon as possible after it is made, but cover and chill in the fridge in the meantime.

CRUNCHY TOFU FAUX-LAFEL

These falafels are crunchy on the outside and creamy on the inside, but make sure to serve them freshly fried! Kalamata olives can be omitted entirely or substituted with other types of olives, or even with chopped corn kernels, especially in summer.

280 g/1½ cups firm tofu
90 g/½ cup Kalamata olives
2 tablespoons freshly chopped coriander/cilantro leaves or snipped chives
2 tablespoons gram flour
½ teaspoon ground turmeric
salt and freshly ground black pepper, to season
250 ml/1 cup oil, for frying

TO SERVE
roasted vegetables of your choice
Tofu Mayonnaise (see page 11) or good-quality ketchup

MAKES 16–18 FALAFELS

In a food processor fitted with an 'S' blade, process the tofu until creamy. Transfer it into a mixing bowl.

Drain, pat dry and finely chop the Kalamata olives and add them to the tofu with coriander/cilantro or chives, gram flour, turmeric, salt and pepper. Combine well with a silicone spatula.

Roll into 16–18 even-sized balls, wetting your hands once in a while to prevent the mixture sticking to your hands. Deep-fry the falafels in hot oil for 2–3 minutes or until golden brown.

Serve hot or warm with plenty of veggies, cooked and raw and with some tofu mayonnaise or good-quality ketchup.

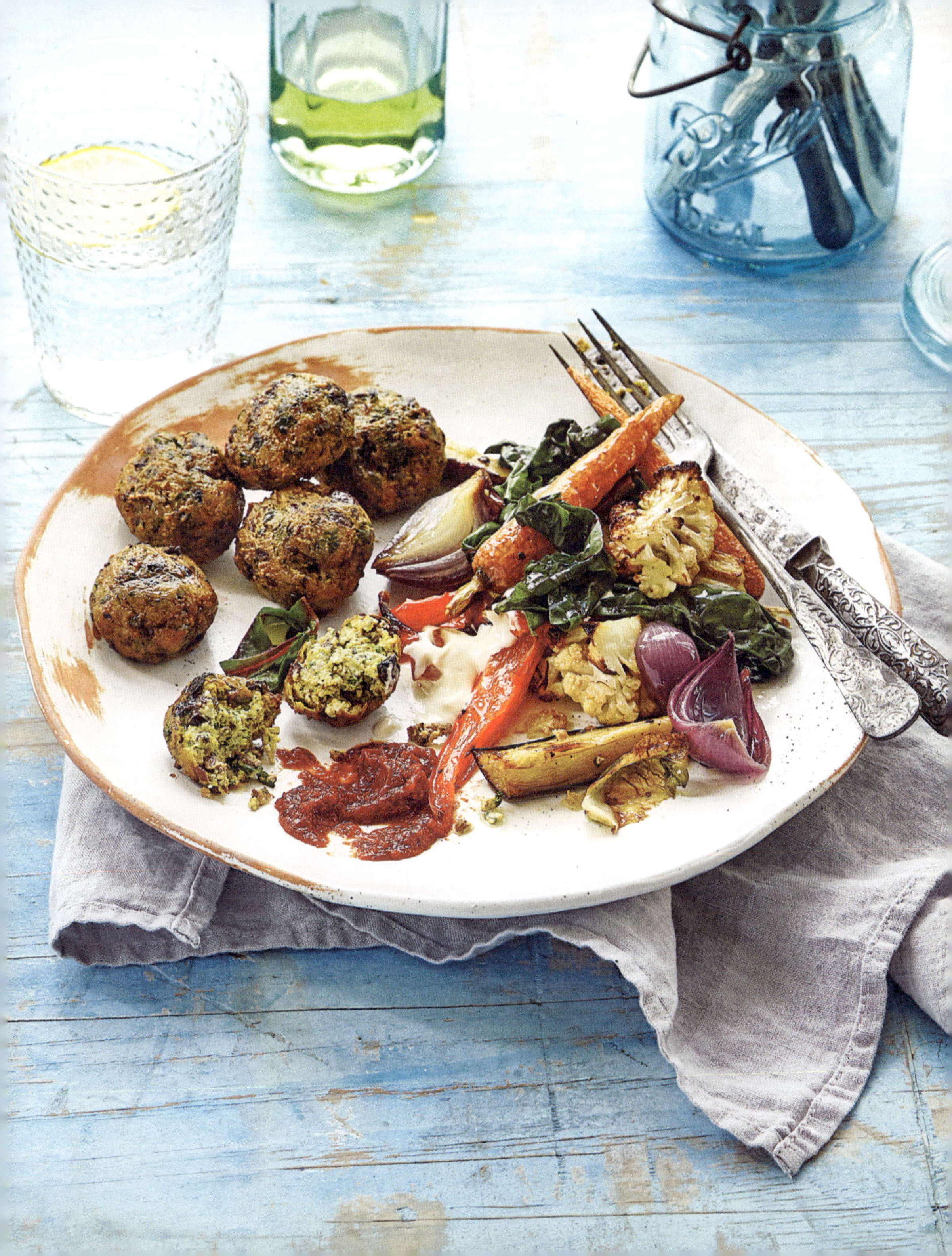
IDEAL

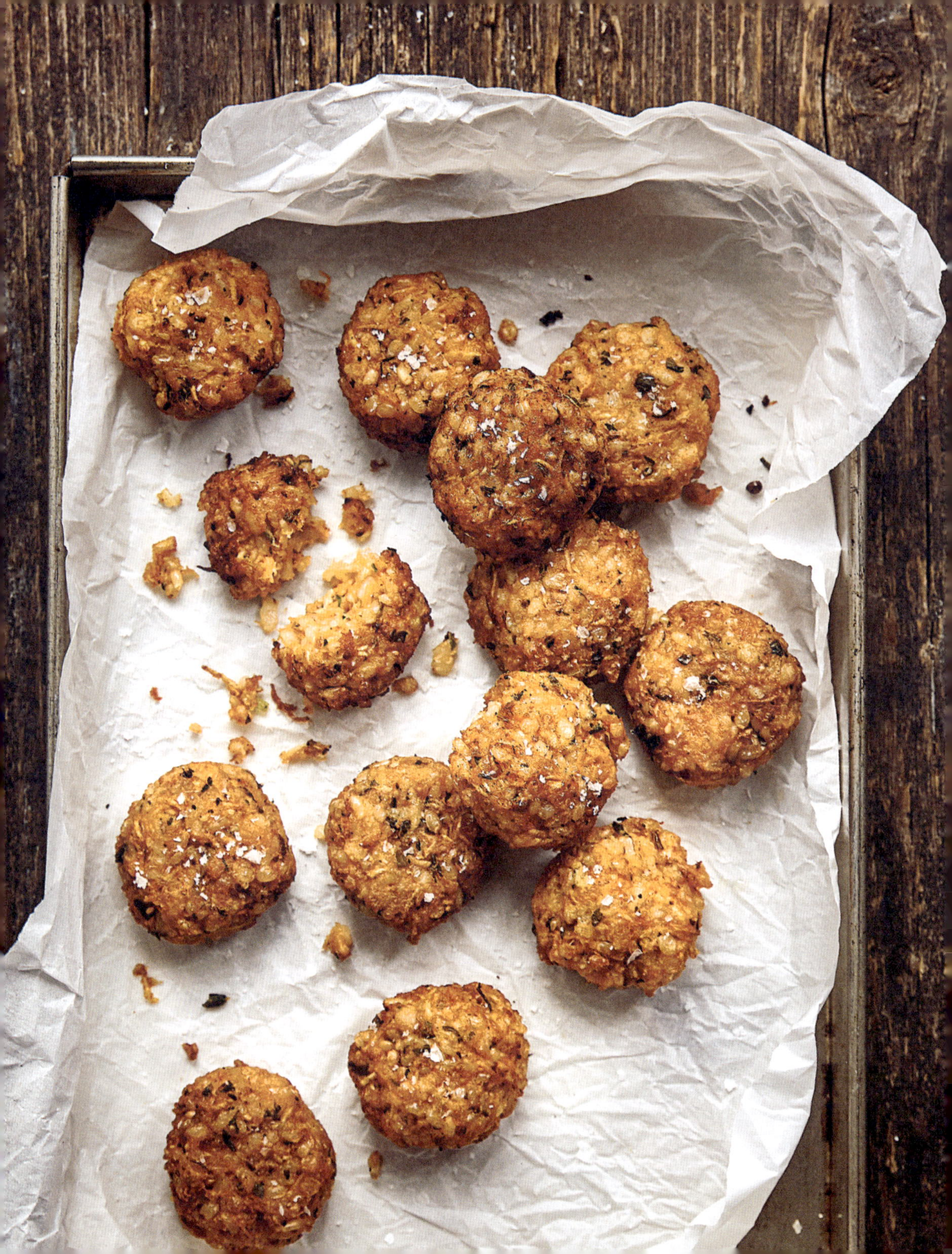

BROWN RICE & SMOKED TOFU FAUX-LAFEL

This is a very simple yet delicious recipe made with wholegrains, veggies and smoked tofu. Serve with any dip you fancy and a green salad.

420 g/3 cups cooked short-grain brown rice
70 g/½ cup very finely grated carrot
40 g/½ cup very finely grated celeriac
80 g/½ cup very finely grated onion
4 garlic cloves, crushed
40 g/¼ cup finely grated smoked tofu
2 tablespoons freshly chopped parsley or spring onion/scallion greens
dried oregano, chilli/chili powder and sweet paprika, to taste
salt and freshly ground black pepper, to season
olive oil, for greasing and brushing

TO SERVE
mixed greens
Tofu Mayonnaise (see page 11), or any dip of your choice

baking sheet, lined with baking paper

MAKES ABOUT 24 FALAFELS

For this dish the rice has to be carefully cooked: it should be neither soggy nor hard. For best results use freshly cooked rice, but if using leftover rice from the fridge, bring to room temperature first.

Put the cooked rice, grated veggies, garlic, tofu, parsley and some salt, pepper, oregano, chilli/chili powder and paprika in a big bowl. Use your hands to knead the mixture until the ingredients are well combined. Taste and add more salt, pepper, oregano, chilli/chili powder or paprika, if needed.

Wet your hands and try to make a small burger shape from the mixture – if it is a little sticky and soft, but the burger keeps its shape, it should be ready. Leave the mixture to sit in the fridge for 1 hour, or longer.

Preheat the oven to 180°C/350°F/Gas 4.

Wet your hands and make about 24 small burger shapes for the falafel balls. Grease the baking paper with oil and oil each ball with a silicone brush when you place them on the baking sheet.

Bake in the preheated oven for 12–16 minutes or until golden and compact, with a thin, crunchy crust and a juicy inside. Depending on the oven, you might want to turn them halfway through baking.

FRIED TOFU SANDWICHES

A good-quality vegan sandwich can be eaten for breakfast, lunch or dinner, and if the ingredients are well chosen, you'll be getting all the necessary nutrients. The three main components of a satisfying sandwich are: tasty bread, seasoned protein and freshly pickled vegetables – the combinations are endless!

2 fresh baguettes or seeded bread rolls of your choice

FOR THE FILLING
240 g/8¼ oz. tofu, marinated and fried (see page 8)
4 tablespoons spread of your choice (Tofu Mayonnaise, see page 11; Bean & Tofu Dip, see page 15; Whipped Tofu, Avocado & Herb Dip, see page 15)
sliced pickles or kimchi, to taste
2 handfuls of lettuce or other salad greens
4 tablespoons seed sprouts

SERVES 2

To prepare the tofu, cut four 10 x 6-cm/4 x 2½-inch slices, 6 mm/¼ inch thick. Marinate and fry these slices following the instructions in the recipe on page 8. You don't have to deep-fry the slices; just cover the bottom of the pan with oil and fry them on both sides until browned.

Take your baguettes or bread rolls and cut them crossways in the middle, then lengthways to get 2 sandwiches. First add the spread on the bottom slices, then add 2 slices of fried tofu, sprinkle with pickles, salad and seed sprouts and top with the remaining slices of bread.

Eat immediately or wrap in clingfilm/plastic wrap and eat when you're hungry!

SMALL BITES & SNACKS

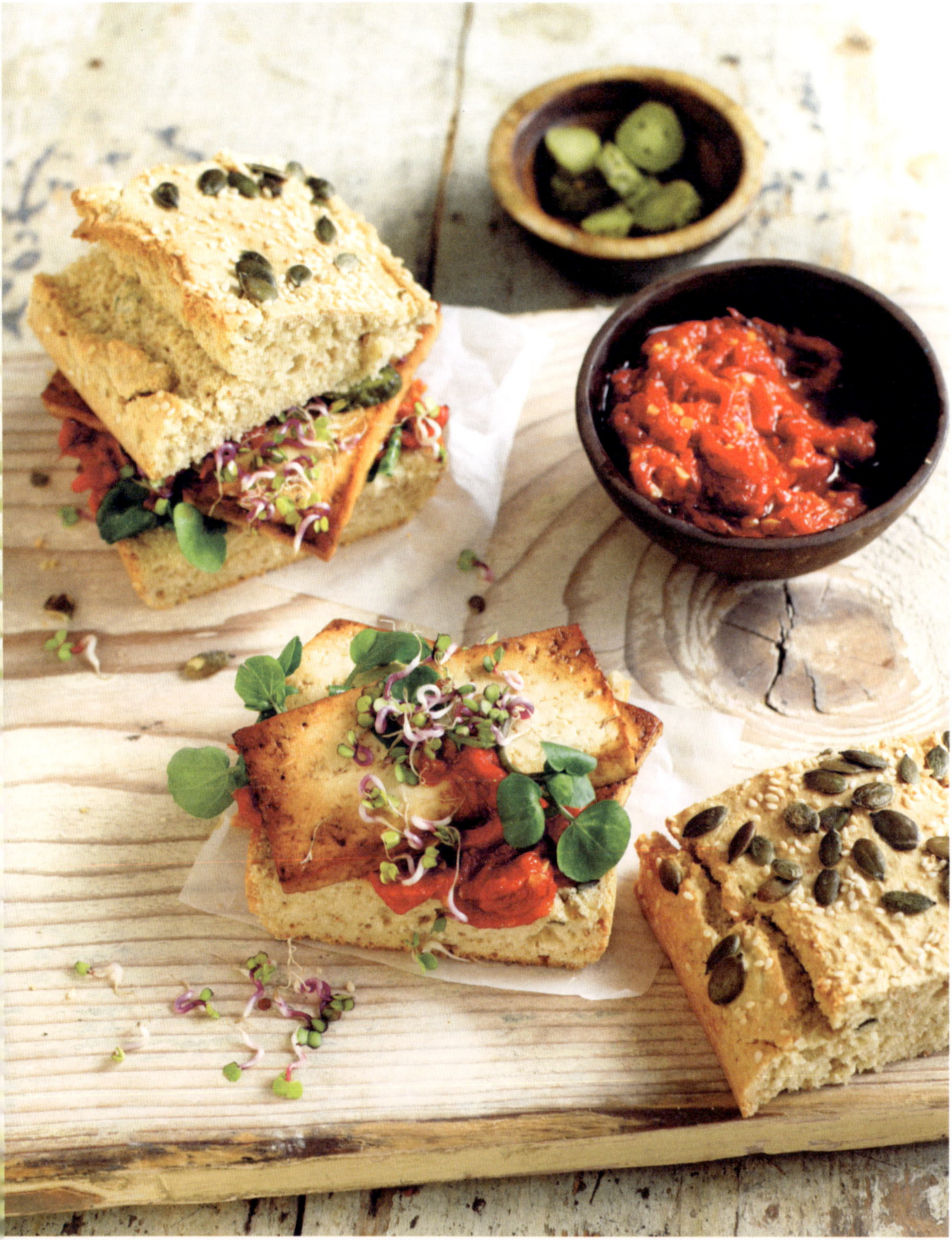

TOFU TACOS WITH FRESH TOMATO SALSA

Tofu is not something that is eaten much in Mexico. However, it's surge in popularity worldwide means that most well-known dishes can and have be given a vegan tofu spin. It is very healthy and its unique texture adds another dimension to classic recipes. It also combines very well with a bit of heat! Pico de Gallo is the perfect accompaniment to these tacos, but you could serve them with sour cream too, if you like.

400 g/14 oz. tofu
½ red onion
1 red (bell) pepper
1 yellow (bell) pepper
2 garlic cloves
1 fresh Jalapeño (or a couple of Thai green chillies for more heat)
20 g/1½ tablespoons butter
½ teaspoon dried oregano
¼ teaspoon sea salt
¼ teaspoon ground white pepper
8 x 15-cm/6-in. corn or flour tortillas

FOR THE FRESH TOMATO SALSA
4 tomatoes
¼ onion
1 medium bunch of coriander/cilantro
¼ teaspoon sea salt

SERVES 4

First, prepare the fresh tomato salsa. Finely chop the tomatoes, onion and coriander/cilantro, and put in a small bowl. Add the salt and mix well. Set aside.

Next, cut the tofu into strips about 5 cm/2 inches long. Cut the onion and (bell) peppers into strips and thinly slice the garlic and Jalapeño.

Melt the butter in a frying pan over high heat, then fry the tofu for about 5 minutes. Add the onion, (bell) peppers, garlic, oregano, salt and pepper and fry for another 5 minutes.

The tofu should be brown and a little crispy at the edges and the (bell) peppers should still have some crunch. Then, stir in the chopped Jalapeño.

Place a dry frying pan over high heat. Warm each tortilla for about 20–30 seconds on each side.

To serve, spoon the ingredients over the tortillas and serve with the fresh tomato salsa.

TOFU 'CHEESE' NACHOS

A typical Tex-Mex snack: fried tortilla chips served with nacho 'cheese' – in this case with a tasty vegan twist!

1 carrot or 1 slice of pumpkin (approx. 100 g/3½ oz. peeled, deseeded and cut into cubes)
60 g/½ cup chopped onion
220 g/1 cup soft tofu
2 tablespoons white tahini
1 tablespoon umeboshi vinegar or apple cider vinegar
1 tablespoon nutritional yeast
½ teaspoon smoked paprika
½ teaspoon chilli/chili powder
1 garlic clove, peeled
2 tablespoons sunflower oil
½ teaspoon salt, or to taste
freshly squeezed lemon juice, to taste
tortilla chips or crunchy vegetables, to serve

MAKES 360 ML/1½ CUPS

Blanch the carrot or pumpkin in a little boiling water or steam, until soft.

Blend all the ingredients into a smooth 'cheese' sauce. Taste and adjust the seasoning.

Pour over tortilla chips or crunchy vegetables, as an appetizer starter or a snack. This 'cheese' can also be served as a party dip, and it tastes even better if left to rest in the fridge overnight.

VIETNAMESE SPRING ROLLS

There are so many names for the ever-popular spring roll, including salad roll, summer roll and crystal roll. Here, in this light and refreshing Vietnamese version, the soft textures of tofu, mushrooms and vermicelli noodles pair wonderfully with the crunch of the cabbage and the freshness of the herbs.

- 55 g/2 oz. rice vermicelli noodles
- 8 rice wrappers (21.5 cm/8½ in. diameter)
- 4–6 shiitake mushrooms, cut into matchstick pieces
- 115 g/½ cup medium–firm tofu, sliced into matchstick pieces
- 30 g/½ cup cabbage, shredded or finely chopped
- 1⅓ tablespoons fresh Thai basil, chopped
- 3 tablespoons freshly chopped mint leaves
- 3 tablespoons freshly chopped coriander/cilantro
- 2 lettuce leaves of your choice, chopped
- 4 teaspoons soy sauce
- 60 ml/¼ cup water
- 2 tablespoons freshly squeezed lime juice
- 1 garlic clove, crushed
- 2 tablespoons white sugar
- ½ teaspoon garlic-chilli/chile sauce
- 3 tablespoons hoisin sauce
- 1 teaspoon peanuts, finely chopped

MAKES 8 SPRING ROLLS

Bring a medium saucepan of water to boil. Boil the rice vermicelli noodles for 3–5 minutes, or until al dente, and drain.

Fill a large bowl with warm water. Dip one rice wrapper into the hot water for 1 second to soften. Lay the wrapper flat. In a row across the centre of the wrapper, place 1 tablespoon of shiitake, 1 tablespoon tofu, a handful of cabbage, basil, mint, coriander/cilantro and lettuce, leaving about 5 cm/2 inches uncovered on each side. Fold the uncovered sides inward, then tightly roll the wrapper, beginning at the end with the lettuce.

Repeat to make another 7 spring rolls.

In a small bowl, mix the soy sauce, water, lime juice, garlic, sugar and garlic-chilli/chile sauce. In another small bowl, mix the hoisin sauce and peanuts.

Serve the spring rolls at room temperature and dip them into both sauces at will!

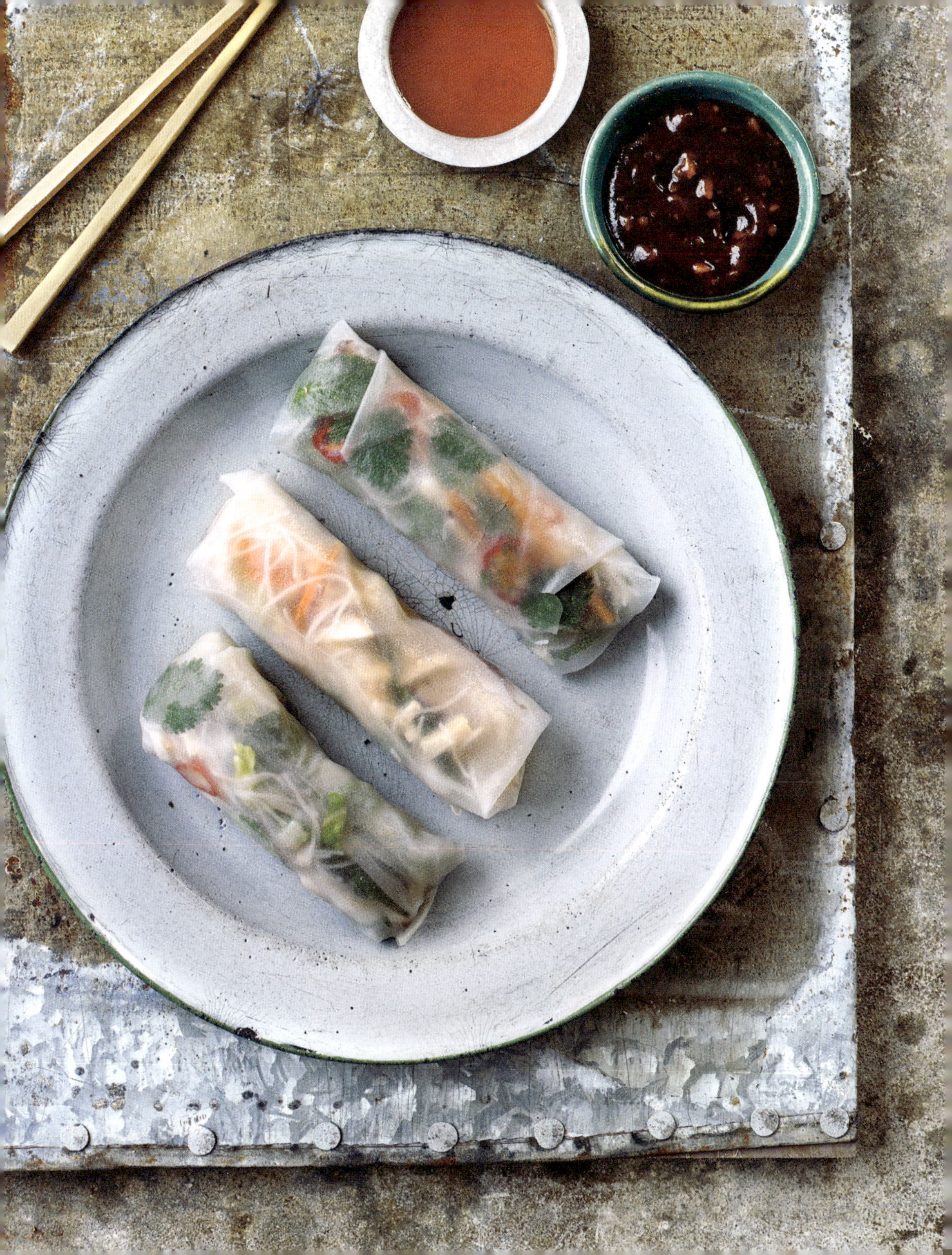

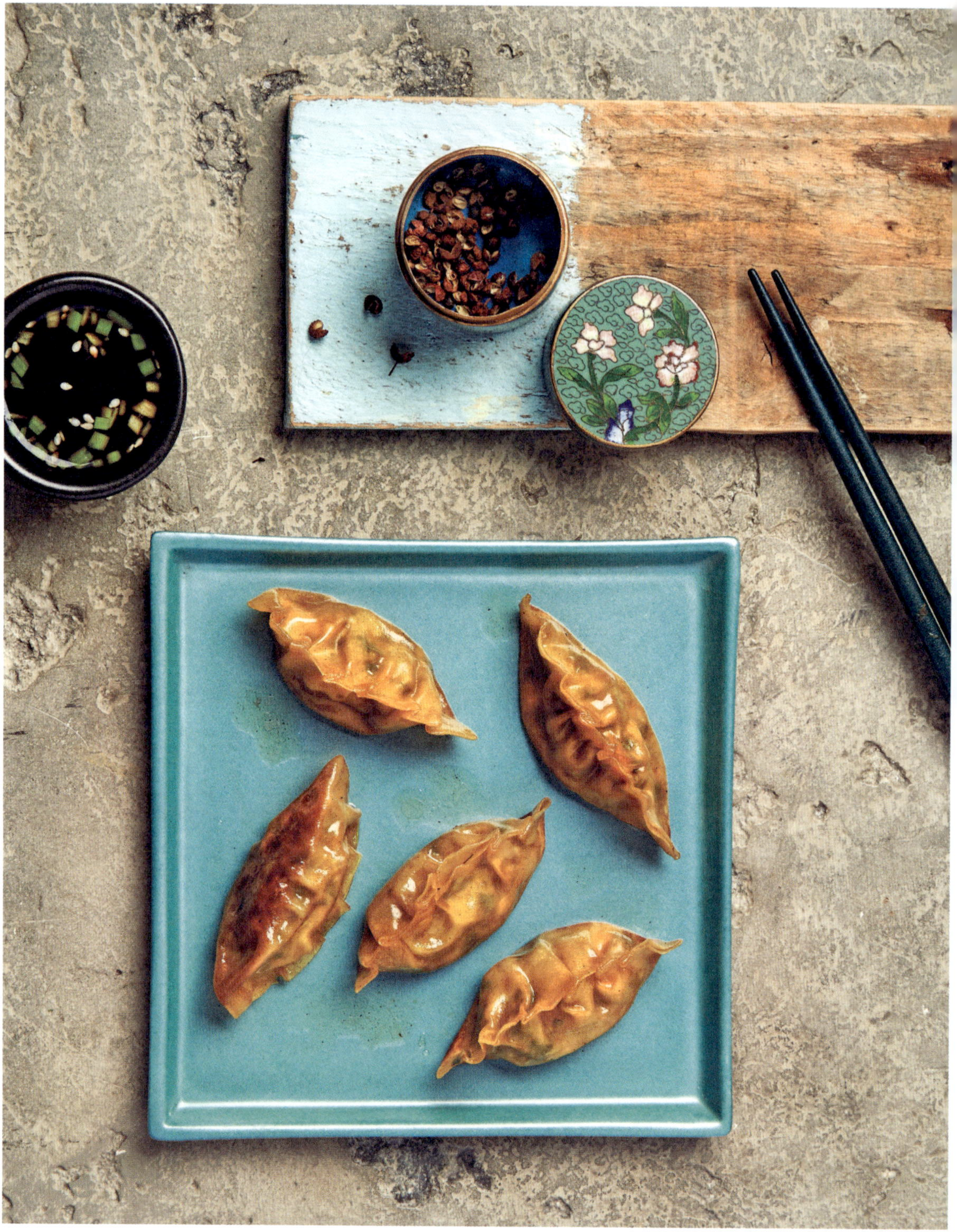

PUMPKIN, LEEK & TOFU DUMPLINGS

Vegetables take centre-stage in these warming and golden pumpkin and leek parcels. The interior of the dumpling should be soft in texture, flavoured beautifully with Chinese chives, ginger and Sichuan pepper. The egg dumpling wrappers provides just a little bite.

16 fresh dumpling wrappers
black vinegar, for dipping

FOR THE FILLING
40 g/¼ cup steamed pumpkin
100 g/3½ oz. firm tofu, sliced into small cubes
pinch of salt
1 leek, finely chopped
2 Chinese cabbage leaves, finely chopped
2 Chinese chive stalks, white parts removed, finely chopped
handful of fresh coriander/cilantro, chopped
1 teaspoon peeled and freshly chopped ginger
1 teaspoon Sichuan pepper
1 teaspoon freshly ground black pepper
2 tablespoons stir-fry sauce of your choice
2 tablespoons sesame oil

MAKES 16 DUMPLINGS

First, make the filling. Lightly salt the tofu slices and set them aside for 30 mins. After that, squeeze out the excess water.

In a large bowl, mix together the steamed pumpkin with the tofu, chopped vegetables, coriander/cilantro, ginger, Sichuan pepper, black pepper, stir-fry sauce and sesame oil. Chill in the fridge for 30 minutes.

Put a large teaspoon of filling into the centre of each dumpling wrapper. Dab a little water on one edge of the skin, fold in half over the filling and pinch the corners together to seal. Fold small pleats to seal up the middle. Continue with the rest of the batch, leaving the prepared dumplings on a tray lightly dusted with flour and covered with a damp kitchen cloth as you work.

Put a large pan of water on to boil. Lower the dumplings into the boiling water and cover with a lid. As soon as they start to float, they are cooked. Serve hot with black vinegar for dipping.

TOFU, SUN-DRIED TOMATO & OLIVE DUMPLINGS

Sun-kissed Mediterranean ingredients fill this stylish little dumpling, resulting in a tasty clash of cultures. The strong tang of sun-dried tomatoes and olives are cooled by the mellow tofu. Pan-frying to get a crispy bottom is a nice finishing touch.

16 fresh dumpling wrappers
dipping sauce, to serve (see below)

FOR THE FILLING
200 g/7 oz. firm tofu, sliced into small cubes
pinch of salt
1 leek, thinly sliced
60 g/½ cup sun-dried tomatoes, finely chopped
50 g/scant ½ cup black pitted olives, finely chopped
2 button mushrooms, finely chopped
2 Chinese chive stalks, white parts removed and finely chopped
handful of freshly chopped Chinese parsley
1 teaspoon Sichuan pepper
1 teaspoon freshly ground black pepper
2 tablespoons stir-fry sauce of your choice
2 tablespoons sesame oil

FOR THE DIPPING SAUCE
1 tablespoon balsamic vinegar
2 tablespoons olive oil
red shallot, finely chopped
handful of freshly chopped basil leaves

MAKES 16 DUMPLINGS

First, make the filling. Sprinkle a little salt over the tofu slices and set them aside for 30 minutes before squeezing out the excess water.

In a bowl combine the tofu with the chopped vegetables, parsley, seasonings, stir-fry sauce and sesame oil. Mix well and place in the fridge for 30 minutes to chill.

Put a large teaspoon of filling into the centre of each dumpling wrapper. Dip your fingertips in a small dish of water and slightly moisten the edge of half the skin. Fold in half and pinch the edges together to form a simple crescent shape. Fold the two ends of the dumpling together and overlap to create a Chinese ingot shape. Seal with another dab of water if needed. Repeat until all the mixture and skins have been used.

Gently lower the dumplings into a pan of boiling water and cover with a lid. As soon as the dumplings start to float they should be ready. Alternatively, you can lightly pan-fry the boiled dumplings to make the bottoms crispy and golden.

To make the dipping sauce, mix the ingredients together in a small bowl.

Serve the dumplings hot with the dipping sauce on the side.

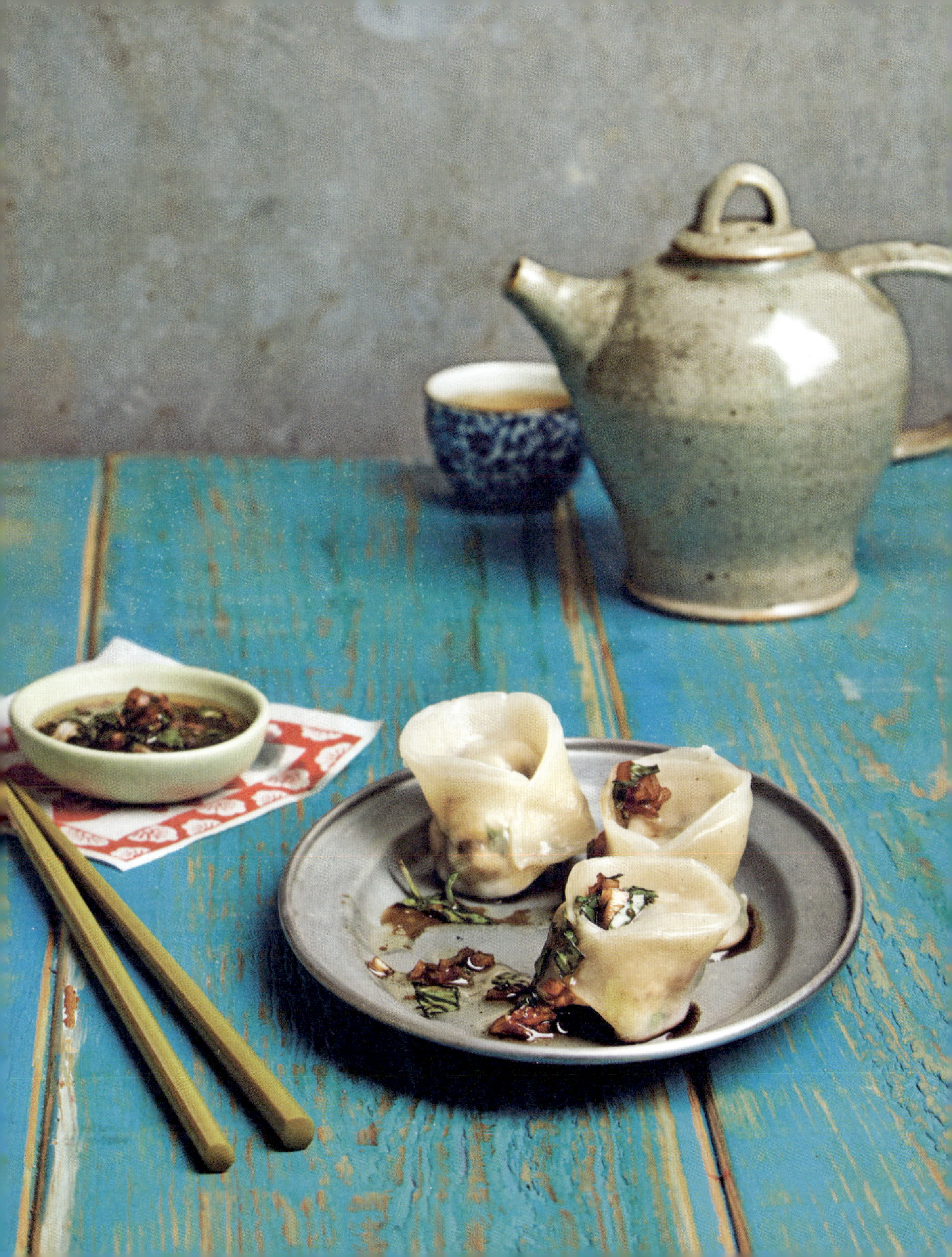

TOFU & VEGETABLE GYOZA

This recipe uses firm tofu rather than the soft type. To avoid having a watery taste, wrap the tofu in paper towels and put a weight on top to remove excess water. It creates a firmer finish to the filling, and is a common way to drain off tofu in a lot of the recipes in this book. You can also use cooked quinoa to substitute the renkon (lotus root) for a unique texture to the overall dish. When cooking, the water evaporates to leave the bottom of the dumplings crispy.

20–22 fresh dumpling wrappers
½ tablespoon vegetable oil, for frying
½ tablespoon toasted sesame oil, for frying
Su-Joyu dipping sauce, to serve (see right)

FOR THE FILLING
125 g/4½ oz. firm tofu
120 g/4¼ oz. Chinese cabbage, very finely chopped
¼ teaspoon fine sea salt
2 spring onions/scallions, finely chopped
50 g/¾ oz. chopped frozen renkon (lotus root)
1 dried shiitake mushroom (soaked in a cupful of water for 30 minutes, then drained, stem removed and finely chopped)
1 teaspoon freshly grated ginger
1 teaspoon freshly grated garlic
1 teaspoon light soy sauce
1½ teaspoon mirin
1 teaspoon toasted sesame oil
1 teaspoon stock powder (kombu)
¼ teaspoon fine sea salt

FOR THE SU-JOYU DIPPING SAUCE
2 tablespoons soy sauce
2 tablespoons rice vinegar
2 tablespoons mirin
4 drops of la-yu (spiced sesame chilli oil)

MAKES 20–22 DUMPLINGS

For the filling, wrap the tofu in paper towels and compress under a heavy weight to remove any excess water. Put the chopped cabbage in a large bowl, add the salt and mix well. Leave for 10 minutes to draw out the excess water.

Smash up the tofu with a wooden spoon in a mixing bowl or use a food processor to break it up into a paste, then add to a large mixing bowl. Briefly rinse the cabbage, then squeeze it to extract as much liquid as possible. Add the drained cabbage to the tofu along with the rest of the ingredients and mix until well combined.

Put 1 teaspoon of filling in the middle of each wrapper. Wet the edges of the wrappers with a dab of water. Fold the wrappers in half over the filling and make seven pleats where the edges connect, squeezing them together to seal well.

To cook the gyoza, heat the large frying pan/skillet over a high heat with the vegetable and toasted sesame oil. Working quickly, put half the gyoza into the pan. Fry for about 2 minutes until the bottoms of the gyoza start to turn brown.

Pour 100 ml/⅓ cup plus 1 tablespoon of water into the pan from the rim, then quickly cover with the lid so that not too much steam is lost. Reduce the heat to medium and steam the gyoza for 4 minutes.

Serve with the su-joyu dipping sauce.

SMALL BITES & SNACKS

TOFU, GINGER & LIME SPOONS

With refreshing, delicate flavours, this canapée is the perfect accompaniment to a glass of fizz to kick off a summer party. You get a light, zing of a lime or a splash of yuzu, but you could substitute with a little soy or tamari if you'd like something richer. You can use silken tofu, but the most important thing is that it is fresh and great quality. The best kind to go for is the tofu you find stored in a tub of water in Asian supermarkets.

500 g/1 lb. 2 oz. firm tofu
90 g/3 oz. freshly grated ginger
2 spring onions/scallions, thinly sliced
freshly squeezed lime juice, to serve

32 canapé spoons

MAKES 32 CANAPÉS

Place the tofu on a few layers of paper towels to absorb the excess liquid. Slice the tofu into small cubes that fit nicely onto your spoons (roughly 2.5 x 3 cm/1 x 1¼ inches).

Place a piece of tofu on each spoon and gently place a pinch of grated ginger on top. Place a pinch of the spring onions/scallions on top of the ginger and, just before serving, sprinkle a little lime juice over each spoon.

SMALL BITES & SNACKS

SPICY TOFU SATAY WITH SOY DIPPING SAUCE

Here is a very tasty dish that does wonderful things to tofu, which works as a blank canvas to soak up these rich ingredients. Full of the flavours of Vietnam, this dish is sold at street stalls there as a snack, but you can serve it as an appetizer or with noodles as a main dish.

300 g/10 oz. firm tofu, cut into bite-sized cubes
leaves from a small bunch of fresh basil, shredded, to serve
sesame oil, for frying

FOR THE MARINADE
3 lemongrass stalks, trimmed and finely chopped
1 tablespoon peanut oil
3 tablespoons soy sauce
1–2 fresh red chillies/chiles, deseeded and finely chopped
2 garlic cloves, crushed
1 teaspoon ground turmeric
2 teaspoons sugar
sea salt, to season

FOR THE SOY DIPPING SAUCE
4–5 tablespoons soy sauce
1–2 tablespoons vegetarian Thai 'fish' sauce
freshly squeezed juice of 1 lime
1–2 teaspoons sugar
1 fresh red chilli/chile, deseeded and finely chopped

3–4 wooden or bamboo skewers, soaked in water

SERVES 3–4

Wrap the tofu in paper towels and press firmly to remove any excess water.

To make the marinade, mix the lemongrass, peanut oil, soy sauce, chilli/chile, garlic and turmeric with the sugar until it has dissolved. Add a little salt to taste and toss in the tofu, making sure it is well coated. Leave to marinate for 1 hour.

Prepare the soy dipping sauce by whisking all the ingredients together. Set aside until ready to serve.

To cook the tofu, you can stir-fry the cubes in a wok with a little sesame oil and then thread them onto sticks to serve, or you can skewer them and grill them over charcoal or under a conventional grill for 2–3 minutes on each side.

Serve the tofu hot, garnished with the shredded basil and with the dipping sauce on the side.

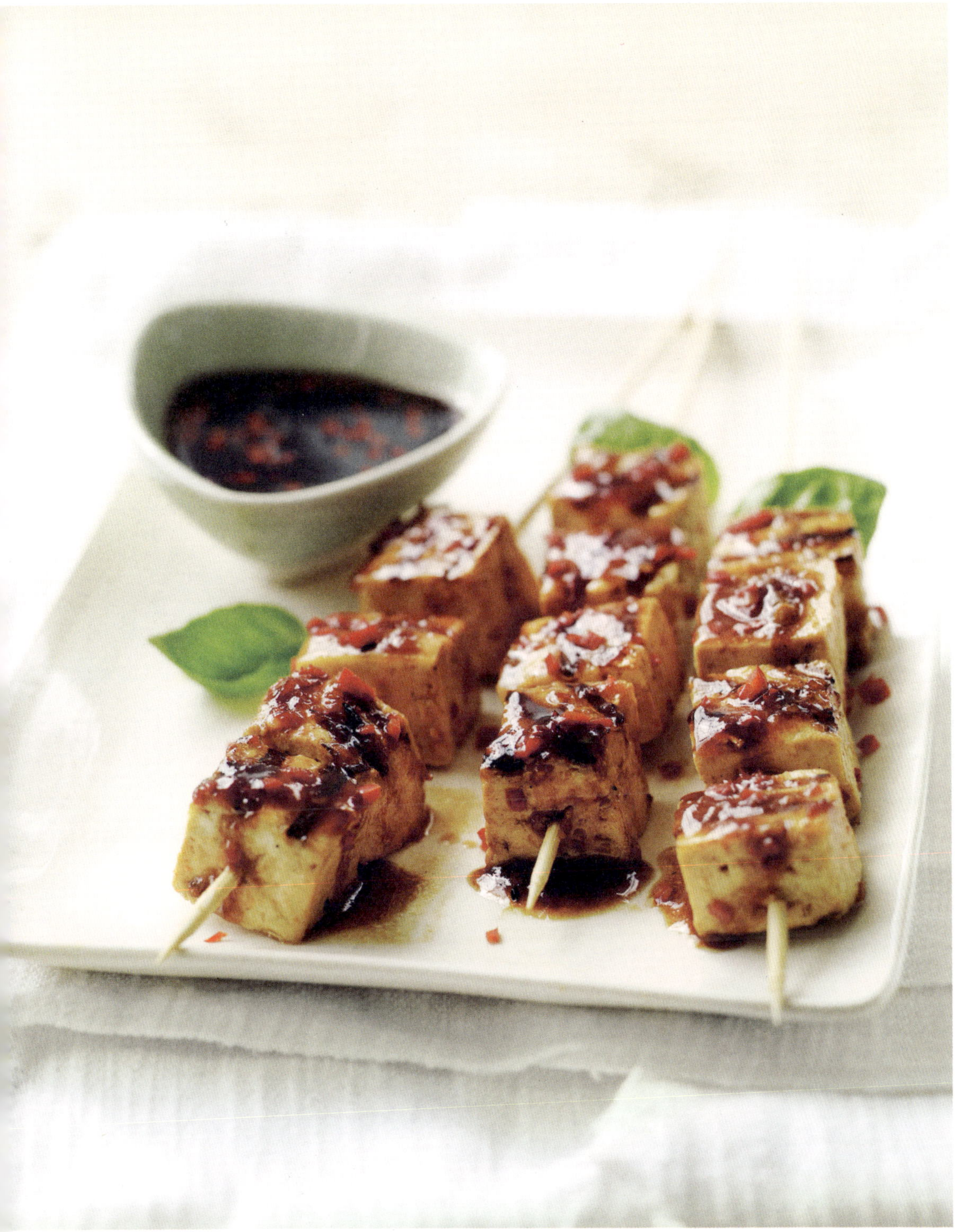

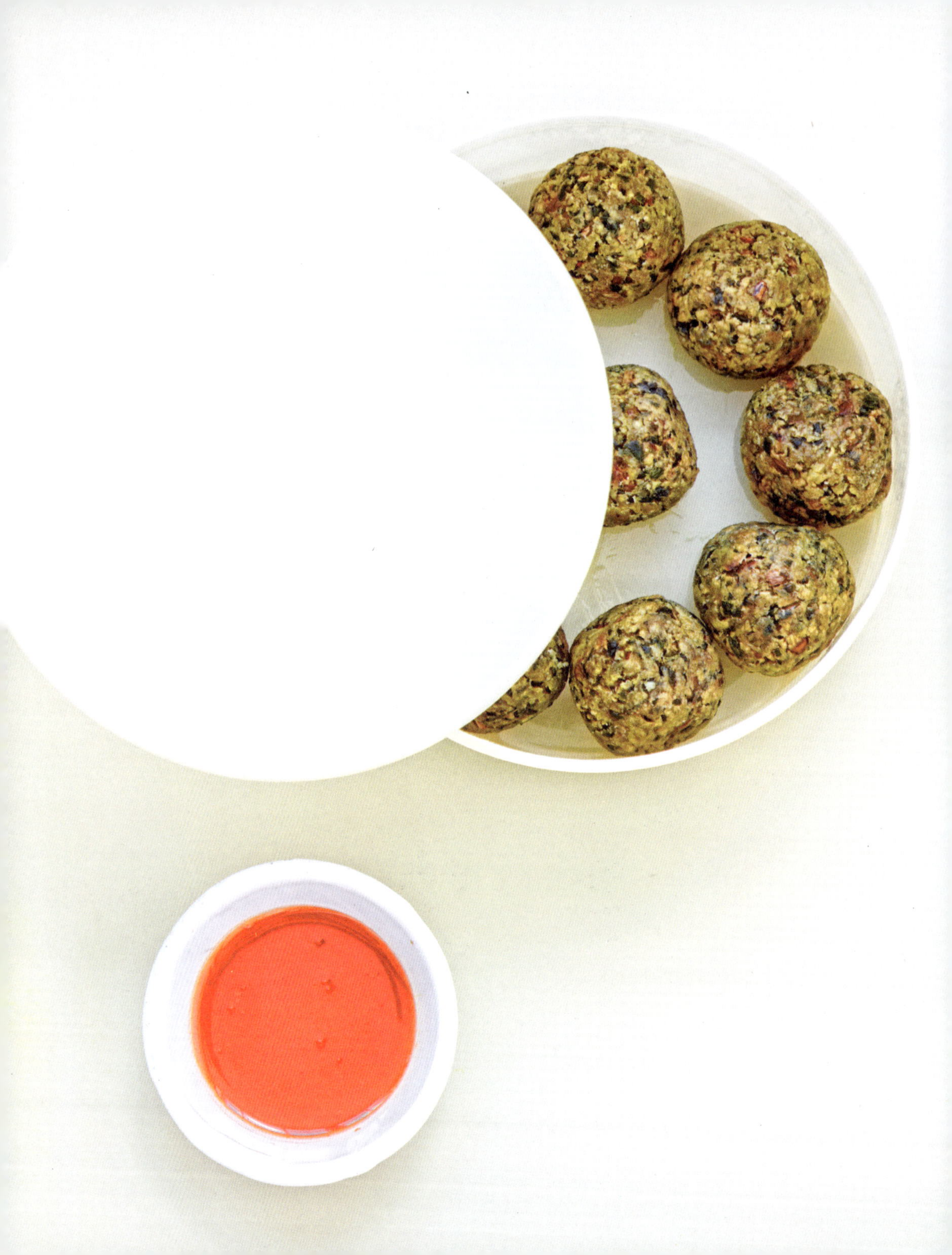

TOFU, GINGER & CHILLI BALLS

Light in flavour but not in nutritional value, these tofu balls benefit from the zingy additions of chilli flakes/hot red pepper flakes, spring onions/scallions, garlic, ginger, turmeric and coriander/cilantro leaves. Serve the balls plain or with a sweet chilli/chili dipping sauce to accompany on the side.

225 g/8 oz. tofu
2.5-cm/1-in. piece of fresh ginger, peeled and finely grated
1 teaspoon dried chilli flakes/hot red pepper flakes
2 garlic cloves, grated
2 large spring onions/scallions, very finely chopped
1 teaspoon ground turmeric
handful of freshly chopped coriander/cilantro leaves
½ teaspoon sea salt
1 tablespoon dried nori flakes
2 tablespoons cornflour/cornstarch
cold-pressed rapeseed oil, for frying

MAKES 12 BALLS

Wrap the tofu in paper towels and press firmly to remove as much water as possible. Coarsely grate the tofu and squeeze out any surplus water still in the tofu.

Put the grated tofu in a mixing bowl with the ginger, chilli flakes/hot red pepper flakes, garlic, spring onions/scallions, turmeric, coriander/cilantro, salt and nori flakes. Mix well, then sprinkle over the cornflour/cornstarch and stir until combined.

With damp hands, shape the mixture into 12 walnut-sized balls and place in the fridge for 30 minutes or until ready to cook, to firm them up.

Heat a generous amount of rapeseed oil in a large frying pan/skillet and cook the balls in batches of four for 8–10 minutes, turning them occasionally until golden all over. Drain on paper towels and serve warm or at room temperature. The balls can be left to cool and then stored in the fridge in an airtight container for up to 3 days.

TOFU & RICE HUMMUS

It's so easy to blend these simple ingredients into a creamy hummus-like dip, and it can be used in variety of ways: as a healthy snack with raw veggie sticks or crackers, as a topping for pizza, or like here, as an open sandwich spread.

150 g/^{2}/$_3$ cup short-grain brown rice, cooked
200 g/1^1/$_3$ cup soft tofu
60 g/^{1}/$_2$ cup finely chopped onion
1 tablespoon white tahini
1 tablespoon umeboshi vinegar or 2 teaspoons umeboshi paste
1 tablespoon nutritional yeast (optional)
^{1}/$_2$ teaspoon salt, or to taste

TO SERVE
2 tablespoons olive oil
seeded toast
shredded red cabbage
diced avocado
pea shoots
freshly ground black pepper

SERVES 2–3

Blend the cooked rice, tofu, onion, tahini, umeboshi vinegar or paste and about 3 tablespoons of water for 1–2 minutes or until smooth. Depending on how soft your tofu is, you might need to add more water, little by little, to achieve a consistency of thick cream cheese. This hummus tastes better if left to rest in the fridge for 24 hours.

Serve on seeded toast, topped with shredded red cabbage, diced avocado and pea shoots (or other vegetables of your choice), with a drizzle of olive oil and some freshly ground black pepper.

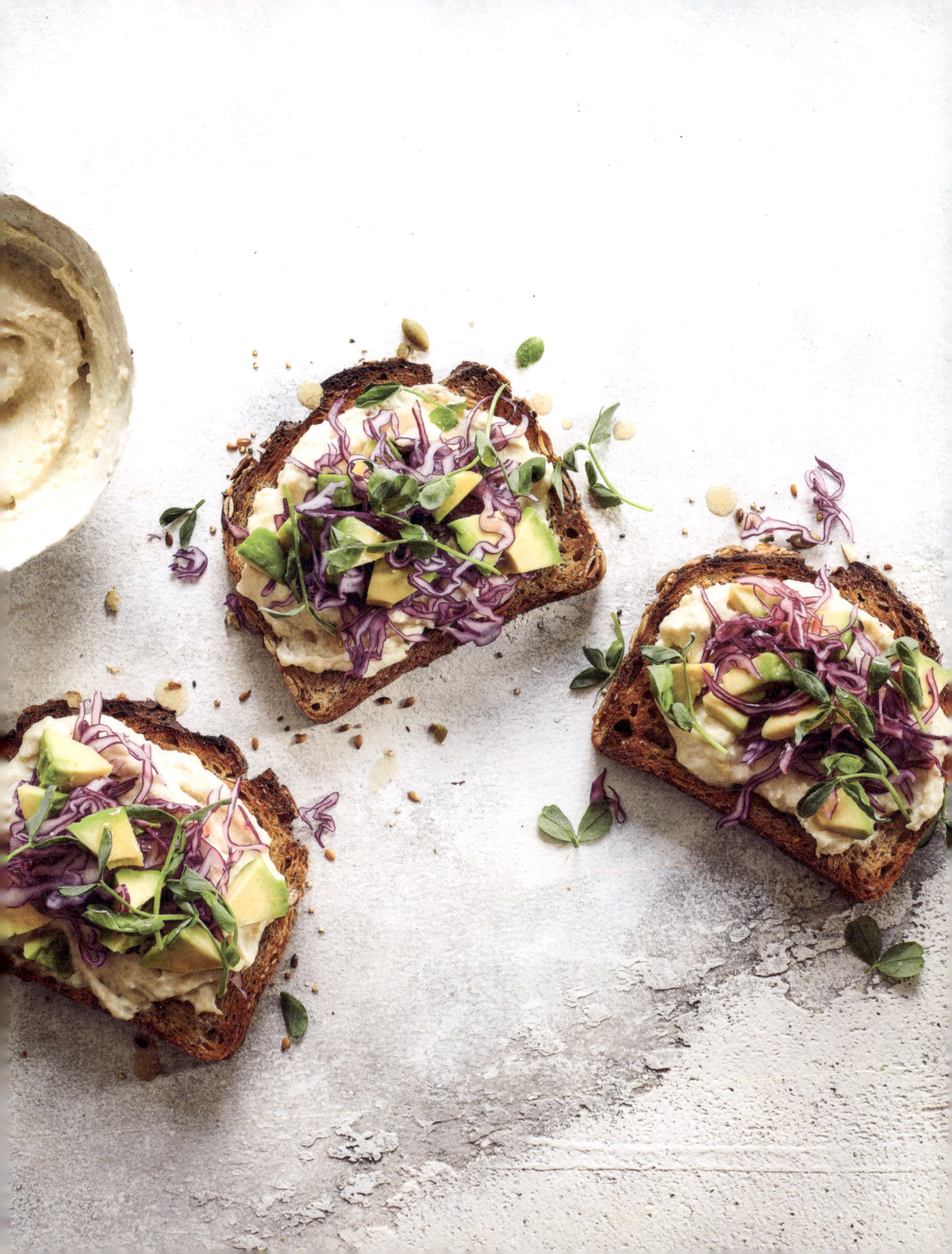

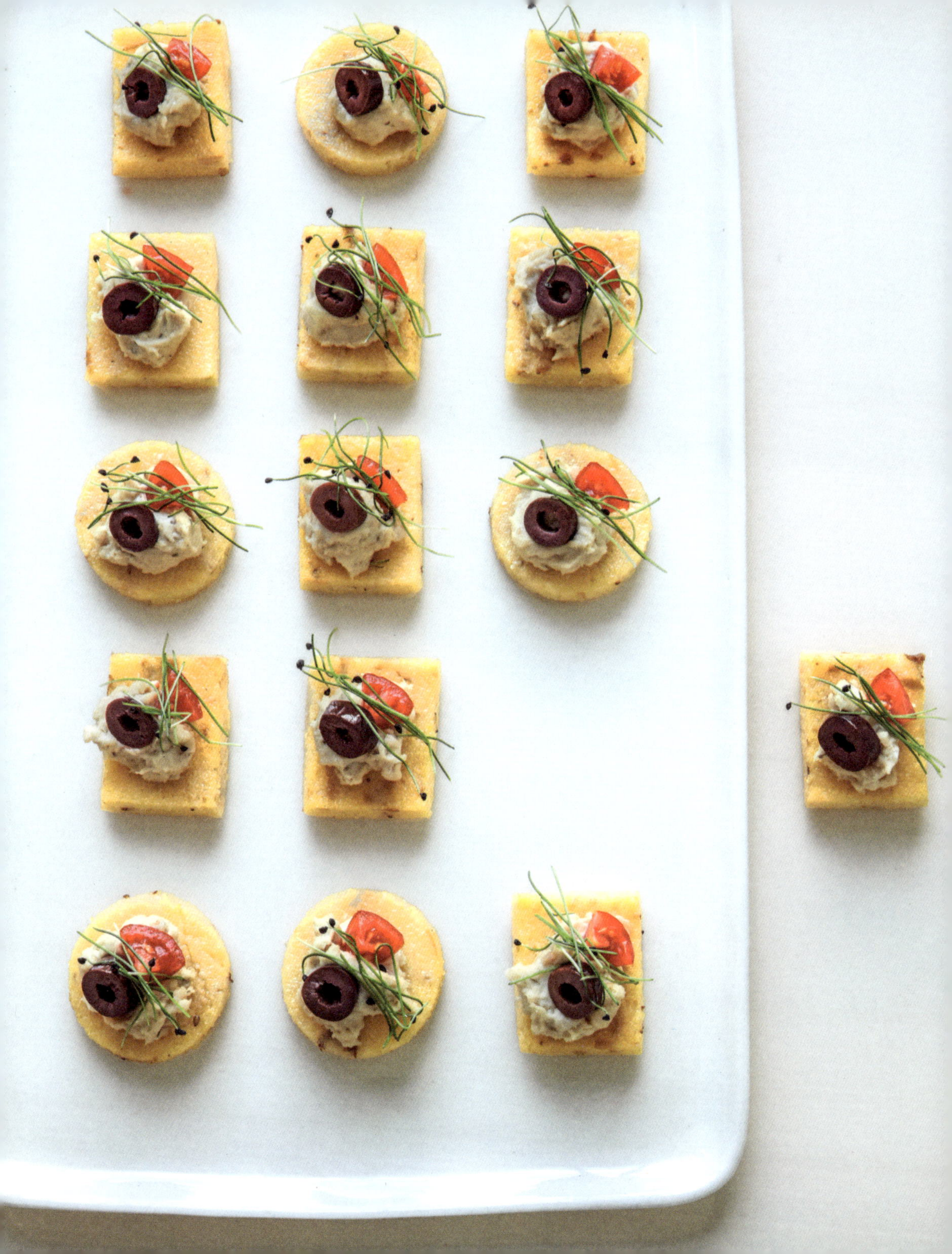

POLENTA & TOFU CANAPÉS WITH BEAN PÂTÉ

Polenta/cornmeal is such a simple, rustic ingredient that has been rediscovered recently, especially with gluten-free products becoming more in demand. It has a great texture and taste, and can be used as a starting point for many recipes, whether it's served as a porridge, a side dish or, as in this recipe, combined with smoked tofu to make a tasty canapé base.

FOR THE POLENTA & TOFU BASE
90 g/½ cup polenta/cornmeal
¼ teaspoon salt
50 g/⅓ cup smoked tofu, finely grated/shredded
olive oil, for oiling and drizzling

FOR THE BEAN PÂTÉ
160 g/1 cup cooked unsalted haricot/navy beans, well drained
60 g/¼ cup tahini
3 garlic cloves, peeled
1 tablespoon nutritional yeast (optional)
½ teaspoon salt, or to taste
2 tablespoons olive oil
¼ teaspoon dried oregano
freshly ground black pepper, to season

TO SERVE
cherry tomatoes, chopped
pitted black olives, halved
snipped chives

23 x 30-cm/9 x 12-in. baking pan

MAKES 24 CANAPÉS

For the base, in a heavy-bottomed saucepan, bring 360 ml/1½ cups water to the boil and whisk in the polenta/cornmeal and salt. Cover, lower the heat to minimum and then simmer for 10 minutes. Stir, add the grated tofu, remove from the heat and let it stand, covered for 10 minutes.

Oil the baking pan and spoon in the cooked polenta/cornmeal, spreading it into an even layer. Drizzle with a little oil and smooth out with a spatula. Leave to cool completely, then cut into small squares or use a well-oiled round cookie cutter to cut out circles.

For the pâté, blend the beans and tahini with the other ingredients into a chunky pâté. Taste and adjust the seasoning.

To assemble the canapés, lay out the polenta/cornmeal pieces on a plate or serving tray. Using two teaspoons, top each bite with a teaspoon of pâté, then top with a small piece of cherry tomato, half a black olive and a few snipped chives. These canapés can be made in advance as the polenta/cornmeal base does not get soggy as quickly as bread or crackers.

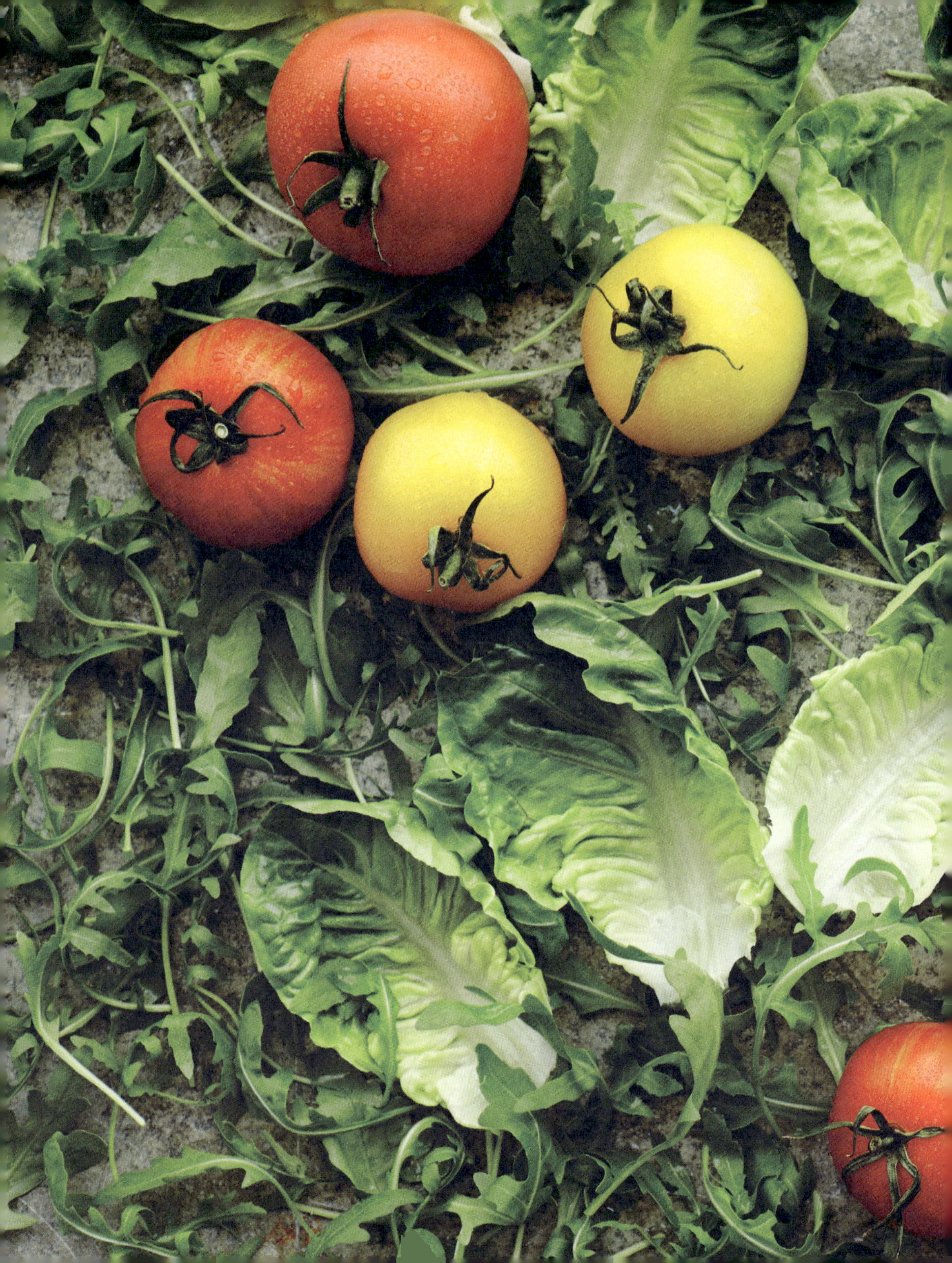

Salads

VEGAN GREEK SALAD WITH TOFU FETA

The key to this beautiful Greek salad is the blend of bold flavours from fresh seasonal vegetables, high-quality olives and olive oil, and creamy fermented tofu. Try to use organic ingredients since they usually taste so much better, and you won't need to peel the cucumber!

FOR FERMENTING THE TOFU
4 slices extra-firm tofu, (around 440 g/14 oz. total weight)
300 g /1¼ cups barley or rice miso

FOR THE SALAD
2 ripe tomatoes (around 340 g/ 12 oz. total weight)
1 green (bell) pepper, deseeded
1 cucumber (around 200 g/7 oz. total weight)
100 g/⅔ cup ripe cherry tomatoes
1 medium red onion, peeled
20 g/½ cup fresh basil leaves
90 g/½ cup oven-dried black olives, stoned/pitted
1 teaspoon dried Mediterranean herbs
4 tablespoons extra virgin olive oil
salt and freshly ground black pepper, to season
apple cider vinegar, to taste

SERVES 4

Slice the block of tofu lengthwise into four equally thick slices. Spread 75 g/⅓ cup of miso over each slice, covering it entirely. Place the tofu slices in a glass container. Cover and let sit at room temperature for 24 hours. The tofu will absorb the saltiness and taste of the miso paste. Scrape off the miso (save it to make soup) and rinse quickly under running water, if necessary.

You can ferment tofu in advance and pack it in jars, covered in olive oil, adding Mediterranean herbs, garlic, olives, dried tomatoes and chilli/chile for an extra flavour. Use it throughout that month to make this vegan Greek salad, or serve it as an appetizer.

Cut the tomatoes and (bell) pepper into large rounds. Cut the cucumber, with the skin on, in half lengthwise and slice into wedges. Cut the cherry tomatoes in half, and chop the onion into thin half-moons. Roughly chop the basil, leaving a couple of leaves whole, for decoration. Put all the vegetables into a large salad bowl, add the olives, basil, dried herbs, olive oil, a pinch of salt, crushed black pepper and vinegar, to taste. Quickly toss the ingredients together, preferably with your hands.

To serve, divide among plates or shallow bowls, top with the fermented tofu cubes, and finish with a sprinkling of dried herbs and a drizzle of olive oil. Garnish with basil leaves and enjoy immediately!

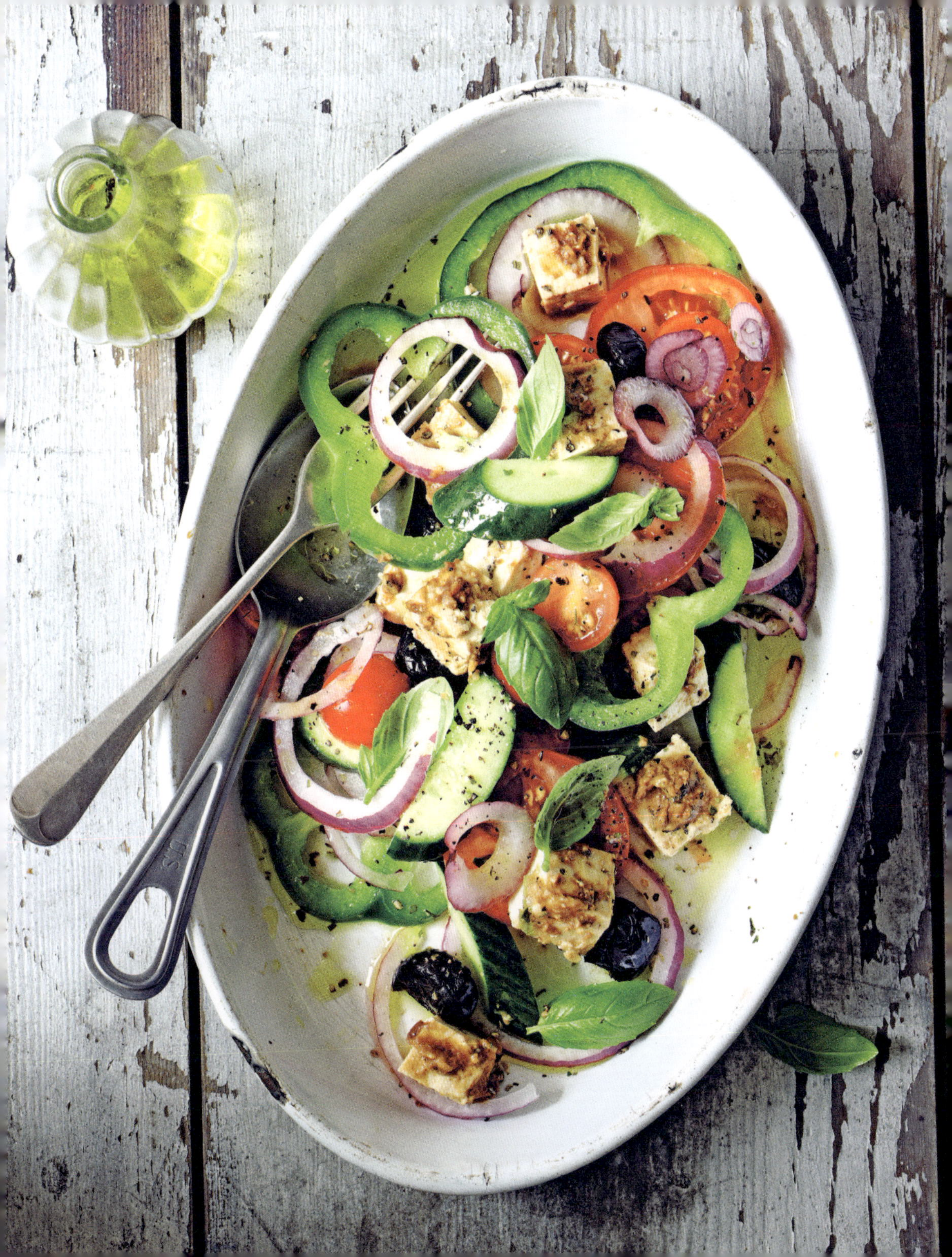

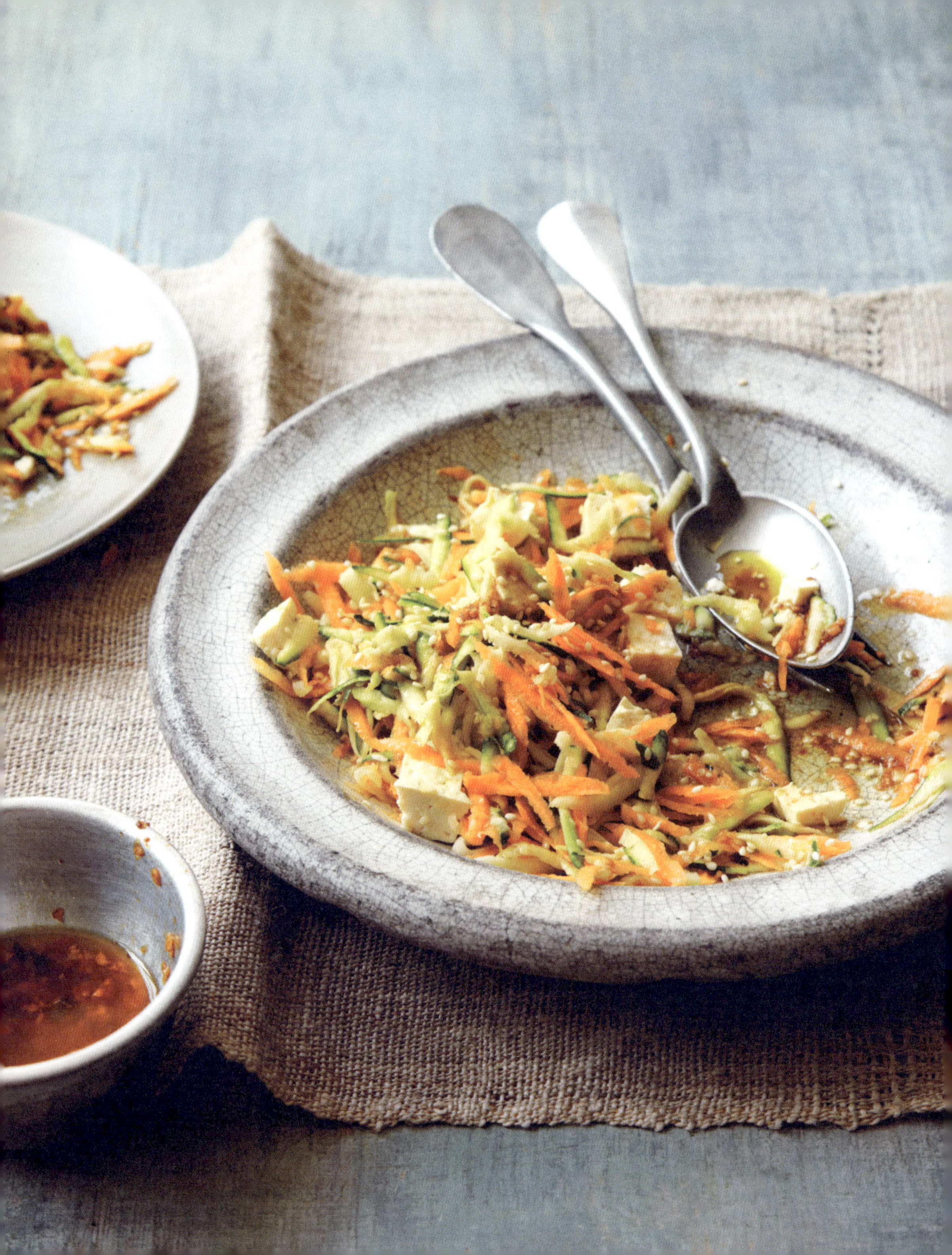

SHREDDED VEGETABLE & TOFU SALAD WITH A SESAME-MISO DRESSING

Vegetables take on a new personality when they are prepared differently. Japanese cuisine can turn a simple radish into a piece of art. The simple act of shredding veggies and mixing in a delicious dressing is a tasty treat. The tofu works particularly well with the miso dressing.

2 carrots, grated/shredded
3 courgettes/zucchini, grated/shredded
30 g/¼ cup sesame seeds
150 g/1 cup firm tofu, chopped

FOR THE SESAME-MISO DRESSING
2 tablespoons miso paste
1 tablespoon rice wine vinegar
1 tablespoon sesame oil
2 tablespoons flaxseed oil
1 teaspoon peeled and finely sliced fresh ginger
2 teaspoons clear honey

SERVES 2–4

Place the carrots, courgettes/zucchini into a large bowl. Add the sesame seeds and chopped tofu.

To make the sesame-miso dressing, whisk all of the ingredients together to an emulsion. Pour over the mixed salad, toss to coat in the dressing and serve. The salad can be prepared in advance and stored in the refrigerator for up to 2 days.

ASIAN TOFU & RAW KALE SALAD

This plant-based recipe is jam-packed full of ingredients that will provide non-dairy eaters with the calcium that might otherwise be lacking from their diet. Kale and other dark, leafy green vegetables are surprisingly an excellent source of calcium, and tofu is a great natural source of vitamin D. A win-win, especially when the end result is having a healthy, delicious salad to enjoy! Perfect as a lunch for two, or as a side when feeding a crowd.

bunch of kale
3 spring onions/scallions, finely chopped
2 tablespoons freshly chopped coriander/cilantro
2 tablespoons freshly chopped mint
2 tablespoons toasted sesame seeds
220 g/7 oz. firm tofu
2 tablespoons vegetable oil (optional), for frying
2 tablespoons dried fried onions, to serve

FOR THE DRESSING
freshly squeezed juice of 1 lime
1 teaspoon sesame oil
1½ tablespoons olive oil
1 tablespoon finely chopped fresh ginger
1 tablespoon agave syrup
pinch each of salt and freshly ground black pepper

SERVES 2

To prepare the kale, cut away the tough stems. Wash all the leaves to get rid of any grit, then fold the leaves together and slice thinly. Put in a large mixing bowl.

Whisk all the dressing ingredients together in a small bowl. Pour two thirds of the dressing over the kale and massage and squeeze the kale with the dressing using your hands, this helps to soften the kale. Leave the kale to sit in the refrigerator for an hour, or even overnight. Keep the spare dressing for serving.

Toss the kale with the spring onions/scallions, coriander/cilantro, mint and sesame seeds.

Drain the tofu and wrap in paper towels. Put something heavy on top to help press out any excess water. If you like, you can have the salad with the tofu cold and raw, simply unwrap it and cut into slices to top the salad.

If you prefer cooked tofu, slice into 1-cm/½-inch thick pieces, add the 2 tablespoons of oil to a frying pan/skillet and set over medium heat. When hot, lay the slices of tofu in the pan. Fry for 2–3 minutes on each side, until it crisps up a bit.

Serve the kale with slices of tofu on top, a drizzle of the leftover dressing and a sprinkle of dried fried onions.

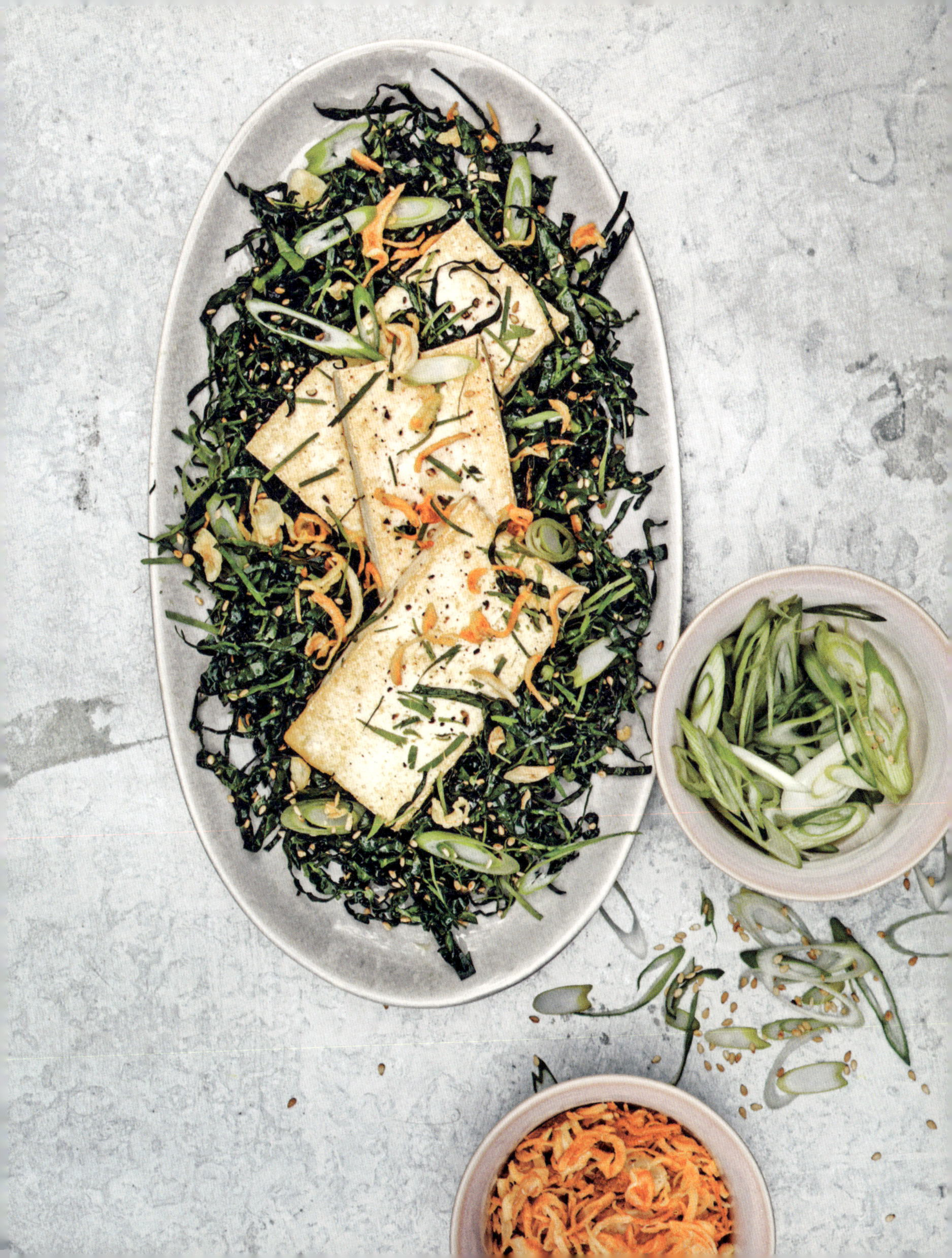

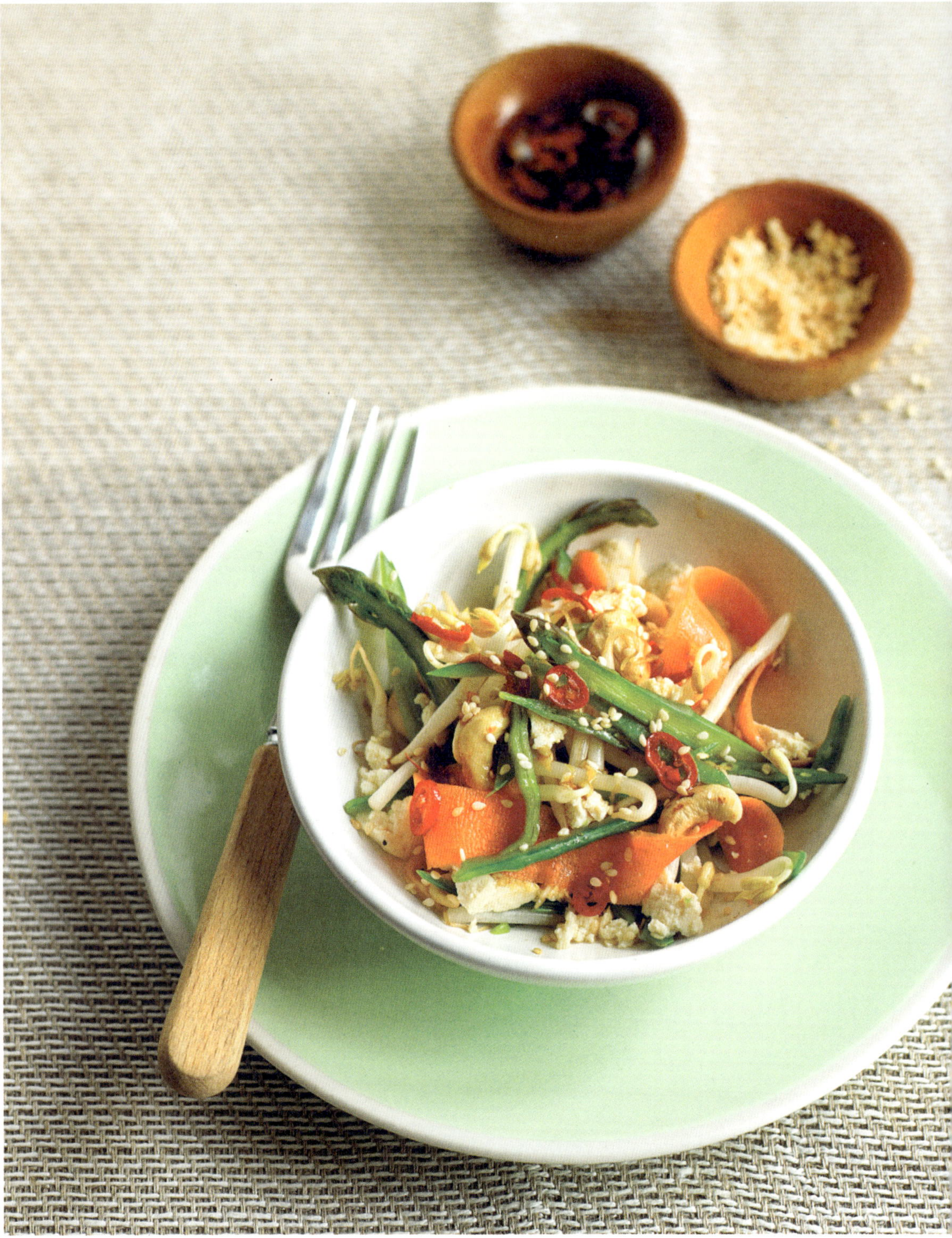

ASIAN-STYLE HOT & SOUR SALAD WITH MARINATED TOFU

This crunchy salad makes a great lunch or as a small dish to serve as part of an Asian meal. You can use any fresh vegetables that you have to hand.

100 g/1 cup asparagus tips
100 g/1 cup mangetout/snow peas
50 g/⅓ cup toasted cashews
100 g/2 cup fresh beansprouts
100 g/3½ oz. rice noodles (optional)
1 carrot, sliced into ribbons
1 tablespoon toasted sesame seeds, to serve

FOR THE MARINATED TOFU
200 g/7 oz. tofu
2 tablespoons sesame oil
1 tablespoon dark soy sauce or tamari
½ fresh red chilli/chile, deseeded and finely chopped
1 teaspoon grated fresh, peeled ginger
grated zest and freshly squeezed juice of ½ lime
½ teaspoon sugar

FOR THE DRESSING
½ teaspoon salt
2 teaspoons sugar
grated zest and freshly squeezed juice of 1 lime
1 teaspoon white wine vinegar
½ fresh red chilli/chile

SERVES 4

For the marinated tofu, put all of the ingredients except the tofu in a bowl and stir until well combined. Put the tofu in a separate bowl, pour the marinade over it and set aside to marinate for 30 minutes.

Bring a saucepan of water to the boil and cook the asparagus and mangetout/snow peas for 3 minutes, until they soften slightly but still have a crunch to them. Remove them from the boiling water and put them into a bowl of ice-cold water to stop the cooking process. Drain, then slice in half lengthways and put them in a serving bowl. Add the cashews to the serving bowl.

If you are using rice noodles, cook them according to the packet instructions, usually by covering them with boiling water for about 6 minutes to soften, then rinsing with cold water and draining.

Put all of the dressing ingredients in a bowl and stir until well combined. Place the rest of the salad ingredients in the serving bowl, add the dressing and toss to coat the salad. Crumble the marinated tofu over the salad and finish with a sprinkling of sesame seeds.

SESAME-COATED TOFU WITH ADUKI BEAN SALAD

In this Asian-inspired salad, the sesame seeds form a thick, nutty crust around slices of tamari-marinated tofu, which are then served on top of an aduki bean and pea shoot salad.

450 g/1 lb. tofu, patted dry and sliced into 8 slices about 1 cm/½ in. thick
2 tablespoons tamari or light soy sauce
4 heaped teaspoons cornflour/cornstarch
6 heaped tablespoons sesame seeds
125 g/4¼ oz. canned aduki beans, drained and rinsed
11-cm/4-in. piece cucumber, quartered lengthways and thinly sliced
3 spring onions/scallions, thinly sliced diagonally
120 g/4 oz. pea shoots and mixed leaves

2 handfuls of sugar snap peas, sliced diagonally
1 red chilli/chile, deseeded and thinly sliced
sunflower oil, for frying

FOR THE DRESSING
2 tablespoons tamari or light soy sauce
2 tablespoons freshly squeezed lime juice
1 teaspoon caster/superfine sugar
1-cm/½-in. piece fresh ginger, peeled and finely chopped

SERVES 4

Put the tofu in a shallow dish and pour the tamari over. Turn the tofu to coat it in the tamari and leave to marinate for 1 hour, spooning the tamari over the tofu occasionally.

Mix together the cornflour/cornstarch and sesame seeds in a second shallow dish. Add the tofu in batches and turn until evenly coated in the mixture. Pour enough sunflower oil into a large frying pan/skillet to shallow-fry the tofu. Fry the tofu over a medium heat in two batches for 2–3 minutes on each side until golden, then drain on paper towels.

Meanwhile, mix together all the ingredients for the dressing and stir to dissolve the sugar.

Put the aduki beans, cucumber, two of the spring onions/scallions, the pea shoots and mixed leaves, sugar snap peas and half the chilli/chile in a large serving dish. Pour enough of the dressing over to coat and toss gently until combined.

Pile the sesame-coated tofu on top of the salad and sprinkle over the remaining spring onions/scallions and chilli/chile.

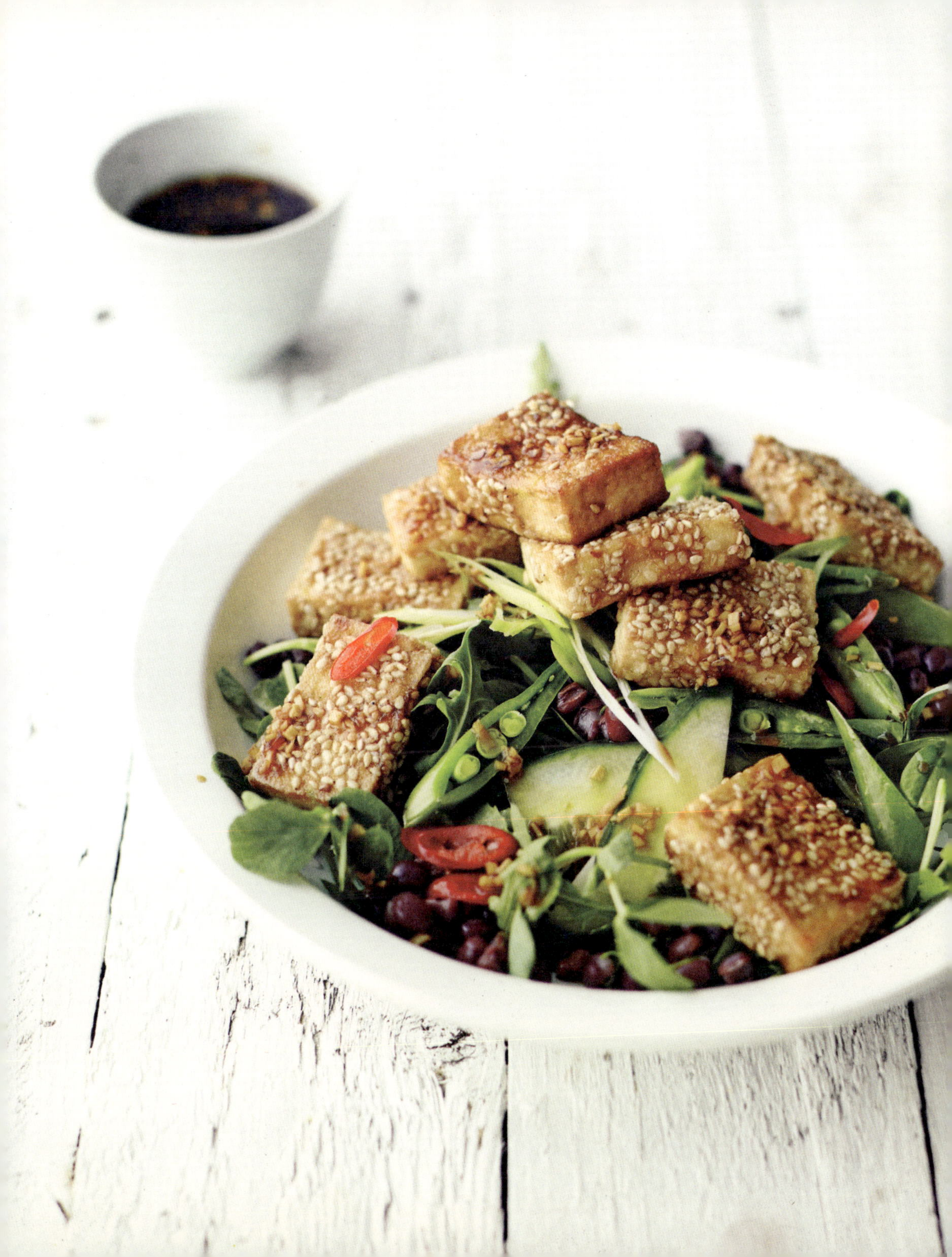

SALAD OLIVIER WITH TOFU MAYONNAISE

This is a vegan version of a very popular festive dish served in many countries, and in Croatia they incorrectly call it Franscuska salata (French salad). It can be served as a side dish or with some crackers or flatbread, it can easily serve as a satisfying light lunch or dinner. See a photograph of this versatile salad on page 11.

2 medium potatoes
750 ml/3 cups water
150 g/1 cup peas, fresh or frozen
3 small carrots, diced
70 g/½ cup diced pickles
200 g/scant cup of Tofu Mayonnaise (see page 11)

SERVES 2–3

In a saucepan, cover the potatoes with cold water and let them boil, uncovered. Lower the heat and cook them until soft, but not overcooked – about 20–25 minutes. Drain and let them cool, and then peel and dice before setting them aside.

In a small saucepan bring 750 ml/3 cups water to a boil, add the peas and cook them until soft but still bright green. To save time, place a steamer basket or a fitting colander on top or the pan while the peas are still cooking and steam the diced carrots, covered, until they're soft. Drain the peas and leave the vegetables to cool.

In a large salad bowl, combine the peas, carrots, potatoes and diced pickles. Pour over the mayonnaise and mix well to cover all the vegetables. Taste and add seasoning; since the mayonnaise recipe isn't overly strong, you might need to add more salt, pepper, vinegar or oil, according to taste.

RICE NOODLE SALAD WITH TOFU & HERBS

This light noodle salad uses a nuoc cham sauce that is similar to a Vietnamese pancake recipe; some of the herbs are the same too, so you could cook dishes like these on consecutive days to make the best use of the ingredients. Be sure to fry the tofu in the vegetable oil until its nicely crisp and golden.

450 g/1 lb. tofu, patted dry and sliced into 8 slices about 1 cm/½ in. thick
2 tablespoons soy sauce
1 garlic clove, crushed
1 stalk lemongrass, outer leaves removed and finely chopped
225 g/8 oz. rice vermicelli noodles
1 tablespoon vegetable oil
½ a red onion, halved and thinly sliced
150 g/5½ oz. cucumber, halved and thinly sliced
1 medium carrot, peeled and julienned or coarsely grated
handful of fresh mint and coriander/cilantro leaves, Thai basil (optional), plus extra to serve
2 tablespoons roasted cashews, plus extra to serve
2 limes, cut into wedges

FOR THE NUOC CHAM SAUCE
2 garlic cloves, peeled and very finely chopped
1 bird's eye chilli/chile, very finely chopped
3½ tablespoons rice vinegar
2 tablespoons freshly squeezed lime juice
3½ tablespoons vegetarian Thai 'fish' sauce
2 tablespoons pure maple syrup
3 tablespoons water

SERVES 4

Make the nuoc cham sauce by combining together the garlic, chilli/chile, rice wine vinegar and lime juice in a small bowl, and set aside for 5 minutes. Add in the rest of the ingredients, mix well and set aside.

In a bowl, combine together the sliced tofu with the fish sauce, garlic and lemongrass and set aside.

Cook the noodles according to the packet instructions, usually by covering them with boiling water for about 6 minutes to soften, then rinsing with cold water and draining.

Heat a frying pan/skillet over a high heat, add in the vegetable oil and when extremely hot add the tofu. Stir-fry for a few minutes until cooked through. Remove and leave to one side.

In a large bowl combine together the noodles, red onion, cucumber, carrot, beef, herbs, nuts and the sauce. Thoroughly mix together and serve in bowls with the lime wedges and remaining herbs and nuts sprinkled on top.

WARM CURRIED LENTIL & MANGO SALAD WITH TOFU & SPICED DRESSING

This mildly spiced and fresh-tasting salad with mango also has plenty of nutty taste and texture from lentils and cashews. It is perfect served with fried marinated tofu on the side. The salad base itself keeps well so can be made in advance, allowing the flavours to develop.

400-g/14-oz. can green lentils
2 sticks/stalks celery, finely sliced
2 carrots, grated/shredded
50 g/heaped 1/3 cup cashews, toasted
1/2 mango, cut in half and sliced lengthways
finely grated zest of 1/2 lime
1 tablespoon vegetable oil
200 g/7 oz. tofu, sliced
handful of freshly chopped mint or coriander/cilantro leaves
lime wedges, to serve

FOR THE SPICED DRESSING
4 tablespoons vegetable oil
1 shallot, finely chopped
1/2 teaspoon mustard seeds
1 teaspoon garam masala
1/2 teaspoon turmeric
pinch of dried chilli/hot red pepper flakes
1 garlic clove, crushed
1 teaspoon sugar
1 tablespoon white wine vinegar
50 g/1/3 cup sultanas/golden raisins
1/2 fresh red chilli/chile, deseeded and finely diced

SERVES 2–4

To make the spiced dressing, heat half the oil in a small saucepan. Add the shallot and cook over low heat for 5 minutes, until it starts to soften but still has a slight bite and has not taken on any colour.

Add the remaining oil, mustard seeds, garam masala, turmeric, dried chilli/hot red pepper flakes, garlic and sugar, and cook for 2 minutes. Turn off the heat and add the vinegar, sultanas and fresh chilli/chile.

For the salad, put the lentils, celery, carrots, toasted cashews, mango and lime zest in a large bowl. Pour in the warm dressing, reserving about 2 tablespoons to serve, and stir until well combined and coated in the dressing.

To cook the tofu, heat the oil in a frying pan/skillet and fry the slices until golden on both sides, using tongs to turn half way through cooking.

Brush the tofu slices with the reserved dressing and serve on top of the salad. Finish the salad with fresh mint or coriander/cilantro, and serve with lime wedges on the side for squeezing.

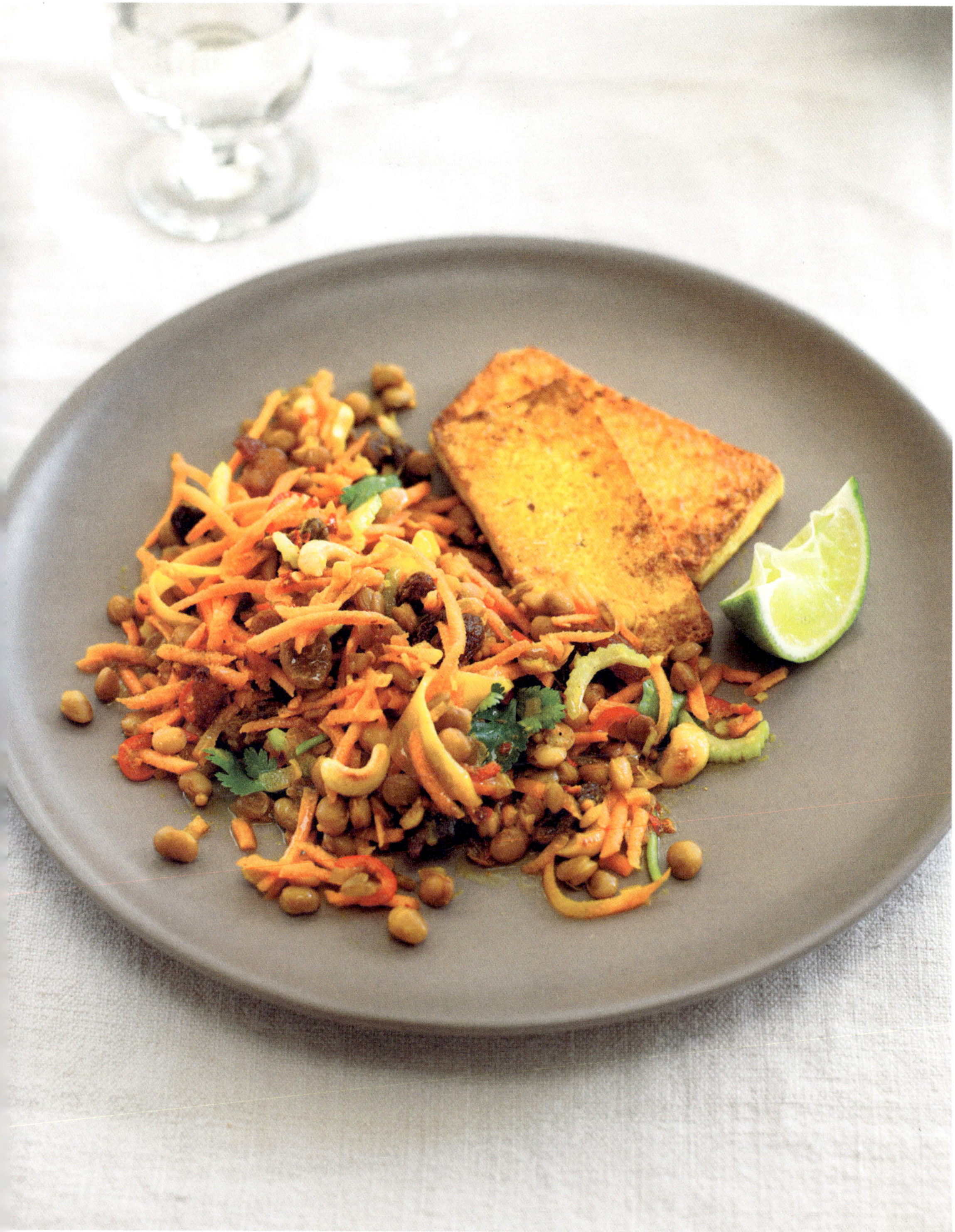

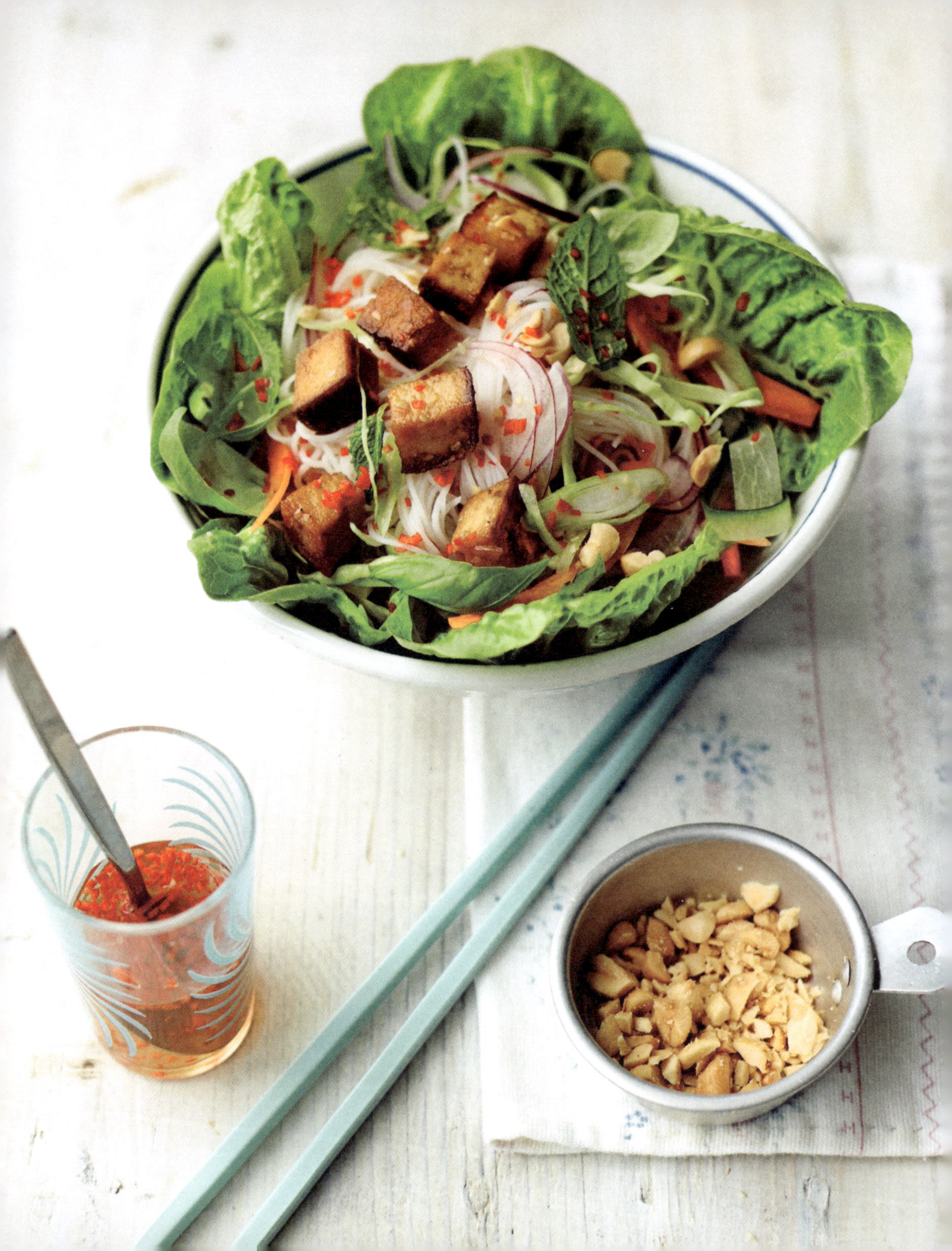

RICE NOODLE & SMOKED TOFU SALAD

The ingredients for this Asian main-meal salad may look on the long side, but it's very easy to prepare and can be made the night before if you are wanting to transport it as a packed lunch. If making in advance, assemble the salad just before serving.

2 tablespoons coconut oil or sunflower oil
275 g/10 oz. smoked tofu, patted dry, and cut into bite-sized cubes
200 g/7 oz. rice vermicelli noodles
1 carrot, halved crossways and thinly sliced into thin strips
10-cm/4-in. piece cucumber, quartered lengthways, deseeded, and thinly sliced into strips
2 handfuls of shredded sweetheart/pointed cabbage
3 spring onions/scallions, thinly sliced
½ red onion, finely sliced
2 handfuls of freshly chopped mint leaves
2 handfuls of freshly torn basil leaves
1 Little Gem/Bibb lettuce, leaves separated
75 g/⅓ cup salted peanuts, roughly chopped

FOR THE DRESSING
5 tablespoons rice wine vinegar
4 teaspoons caster/superfine sugar
1 tablespoon soy sauce
1 red chilli/chile, deseeded and diced

SERVES 4

Heat the oil in a large frying pan/skillet over a medium heat and fry the tofu for 8-10 minutes, turning often, until golden and crisp. Drain on paper towels.

Meanwhile, prepare the noodles according to the packet instructions, then drain and refresh under cold running water and drain again. Transfer the noodles to a large bowl. Mix together all the ingredients for the dressing and pour over the noodles.

Add the carrot, cucumber, cabbage, spring onions/scallions, red onion and half the herbs to the noodles and toss until combined. Arrange the Little Gem/Bibb leaves on a large, flat serving plate and top with the noodle salad, smoked tofu, remaining herbs and peanuts.

WARM NOODLE & TOFU SALAD

This is a fascinating salad where several types of noodles – as well as cooked rice, potato and tofu – are arranged in serving bowls with a whole range of toppings laid on the table for guests to help themselves. It's a fun way to put together just what you want. Use one or as many different types of noodle as you prefer.

100 g/2 cups marinated and fried tofu (see page 8)
200 g/7 oz. egg, rice vermicelli, cellophane or rice stick noodles
100 g/½ cup plus 1 tablespoon basmati rice
1 teaspoon chilli/chili oil
100 g/4 oz. floury potatoes
125 g/about ¼ head iceberg/butter lettuce, thinly sliced
100 g/2 cups soft tofu, crumbled

FOR THE TOPPINGS
25 g/⅓ cup dried shrimp
25 g/⅓ cup chickpea/gram flour
125 ml/½ cup garlic oil
55 g/⅓ Baluchung mix
25 g/1½ tablespoons toasted ground rice
250 ml/1 cup sweet and sour chilli/chili sauce
2 limes, cut into wedges
handful fresh herbs, such as mint, coriander/cilantro and Thai basil

SERVES 4

Start by preparing the fried tofu and then the toppings, as necessary. Take the dried shrimp and, using a pestle and mortar or spice grinder, pound to a 'floss'. Set aside. Toast the chickpea/gram flour in a dry frying pan/skillet set over a medium heat for 2–3 minutes. Set aside. Arrange everything in separate bowls on a tray in the middle of the table.

Prepare the noodles. Cook the egg noodles in a pan of boiling water for 3–4 minutes until al dente. Drain, rinse under cold water, drain again and dry thoroughly with a clean kitchen cloth. Soak the remaining noodles in a bowlful of hot water for 20–30 minutes until al dente. Drain well and dry thoroughly.

Cook the basmati rice according to packet instructions. Transfer to a bowl, stir in the chilli/chili oil and set aside until cold.

Cook the potatoes in a pan of boiling water set over a medium heat for 10–12 minutes, until tender. Leave to cool completely before cutting into cubes.

Set aside in a large mixing bowl.

To serve, spoon the noodles, rice, potatoes and marinated and fried tofu into serving bowls and top each one with some shredded lettuce and soft tofu. Then everyone can help themselves to the different toppings as wished.

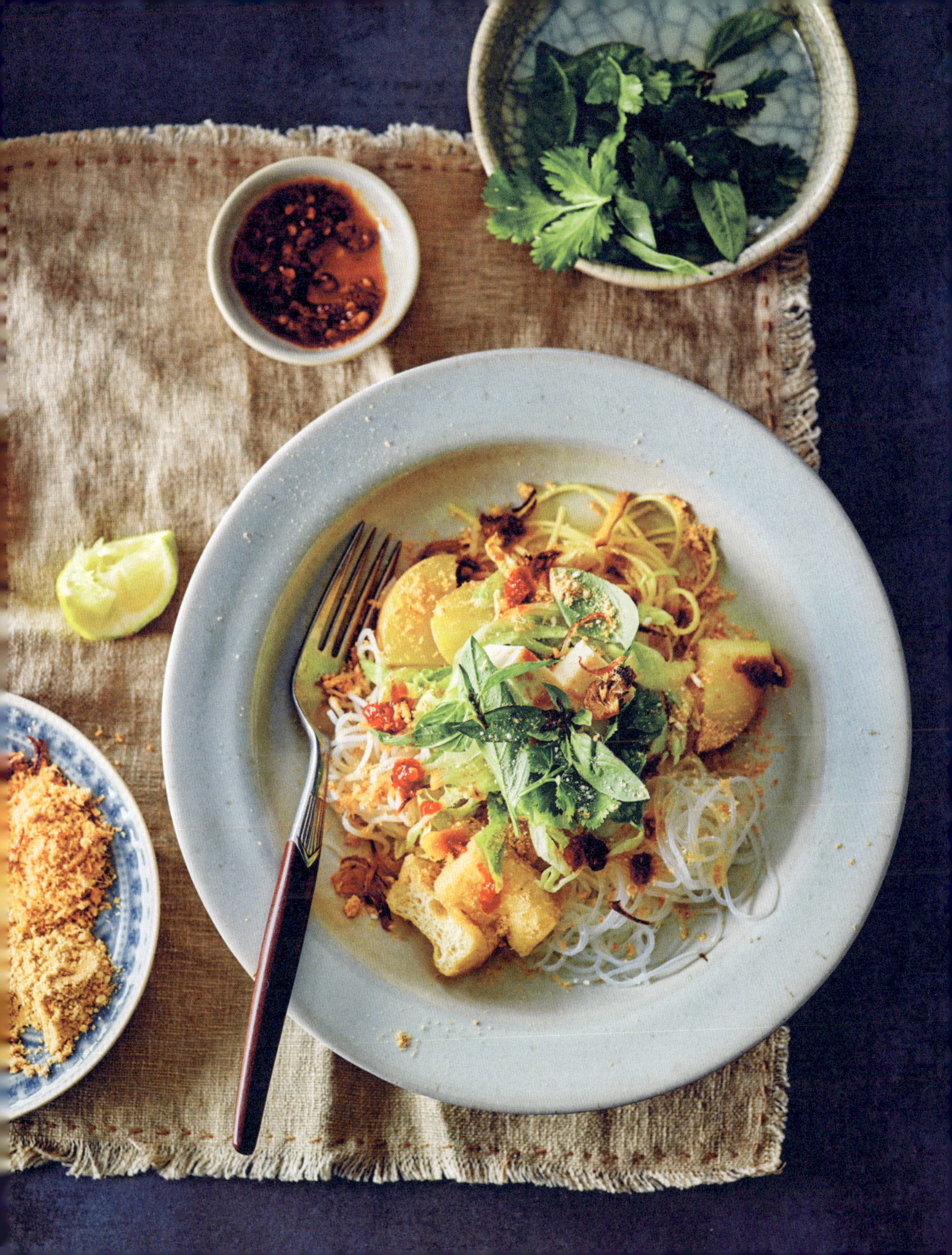

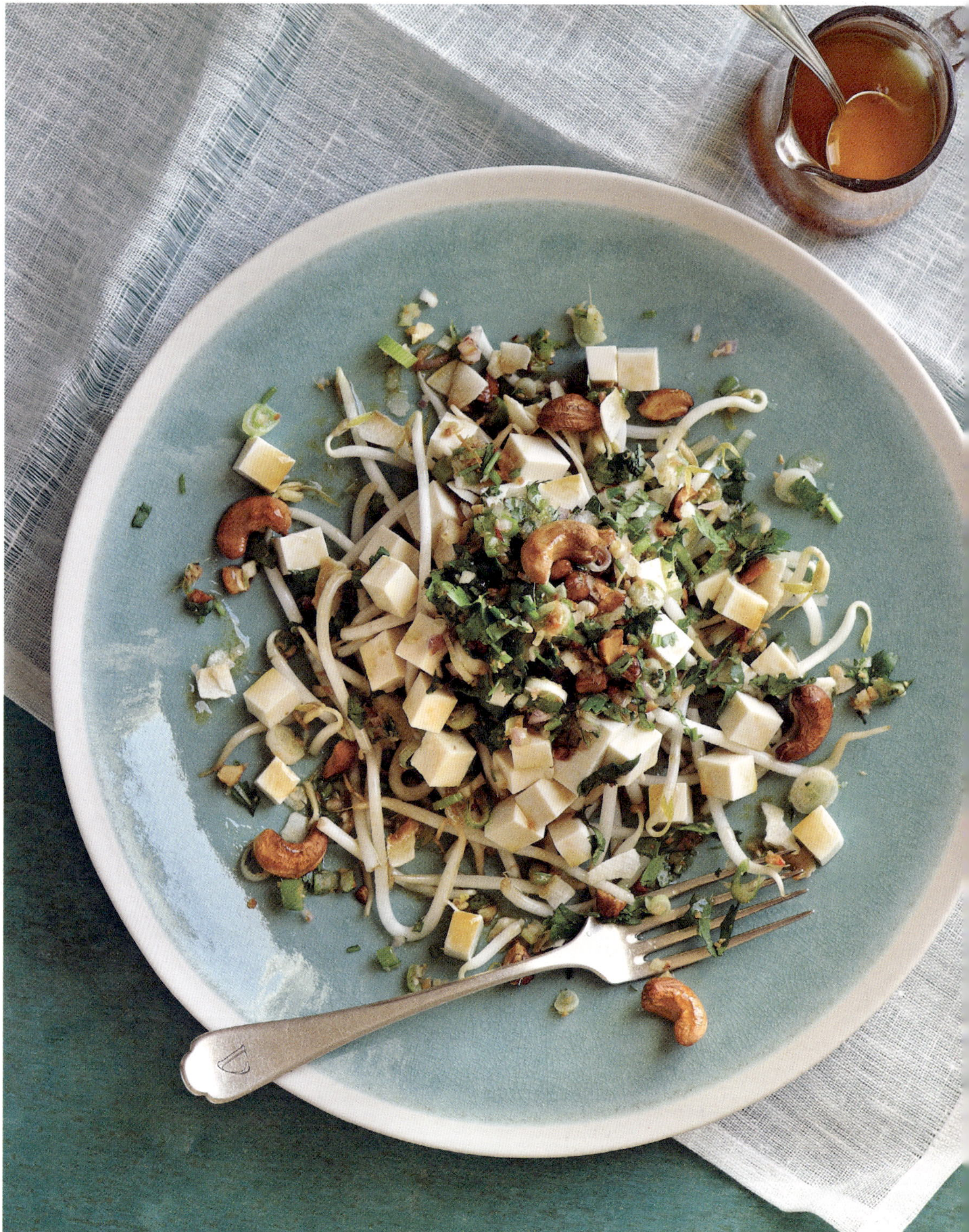

THAI-STYLE SALAD WITH TOFU & CASHEWS

Hot, sweet and sour are the key flavours of a good dish from Thailand and are all present here in this crisp and crunchy tofu salad.

small bunch of fresh coriander/cilantro
bunch of spring onions/scallions, finely chopped
1 stalk fresh lemon grass, finely chopped
2 red Birdseye chillies/chiles, deseeded and finely chopped
2 shallots, finely chopped
50 g/2 oz. fresh galangal (or 30 g/1 oz. fresh ginger), peeled and grated
50 g/1 cup toasted coconut slices
grated zest of 1 lime
200 g/3½ cups beansprouts
75 g/⅔ cup roasted cashew nuts, roughly chopped
200 g/1½ cups cubed firm tofu

FOR THE DRESSING
100 ml/⅓ cup vegetable oil
30 ml/2 tablespoons sesame oil
seeds of 2 red Birdseye chillies/chiles
2 teaspoons palm sugar/jaggery
freshly squeezed juice of 1 lime

SERVES 4

Make the salad dressing by putting all the dressing ingredients in a sealed bottle or jar and shaking vigorously until the sugar is dissolved. Set aside.

Finely chop the coriander/cilantro stalks, setting the leaves aside. Toss with the spring onions/scallions, lemon grass, chillies/chiles and shallots in a large mixing bowl. Add the galangal or ginger, then add the lime zest and half of the cashews.

To serve, divide half of the beansprouts between four plates. Arrange the tofu on top. Mix the remaining beansprouts with the other salad ingredients and pile on top of the tofu. Dress generously with the salad dressing and finish with a sprinkle of coriander/cilantro leaves and the remaining cashew nuts.

EGG NOODLE, BLACK CLOUD EAR FUNGUS & TOFU SALAD

The black cloud ear fungus mushrooms used here add a delightful crunch to this Chinese-style tofu salad. You can use plain tofu if you prefer, but the slight smokiness from marinated tofu works very well, too. Different flavours of tofu can be found in most large supermarkets or health food stores, so try out a few varieties to see which you like best.

15 g/1 cup dried black cloud ear fungus
200 g/7 oz. fresh egg noodles
½ cucumber, peeled
1 large carrot
150 g/1 cup plus 1 tablespoon marinated tofu, thinly sliced
4 spring onions/scallions, trimmed and thinly sliced
100 g/1⅔ cups Chinese cabbage, sliced
small handful each of fresh mint and coriander/cilantro
1 tablespoon sesame seeds, toasted

FOR THE DRESSING
2 tablespoons light soy sauce
2 tablespoons brown rice vinegar
1 tablespoon caster/granulated sugar
1 teaspoon sesame oil
1 teaspoon chilli/chili oil

SERVES 4

Put the black cloud ear fungus in a large mixing bowl, cover with boiling water and soak for 20 minutes until softened. Drain well, pat dry with paper towels and slice thinly, discarding any tough stalks. Set aside.

Meanwhile, cook the noodles by plunging them into a saucepan of boiling water. Return to the boil and simmer for 2–3 minutes until al dente. Drain and immediately refresh under cold water before draining again. Dry using a clean kitchen cloth and set aside.

Cut the cucumber and carrot into thin strips and place in a large mixing bowl.

Add the black cloud ear fungus, tofu, spring onions/scallions, cabbage and herbs and toss well.

To make the dressing, whisk all the ingredients together in a small bowl until the sugar is dissolved.

Stir the noodles into the salad, add the dressing and toss well until evenly combined. Serve in bowls, sprinkled with the toasted sesame seeds.

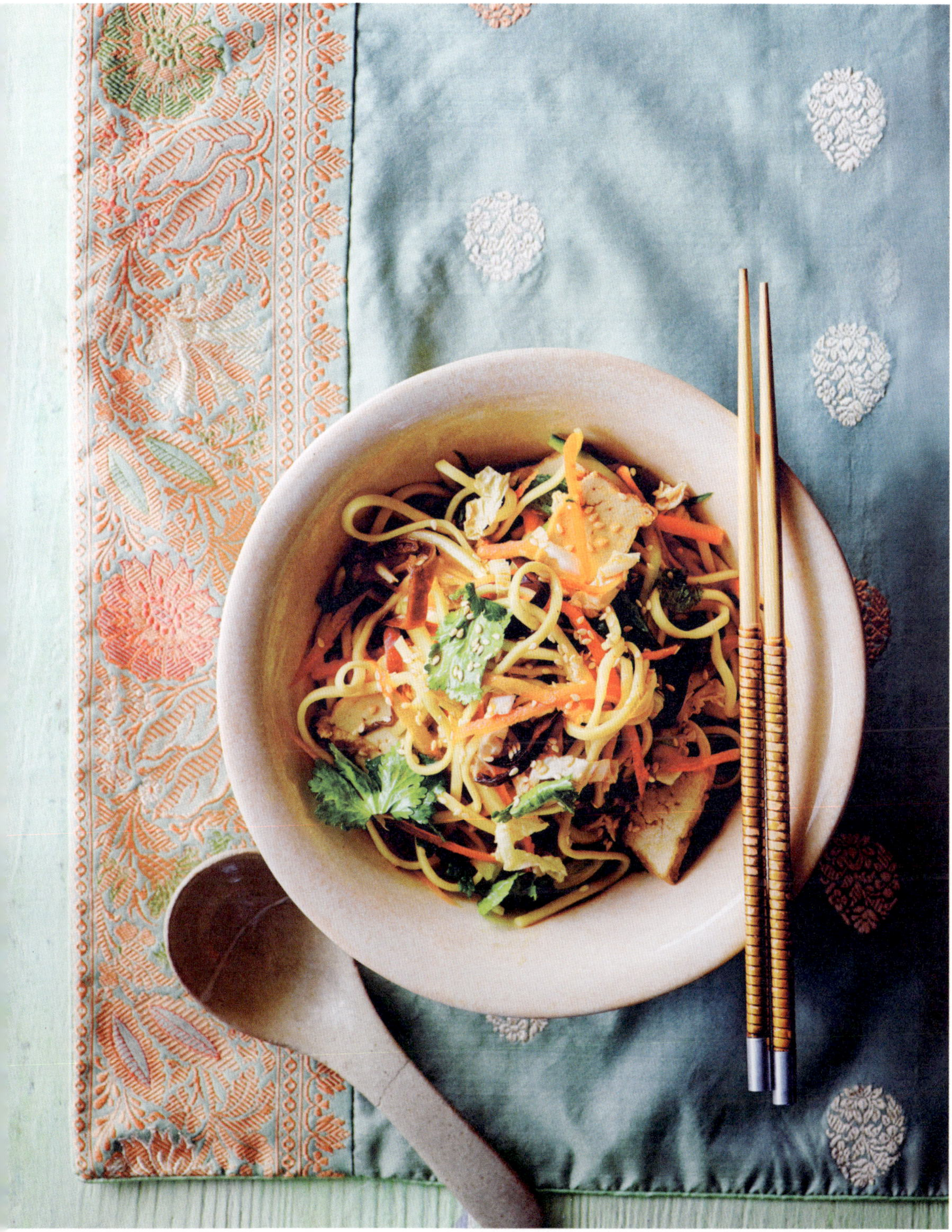

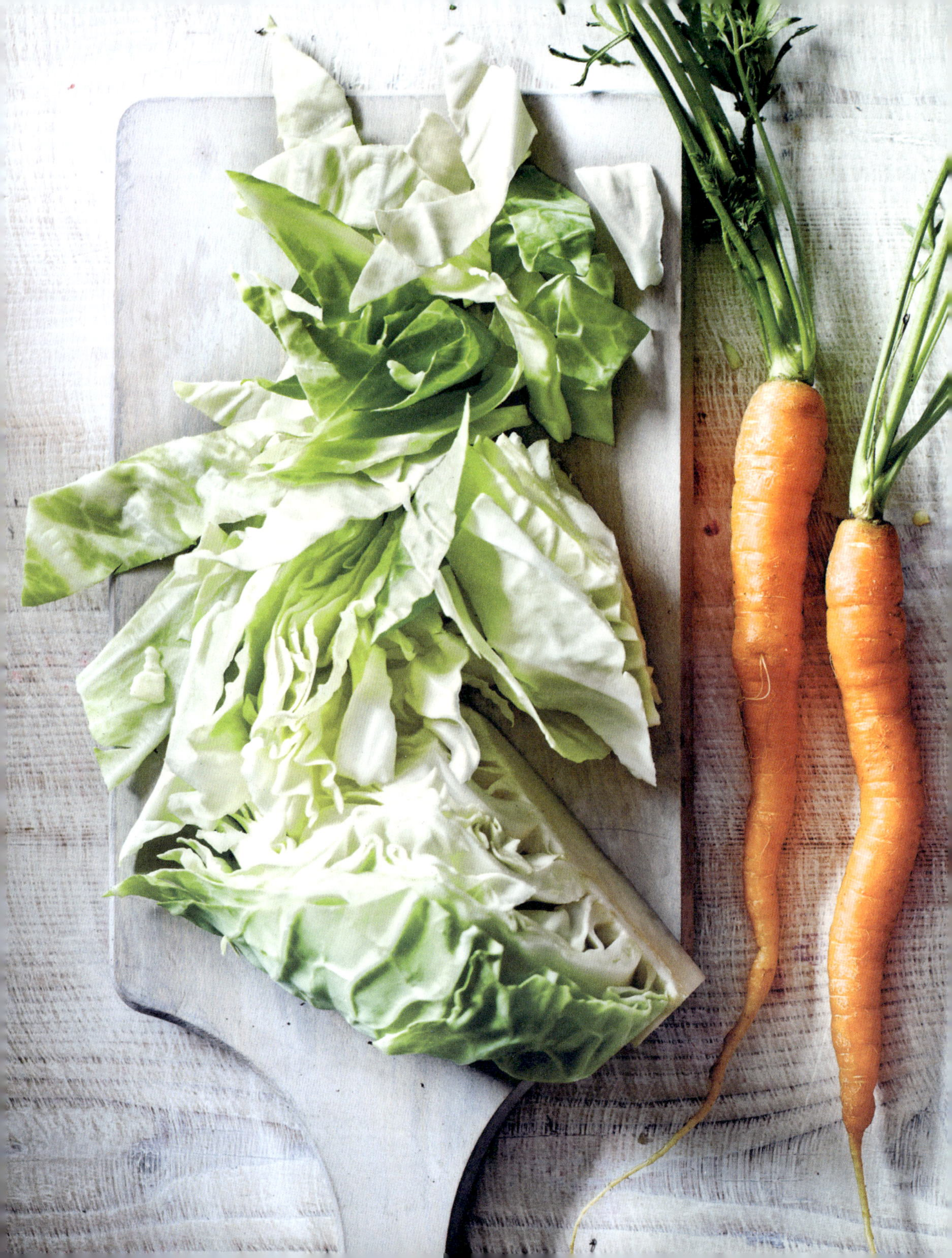

SOUPS, NOODLE BOWLS & stews

THAI SOUP WITH TAHINI & TOFU

If you want to try something different to peanut butter in your Asian cooking, substitute with tahini, and discover great results! Tahini adds thickness, creaminess and taste to the stock and is delicious in combination with plenty of crunchy veggies and the soft bite of tofu.

1 carrot
1 red (bell) pepper, deseeded
3 tablespoons virgin coconut oil
1 onion, chopped
3 tablespoons peeled and finely chopped fresh ginger
160 g/1 cup cubed tofu
1 red chilli/chile, deseeded and thinly sliced, or ½ teaspoon chilli/chili powder
4 tablespoons tamari soy sauce, plus extra to taste
1.2 litres/5 cups boiling water
180 g/4 cups dried flat rice noodles
2–4 tablespoons tahini
2 tablespoons rice or apple cider vinegar
2 tablespoons agave syrup or demerara/turbinado sugar
2 handfuls of greens (spinach, chard, kale, etc.), chopped
2 garlic cloves, thinly chopped
2 spring onions/scallions, finely sliced
2 teaspoons freshly squeezed lemon juice
4 tablespoons salted peanuts or cashews, chopped
salt, to season

SERVES 2

Slice the carrot and (bell) pepper into thick matchsticks. Heat the coconut oil in a heavy-bottomed saucepan and sauté the onion, carrot and (bell) pepper with the ginger, adding a pinch of salt. Add the tofu, chilli/chile slices or chilli/chili powder and tamari and cook until browned.

Add the boiling water and the dried rice noodles and bring to the boil. Whisk in the tahini, vinegar and syrup or sugar, stir well and cook over a medium heat for a couple of minutes. Add the chopped greens and cook for another minute or two, making sure the noodles do not overcook.

Remove from the heat and add the chopped garlic, spring onions/scallions, extra tamari, the lemon juice and salt to season. Divide between two bowls, sprinkle with chopped nuts and dig in. Chopsticks and slurping are mandatory!

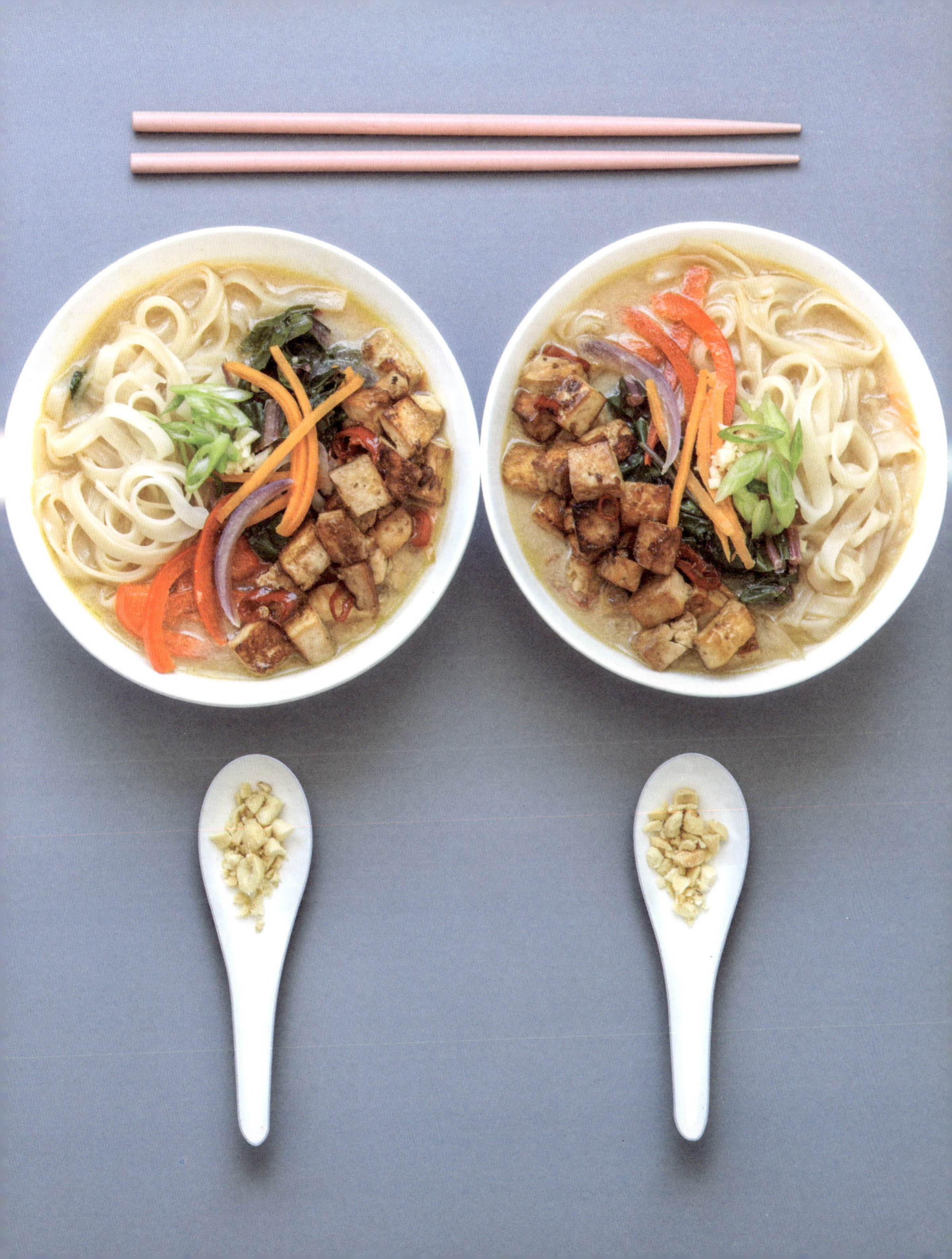

CREAMY COURGETTE & TOFU SOUP

Here is a basic but healthy green recipe for a creamy tofu-based soup, which makes a nice change from typical stock-based ones.

1 onion, finely chopped
1 courgette/zucchini, grated/shredded
1 tablespoon rapeseed oil
1 litre/4 cups vegetable stock
large handful of freshly chopped flat-leaf parsley
250 ml/1 cup soft tofu (or milk, or half and half)
salt and freshly ground black pepper, to season

MAKES 4–6 SERVINGS

Combine the courgette/zucchini, onion and oil in a large saucepan and cook for 3–5 minutes, until soft. Season lightly.

Add the stock and parsley and simmer for 15–20 minutes, until the vegetables are tender. Stir in the tofu and cook to warm through. Taste and adjust the seasoning. Serve immediately.

MAGICAL MISO SOUP

Miso paste is a traditional Japanese seasoning – a fermented soy bean paste, which is also a probiotic that can help boost your overall gut health. For all the umami lovers out there, this is a must-try for a wonderful savoury hit!

220 g/7 oz. firm tofu
1 litre/4 cups vegan dashi (see Note)
4 tablespoons dark miso paste
1 tablespoon dried seaweed
2 spring onions/scallions, thinly sliced

SERVES 2

First, drain the tofu and wrap in a few layers of paper towels. Put something heavy on top to help press out any excess water.

Meanwhile, very gently heat the dashi in a saucepan over low heat – you don't want it to boil! Once it's warm, mix a few tablespoons of the stock into the miso paste in a large mixing bowl. Once smooth, pour it back into the pan with the remaining dashi and stir together.

Unwrap the tofu and chop or break into pieces. Add the seaweed, tofu and spring onions/scallions to the pan. Heat gently until hot but not boiling. Serve hot.

Note Various varieties of Dashi (Japanese stock) are readily available in Asian or health food stores. However some versions contain fish products, such as bonito flakes, so read packaging carefully and choose a vegan or vegetarian brand, as preferred.

HEALING MISO SOUP WITH TOFU

If you've never had soup for breakfast, you should try treating yourself with a bowl of hot miso soup like this one. In Japan, miso soup is traditionally served for breakfast, accompanied by rice and pickled vegetables. Don't forget that you can combine different kinds of miso in the same soup. Or, in the warmer weather, you may want to try substituting darker miso pastes with the milder sweet white miso.

7-cm/3-in. piece dried wakame (seaweed)
2-cm/1-in. piece fresh ginger
4 spring onions/scallions
110 gc cup tofu
2 tablespoons sesame oil
4 garlic cloves, crushed
pinch of salt
540 ml/2¼ cups hot water
1–2 tablespoons barley or rice miso
2 tablespoons freshly chopped flat-leaf parsley
freshly squeezed juice of ½ lemon

SERVES 2

Soak the wakame in a bowl with 120 ml/½ cup cold water until soft. Drain, cut into small pieces and set aside. Peel the fresh ginger and finely mince half of it. Finely grate the other half in a small bowl and keep for later. Chop the spring onions/scallions and cut the tofu into small cubes.

In a frying pan/skillet, sauté the white part of the spring onions/scallions for 1 minute in the sesame oil, then add the garlic, ginger and salt. Sauté a little longer, pour in 480 ml/2 cups of the hot water, add the tofu and set-aside wakame and cover. Bring to the boil, then lower the heat and simmer for 4 minutes. Remove from the heat.

Pour the remaining hot water into a small bowl. Add the miso and purée really well with a fork, until completely dissolved. Pour back, cover and let sit for 2–3 minutes. Take the grated ginger in your hand and squeeze it to release the juice directly into the hot soup. Discard the remaining ginger pulp. Add the chopped spring onion/scallion greens, parsley and lemon juice and serve immediately.

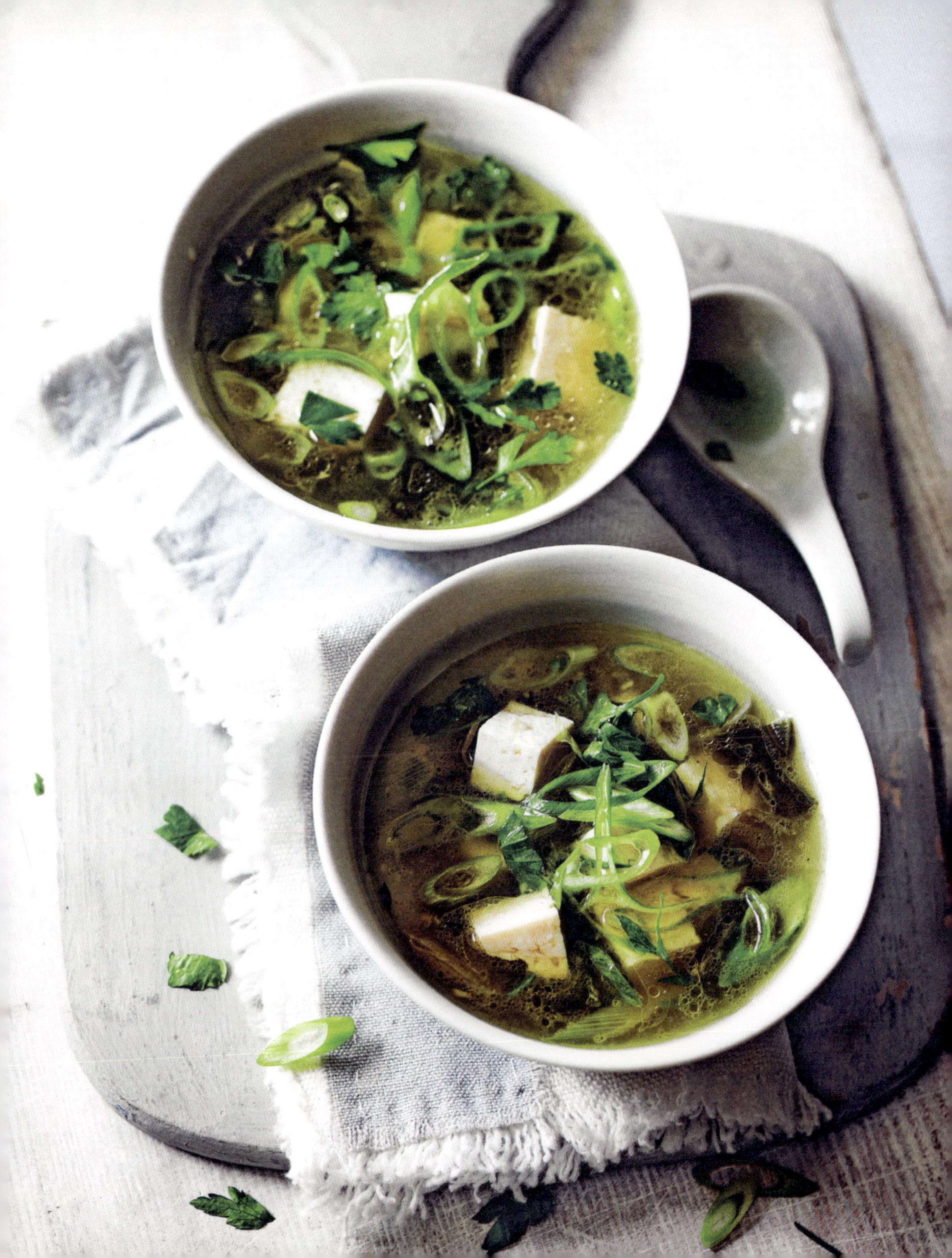

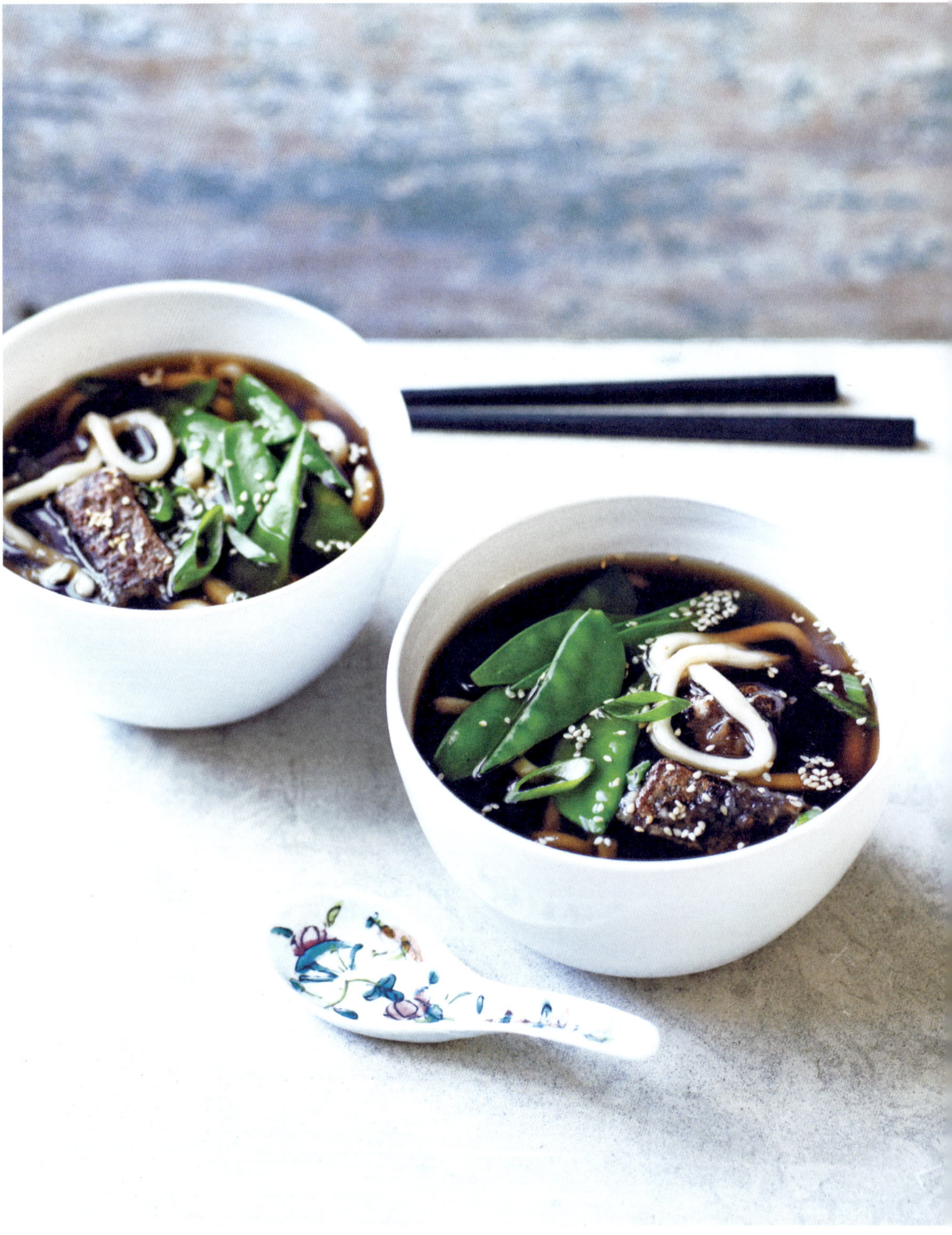

UDON NOODLE SOUP WITH CRISPY TOFU

This is one of those simple, comforting and totally delicious Japanese noodle soups that you could make and eat time after time. If you're pushed for time you don't even have to bother leave the tofu for half an hour, simply marinate it briefly before frying. Good-quality Japanese udon noodles are available in most supermarkets; they are made with wheat flour, so if you are avoiding wheat, use rice noodles instead.

200 g/6½ oz. firm tofu
5 tablespoons tamari or dark soy sauce
3 tablespoons mirin
2 tablespoons coconut palm sugar
salt, to season
200 g/6½ oz. mangetout/snow peas
400 g/14 oz. udon noodles or rice noodles
1.5 litres/quarts vegetarian or vegan dashi (see Note on page 69)
5-cm/2-in. piece of fresh ginger, peeled and cut into chunks
sunflower oil
2 spring onions/scallions, sliced
sesame seeds, to serve

SERVES 4

Drain and wrap the tofu in a paper towels and very gently squeeze to remove excess water. Remove the towels and slice into 16 pieces of equal size.

In a wide bowl, combine together the tamari or dark soy sauce, mirin and coconut palm sugar. Add in the tofu, cover with the marinade and leave to infuse for 25 minutes.

Bring a pot of salted water to the boil, add in the mangetout/snow peas and cook for 2 minutes, then remove (reserving the water for the udon) and plunge into cold water.

Cook the udon noodles according to the packet instructions, then rinse under running cold water.

Remove the tofu from the marinade (reserve the marinade) and shake off any excess. Add the dashi and ginger to a small saucepan, almost bring to a boil and add in the reserved tofu marinade, then reduce the heat to a gentle simmer.

Place a frying pan/skillet over a medium-high heat, and add in 1 tablespoon of sunflower oil. When hot, add in the tofu and fry for 1 minute on each side until golden. Remove, drain and keep warm.

When ready to serve, add the udon and mange tout/snow peas to the stock until warmed through, then immediately ladle into bowls (avoiding the ginger), top with the tofu, spring onions/scallions and sesame seeds and serve.

SPICY MISO SOBA NOODLE SOUP WITH GINGER TERIYAKI TOFU

This dish is healthy and quick to prepare, plus full of punchy flavours. The perfect no-fuss meal for hungry people! Japanese cuisine tends to be mild on the whole, but this dish has a real kick. The chilli/chile will certainly lift your spirits and boost your energy on a cold day.

FOR THE GINGER TERIYAKI TOFU
200 g/7 oz. firm tofu
1 tablespoon vegetable oil
1 teaspoon peeled and very finely chopped fresh ginger
2 tablespoons soy sauce
2 tablespoons mirin

FOR THE NOODLE SOUP
1 tablespoon vegetable oil
2 garlic cloves, peeled and finely chopped
2 spring onions/scallions, whites only, finely chopped
800 ml/3$\frac{1}{3}$ cups vegetarian or vegan dashi (see Note on page 69)
160 g/5$\frac{1}{2}$ oz. dried soba (buckwheat) noodles
3 tablespoons red miso
1 tablespoon gochujang (Korean red chilli/chili paste)

TO SERVE (OPTIONAL)
2 tablespoons dried wakame seaweed, soaked in water to reconstitute, then drained
1 tablespoon toasted mixed black and white sesame seeds
dried red chilli/chile strips
1 spring onion/scallion, thinly sliced

SERVES 2

For the ginger teriyaki tofu, wrap the tofu in paper towels and place under a heavy kitchen utensil for 30 minutes to remove excess water.

Dice the tofu into cubes. In a medium frying pan/skillet, heat the vegetable oil over a medium heat and fry the tofu until browned on all sides. Add the ginger and stir in. Add the soy sauce and mirin and fry for 2 minutes until the tofu becomes caramelized. Set aside.

For the noodle soup, put the vegetable oil in a saucepan over a medium heat. Add the garlic and spring onions/scallions and fry for 1 minute to infuse some flavour into the oil. Add the dashi and bring to the boil. Once boiling, turn down the heat and simmer for 5 minutes.

Meanwhile, cook the dried soba (buckwheat) noodles in a separate pan of boiling water following the packet instructions. Drain well and divide between serving bowls.

Combine the red miso and gochujang in a cup and stir in a ladleful of the dashi until dissolved. Add the miso mixture back into the saucepan with the soup and stir well to combine. Heat through for another minute, if needed, before serving.

Pour the hot miso soup over the cooked soba (buckwheat) noodles in the serving bowls, then top with the ginger teriyaki tofu, wakame, sesame seeds, dried chilli/chile strips and spring onion/scallion, if liked.

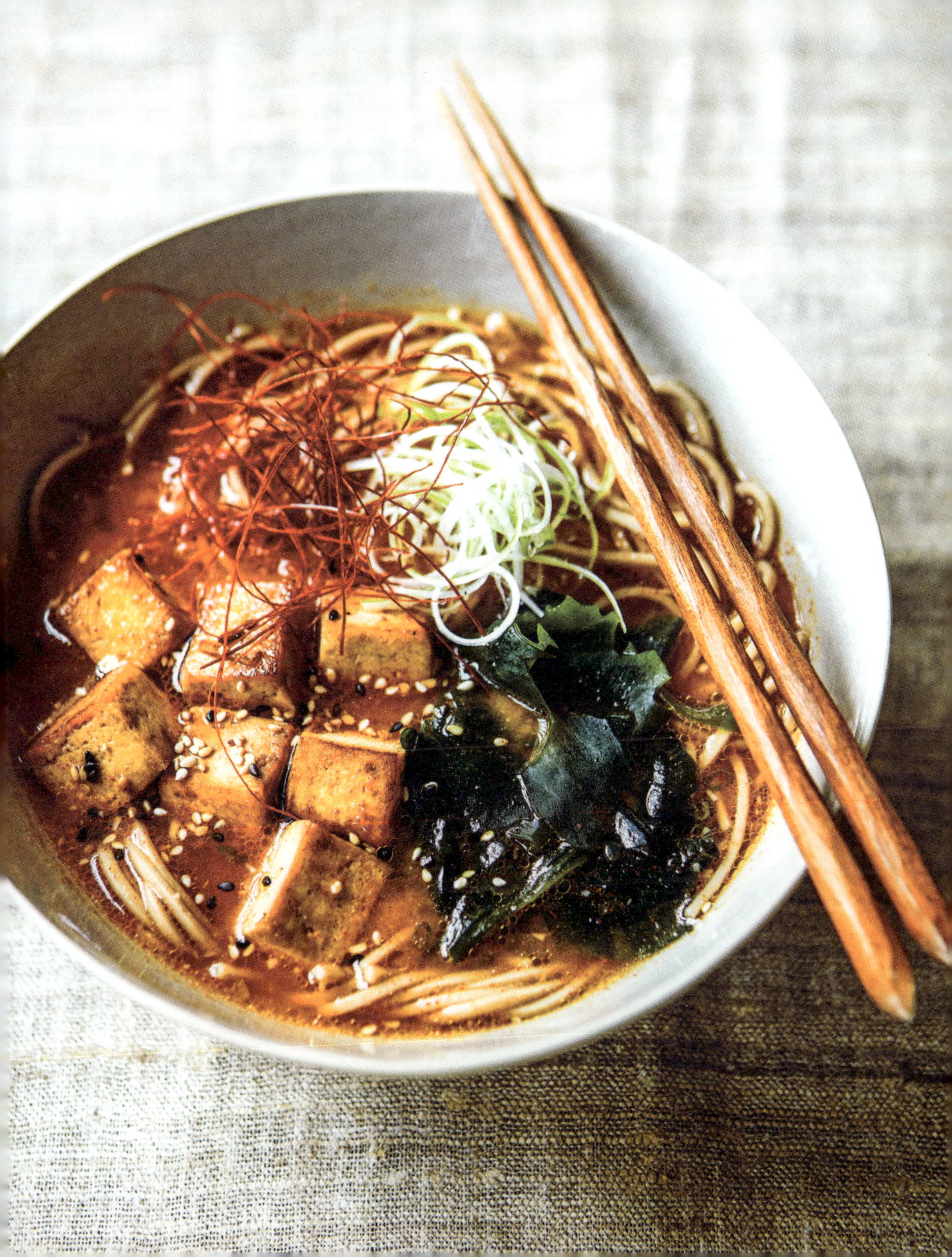

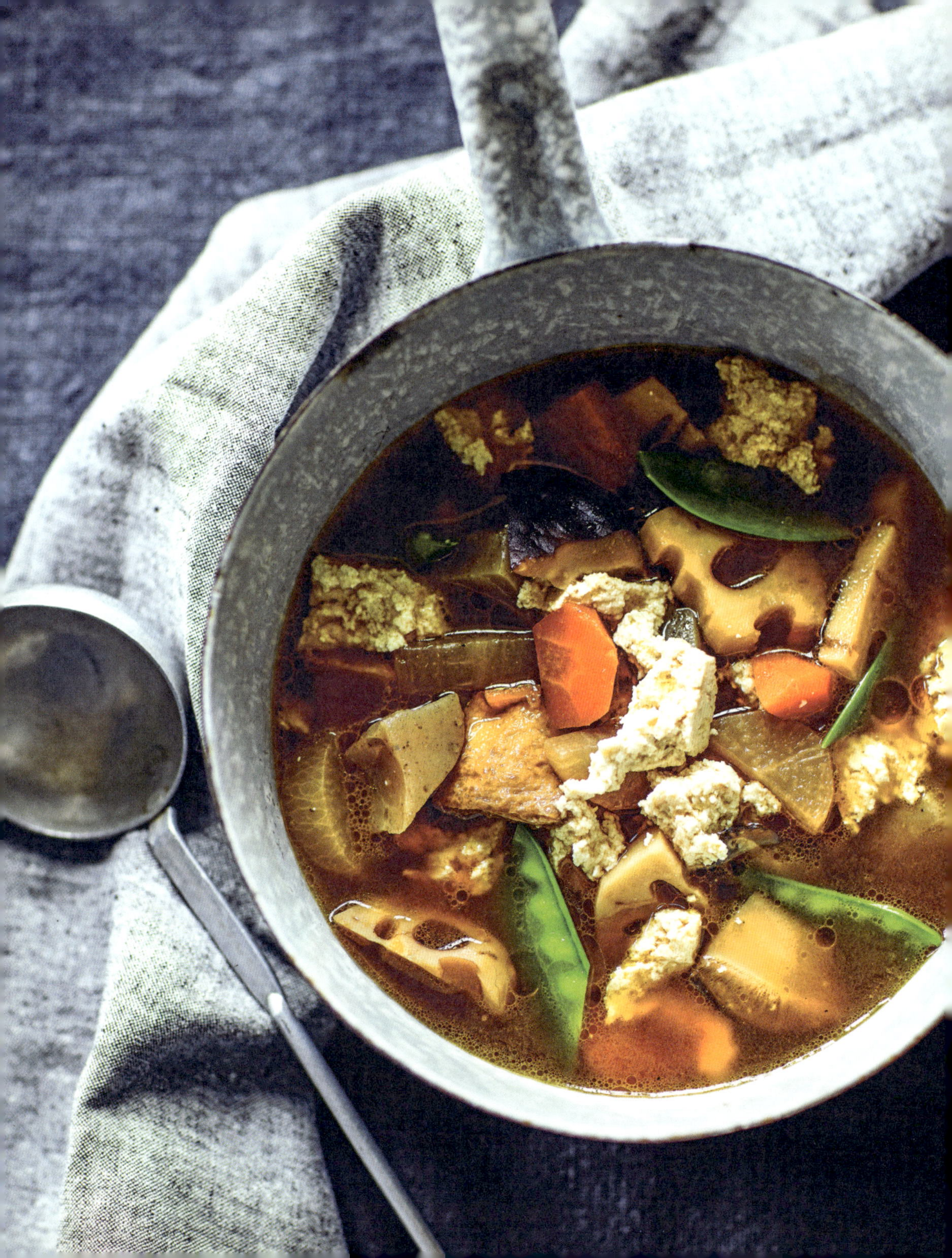

JAPANESE BUDDHIST VEGETABLE & TOFU SOUP

This recipe is a great example of Shojin Ryori (Buddhist temple cuisine). Like all Shojin Ryori dishes, this is vegan, but if you're cooking for someone who isn't a fan of the 'v' word, don't let this deter you from serving this! It is a really hearty, comforting soup on a wintry day, but it won't weigh on your stomach for hours. The story of goes that a young monk dropped a fresh block of tofu onto the kitchen floor. The floor was clean, so they added the smashed tofu into the soup rather than waste it. This became the same recipe that you see today!

½ konnyaku block, about 100 g/3½ oz.
1 teaspoon sea salt
1½ tablespoons toasted sesame oil
1 carrot, peeled and chopped into rounds
10-cm/4-in. renkon (lotus root), peeled and chopped into bite-sized pieces
100 g/3½ oz. sweet potato, peeled and chopped into bite-sized pieces
100 g/3½ oz. daikon radish, or turnip, peeled and chopped into bite-sized pieces
3 shiitake mushrooms, cut into bite-sized pieces
4 tablespoons soy sauce
800 ml/3⅓ cups vegetarian or vegan dashi (see Note on page 69)
2 tablespoons sake
200 g/7 oz. firm tofu
16 mangetout/snow peas, trimmed and cut in half diagonally

SERVES 4

Boil the konnyaku in water with the 1 teaspoon salt for 3 minutes to remove the smell. Drain and leave to cool, then cut into small pieces with a teaspoon to create an uneven surface, which will absorb more of the flavours. Set aside.

Add the toasted sesame oil to a large saucepan over a medium heat. Fry the chopped carrot, renkon (lotus root), sweet potato, daikon radish and konnyaku for 2 minutes. Stir in the shiitake and let the oil coat all the ingredients. Add 2 tablespoons of the soy sauce to season.

Pour in the dashi and bring to the boil with the lid on.

Once boiling, add the sake and the remaining 2 tablespoons of soy sauce. Turn down the heat, cover with the lid again and simmer for a final 20 minutes until the vegetables are tender and cooked through.

When ready to serve, crush up the tofu by hand and add with the mangetout/snow peas to the soup. Stir and bring to the boil again to serve hot.

TOFU & MUSHROOM CHINESE HOTPOT

Mushrooms and tofu have a natural affinity as ingredients, and they are combined here in a fresh vegetarian take on a classic Chinese hotpot. Serve with steamed rice or boiled noodles for lunch or supper.

400 g/14 oz. firm tofu
8 dried shiitake mushrooms
1 tablespoon cornflour/cornstarch
2 tablespoons vegetable oil
½ onion, chopped
1 leek, finely sliced
2.5-cm/1-in. piece of fresh ginger, peeled and finely chopped
1 garlic clove, chopped
¼ head of Chinese leaf/napa cabbage, roughly chopped
3 tablespoons rice wine or Amontillado sherry
a pinch of Chinese five spice powder
150 g/5 oz. assorted fresh mushrooms (oyster, shiitake, eryngii), large ones halved
1 tablespoon light soy sauce
a pinch of sugar
1 teaspoon sesame seed oil
salt, to season
spring onion/scallion, chopped, to garnish

SERVES 4

Wrap the tofu in paper towels and place a weighty item on top to squeeze out the excess moisture.

Soak the dried shiitake mushrooms in 200 ml/1 scant cup of hot water for 20 minutes. Strain through a fine-mesh sieve/strainer, reserving the soaking liquid. Trim and discard the tough stalks from the shiitake and cut them in half.

Cut the tofu into cubes and roll them in the cornflour/cornstarch to coat. Heat 1 tablespoon of the oil in a frying pan/skillet. Fry the tofu for 5 minutes over a medium-high heat, turning over during frying, until lightly browned on all sides.

Heat the remaining oil in a casserole dish or Dutch oven over a medium heat. Add the onion, leek, ginger and garlic and fry, stirring, for 2 minutes.

Add the Chinese leaf/napa cabbage and fry for a further 2 minutes. Mix in the rice wine or sherry and five spice powder and cook for 1 minute. Add the fried tofu, soaked shiitake and the fresh mushrooms.

Pour in the reserved shiitake soaking liquid, soy sauce and add the pinch of sugar. Bring to the boil. Cover and cook over a medium heat for 15 minutes.

Uncover and cook for 10 minutes, stirring gently now and then. Season with salt. Stir in the sesame seed oil. Serve straight away, garnished with chopped spring onion/scallion.

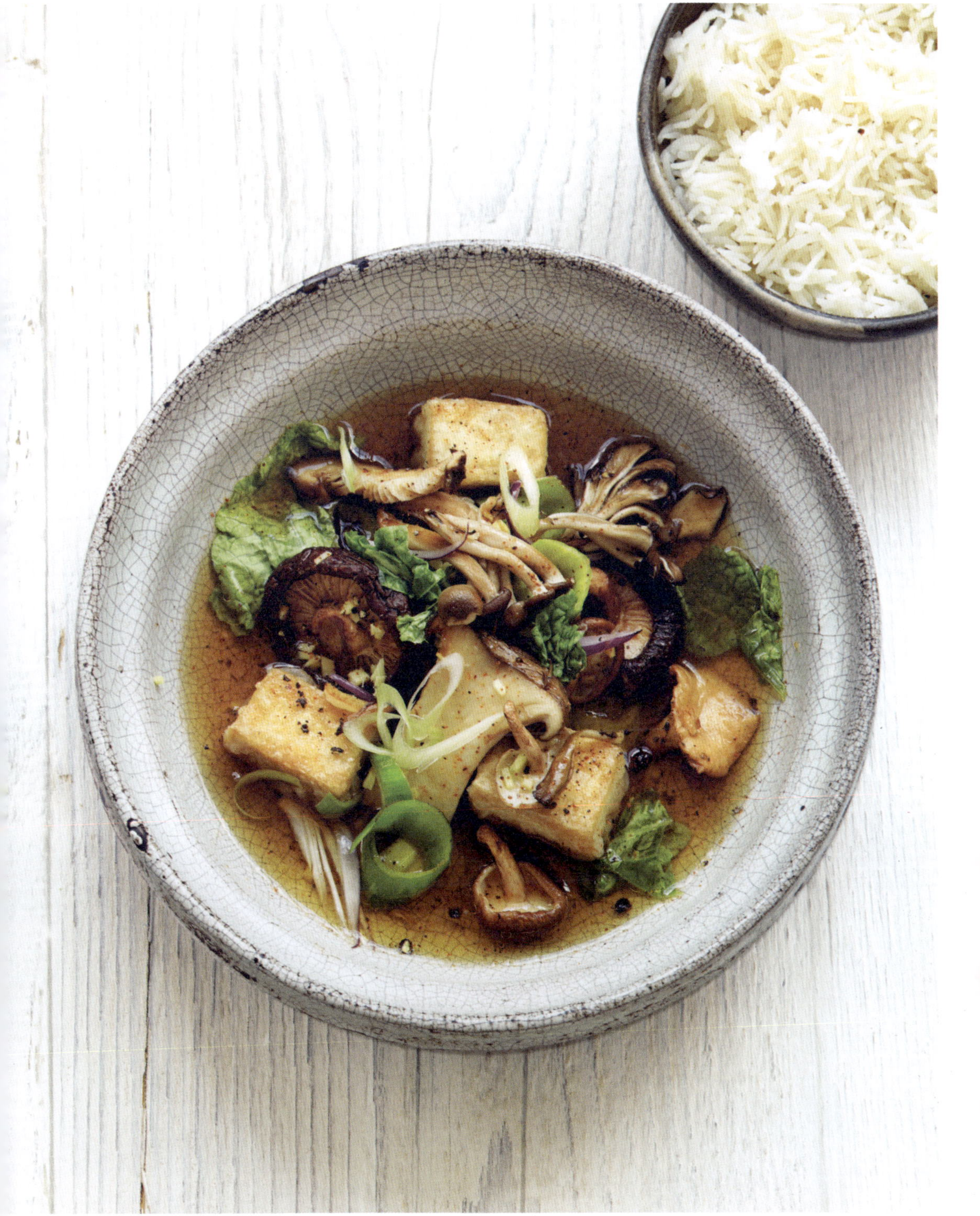

TOFU & MUSHROOM GOULASH

Nothing can beat a plate of this warming goulash on a chilly day to comfort and nourish both body and soul. You can serve it with potato gnocchi, brown rice, millet mash, potato mash or just plain polenta/cornmeal, as preferred. You'll need to marinate and fry the tofu cubes following the instructions on page 8, ahead of preparing this dish.

FOR THE TOFU
290 g/10 oz. tofu, cut into 2-cm/¾-in. cubes

FOR THE GOULASH
10 g/½ cup dried porcini mushrooms or other dried mushrooms
375 ml/1½ cups water
5 tablespoons sunflower or sesame oil
160 g/1¼ cups onions, diced
½ teaspoon sea salt
½ teaspoon ground dried rosemary
2 bay leaves
1 teaspoon sweet paprika
⅛–¼ teaspoon crushed black pepper or chilli powder
tamari, to taste
80 ml/⅓ cup cooking wine
1½ teaspoons kuzu, arrowroot powder or cornflour/cornstarch
2 tablespoons freshly chopped parsley or spring onion/scallion, to garnish
cooked brown rice, to serve

SERVES 2–3

To prepare the tofu, follow the instructions in the recipe on page 8, and for the 2 teaspoons of dry herbs or powdered spices of your choosing, add 1 teaspoon rosemary, ½ teaspoon sweet paprika and ½ teaspoon black pepper. Marinate and fry the tofu as instructed.

Meanwhile, soak the mushrooms in the water for 30 minutes. Drain them, but save the soaking water for later. Next, chop the mushrooms.

Heat the oil in a large frying pan/skillet and sauté the onions with the salt over a medium heat until softened. Add all the herbs and spices and the tamari and stir until everything is slightly browned. Add the mushrooms and stir for another 1–2 minutes. Pour in the wine and let it simmer for another minute. Now stir in the fried tofu cubes, and then add the soaking water and cover. Let the mixture boil, and then stir again, before lowering to a medium heat for 5–10 minutes.

At the end, dilute the kuzu, arrowroot powder or cornflour/cornstarch in a little cold water and add it to the goulash, stirring until it boils again. Serve over your choice of side, sprinkled with the chopped parsley or spring onion/scallion.

DEEP-FRIED TOFU IN TSUYU BROTH

These are little cubes of heaven when they enter the mouth: crispy on the outside, creamy on the inside, and with a dash of umami-rich sauce. The katakuriko gives the coating a distinctive soft, almost jelly-like texture when in contact with the tsuyu. And although it is deep-fried, it's hardly greasy as the coating is so thin. This can become seriously addictive. No wonder it is one of the most popular dishes ordered in Japanese izakaya bars. Everyone must still give this a try!

300 g/10½ oz. soft tofu

500 ml/2 cups plus 2 tablespoons vegetable oil

3 tablespoons katakuriko (potato starch) or cornflour/cornstarch

15 small red radishes (or 15-cm/6-in. white daikon radish), grated and excess juice drained

1 teaspoon peeled and grated fresh ginger, excess juice drained

1 tablespoon freshly chopped chives

FOR THE TSUYU SAUCE

200 ml/generous ¾ cup vegetarian or vegan dashi (see Note on page 69)

2 tablespoons light soy sauce

2 tablespoons mirin

SERVES 4 AS AN APPETIZER

Cut the tofu into four pieces, then wrap in paper towels and leave for 30 minutes to remove as much excess water as possible. Do not skip this step as it will ensure a creamy rather than watery texture on the inside of the tofu and a properly crispy outside.

To make the tsuyu sauce, heat the dashi, soy sauce and mirin in a saucepan until warmed through. Set aside and keep warm with the lid on until ready to serve.

Heat the vegetable oil in a medium-sized, deep frying pan/skillet to 180°C/350°F over a high heat. To check that the oil is ready, you can drop a few breadcrumbs into the oil. If they sizzle and float to the surface and sizzle, then it means the oil is ready. Reduce the heat to medium to maintain the temperature.

Coat all the sides of the tofu in katakuriko (potato starch) or cornflour/cornstarch. Gently put two pieces of tofu into the hot oil and fry for 1–2 minutes, turning once halfway through. The tofu won't turn golden because it is coated in the starch, but it should turn crispy on the outside. Remove with a slotted spoon and drain on paper towels while you cook the other two pieces of tofu.

Divide the warm tsuyu sauce between four serving bowls and then place a piece of tofu into each bowl. Top each piece of tofu with grated radish, ginger and freshly chopped chives.

TOFU YOTA

Yota is a typical Istrian stew, also popular in some parts of Slovenia and northern Italy. The main ingredients are borlotti beans and sauerkraut, which makes this a strong tasting and filling winter dish. An ingredient that is never omitted by Istrian nonnas is spare ribs, so for a vegan yota, a piece of smoked tofu is added instead, but at the end of cooking. Avoid adding all of the sauerkraut at once, but leave a third of the amount to add when the stew is ready, this way, you can benefit from the live cultures in the sauerkraut that are otherwise deactivated with cooking.

340 g/2 cups dried borlotti beans
3 dried bay leaves
1 small dried chilli
1 strip kombu seaweed (optional)
200 g/6½ oz. smoked tofu
2 small potatoes (around 210 g/ 7½ oz. total weight)
300 g/1½ cups sauerkraut
2 garlic cloves, crushed
2 tablespoons olive oil
1 teaspoon sweet paprika
½ teaspoon sea salt
1 vegetable stock/bouilllon cube
freshly ground black pepper, to season

SERVES 4

Soak the beans in 2.4 litres/10 cups water for 24 hours. Bring the beans to the boil in the soaking water, and then discard the water. Put the drained beans, bay leaves, chilli, kombu and 1.7 litres/7 cups of water in a large saucepan with a tight-fitting lid. Securely close the lid and cook for about 45 minutes, covered, over gentle heat until the beans are soft, adding a little extra water during cooking, if necessary.

Meanwhile, peel and cut potatoes into quarters and cut the tofu into small cubes.

Open the lid, remove the bay leaves, take out the kombu (if using), chop it and put it back into the pan. Add the potatoes, 200 g/1 cup of the sauerkraut and smoked tofu and cook covered for 20 further minutes. Take out the potatoes and press them through a potato ricer or mash them with a fork. Return to the pot. Add sweet paprika, freshly ground black pepper, the vegetable stock cube and salt and bring to the boil.

Turn off the heat and add the remaining 100 g/½ cup of sauerkraut, crushed garlic and olive oil. Taste and adjust the seasoning if necessary. The stew should be creamy and thick. If too dense, add a little more hot water. Ideally, yota should sit covered for at least 30 minutes before serving, but if you're in a hurry you can serve it immediately.

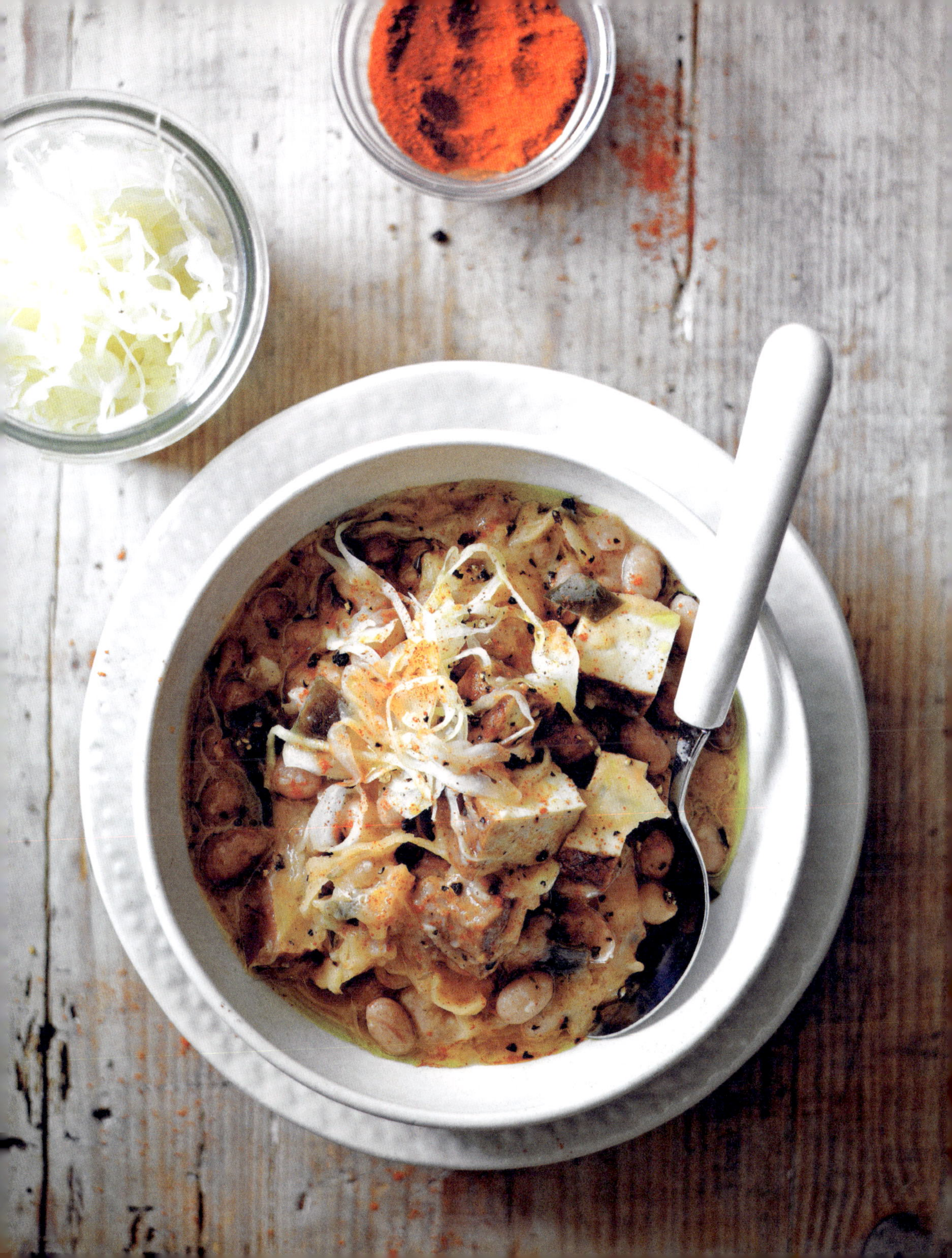

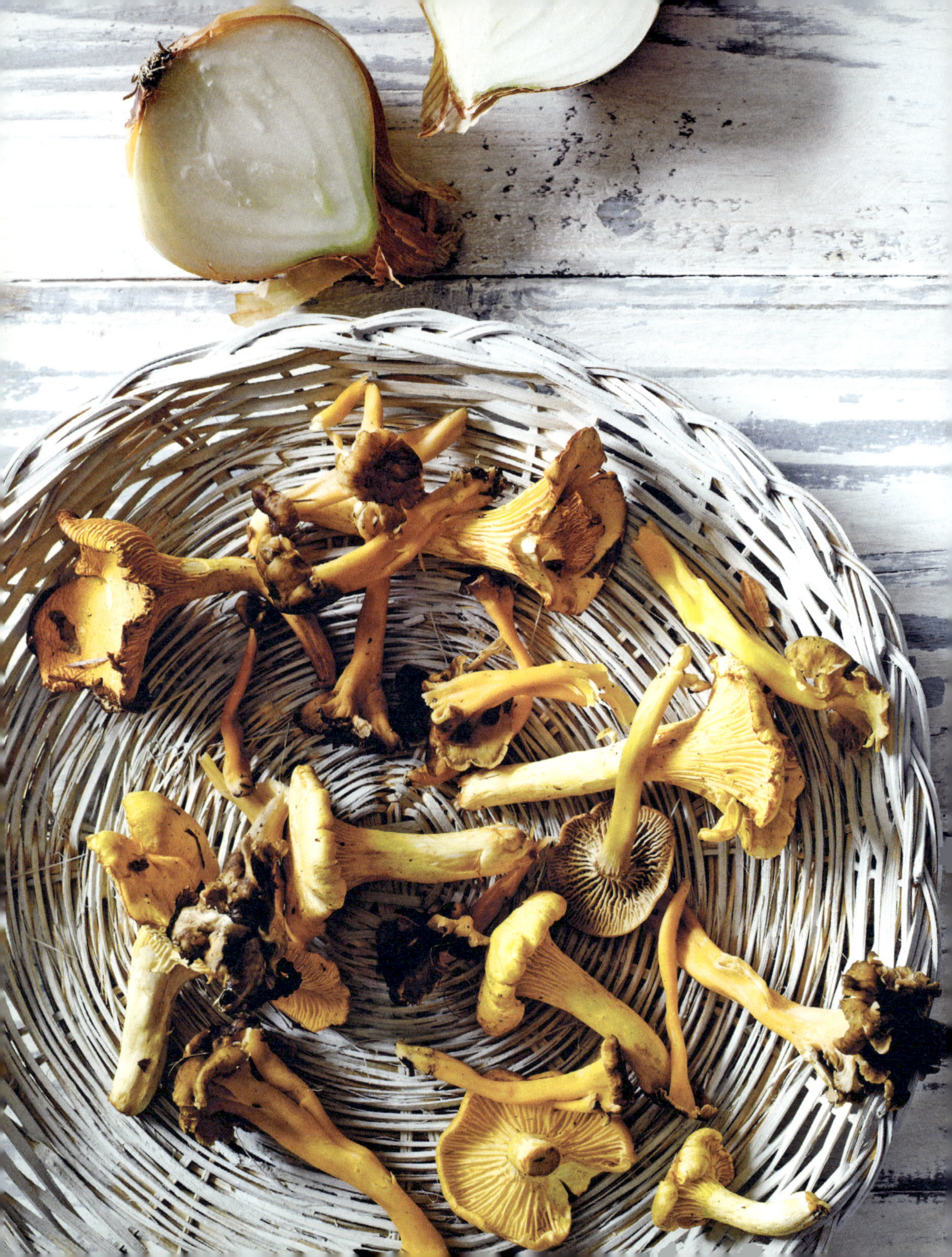

MAIN
Plates

SESAME-FULL TOFU QUICHE

This quiche can be kept in the fridge for a few days – perfect for packed lunches and picnics.

1 onion, chopped
2 garlic cloves, chopped
½ red (bell) pepper, deseeded and cubed
2 tablespoons light sesame oil
1 vegetable stock cube
¼ teaspoon ground turmeric
½ teaspoon smoked paprika
½ teaspoon dried oregano
420 g/2½ cups soft tofu, crumbled
60 g/¼ cup tahini
60 ml/¼ cup soya/soy or oat cream
2 tablespoons nutritional yeast
100 g/1 cup broccoli florets, steamed
2 tablespoons each unhulled sesame seeds and black sesame seeds

FOR THE PASTRY/CRUST
260 g/2 cups plain/all-purpose flour
90 g/⅔ cup finely ground yellow cornflour/cornstarch
1½ teaspoons baking powder
salt and freshly ground black pepper
180 g/1½ cups vegan spread
3 tablespoons unhulled sesame seeds
1 tablespoon rice or agave syrup

30-cm/12-in. loose-based tart pan

SERVES 4–6

Preheat the oven to 180°C/350°F/gas mark 4.

To make the pastry/crust, combine the flour, cornflour/cornstarch, baking powder and ¼ teaspoon salt in a food processor and pulse to mix. Add the vegan spread and sesame seeds and pulse 6–8 times, until the mixture resembles coarse meal, with pea-sized pieces of vegan spread. Add the syrup and 2 tablespoons ice-cold water and pulse again a couple of times. Only if necessary, add more ice-cold water, 1 tablespoon at a time, pulsing until the mixture just begins to clump together. If you pinch some of the crumbly dough and it holds together, it's ready. If the dough doesn't hold together, add a little more water and pulse again. Be careful not to add too much water as this would make the crust tough.

Place the dough in a mound on a clean surface.

Work the dough just enough to form a ball; do not overknead. Form a disc, wrap in clingfilm/plastic wrap and refrigerate for at least 1 hour, or up to 2 days. If you're in a hurry, chill the dough in the freezer for 20 minutes. Roll it out between two pieces of baking parchment about 3 cm/1¼ inches wider than the tart pan. Oil the pan. Using a rolling pin, transfer the dough over the pan and press in to cover the entire surface and the sides. Remove excess dough by pressing it outwards with your fingers and patch up any holes with leftover dough. Prick the base all over with a fork and bake in the preheated oven for 8–10 minutes, until just lightly puffed.

To make the filling, sauté the onion, garlic and red (bell) pepper in the sesame oil with a pinch of salt, until fragrant. Add the stock cube, spices and oregano and sauté until the cube dissolves and the spices start to sizzle. Add the crumbled tofu, tahini, cream, nutritional yeast (if using), broccoli and a pinch of black pepper, and stir well until combined. Taste and adjust the seasoning. Spread evenly over the lightly baked crust. Sprinkle with both types of sesame seeds and bake in the oven for about 30 minutes.

Cool slightly and carefully remove from the pan. Store leftovers in the fridge for up to 2 days. Reheat until hot in the oven.

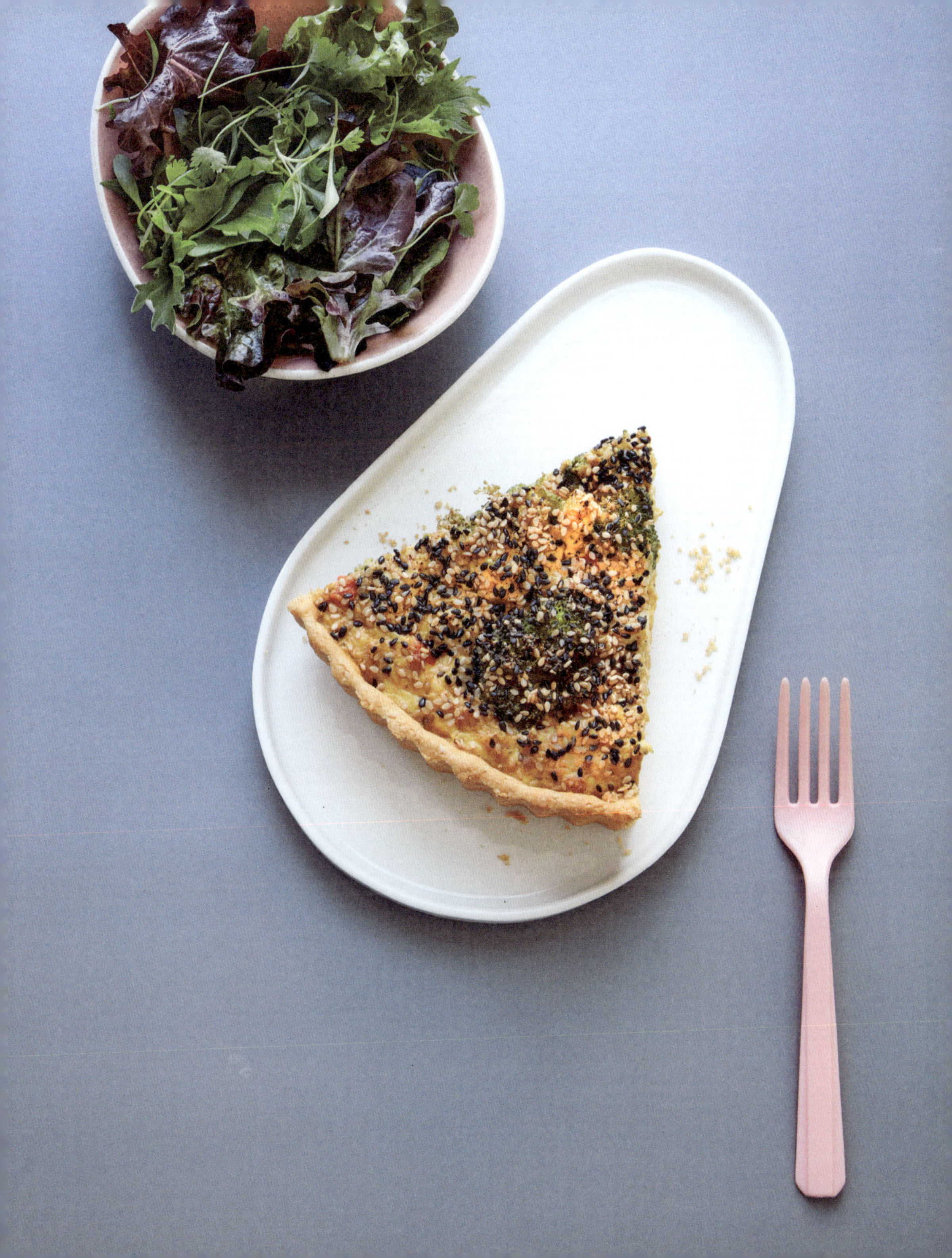

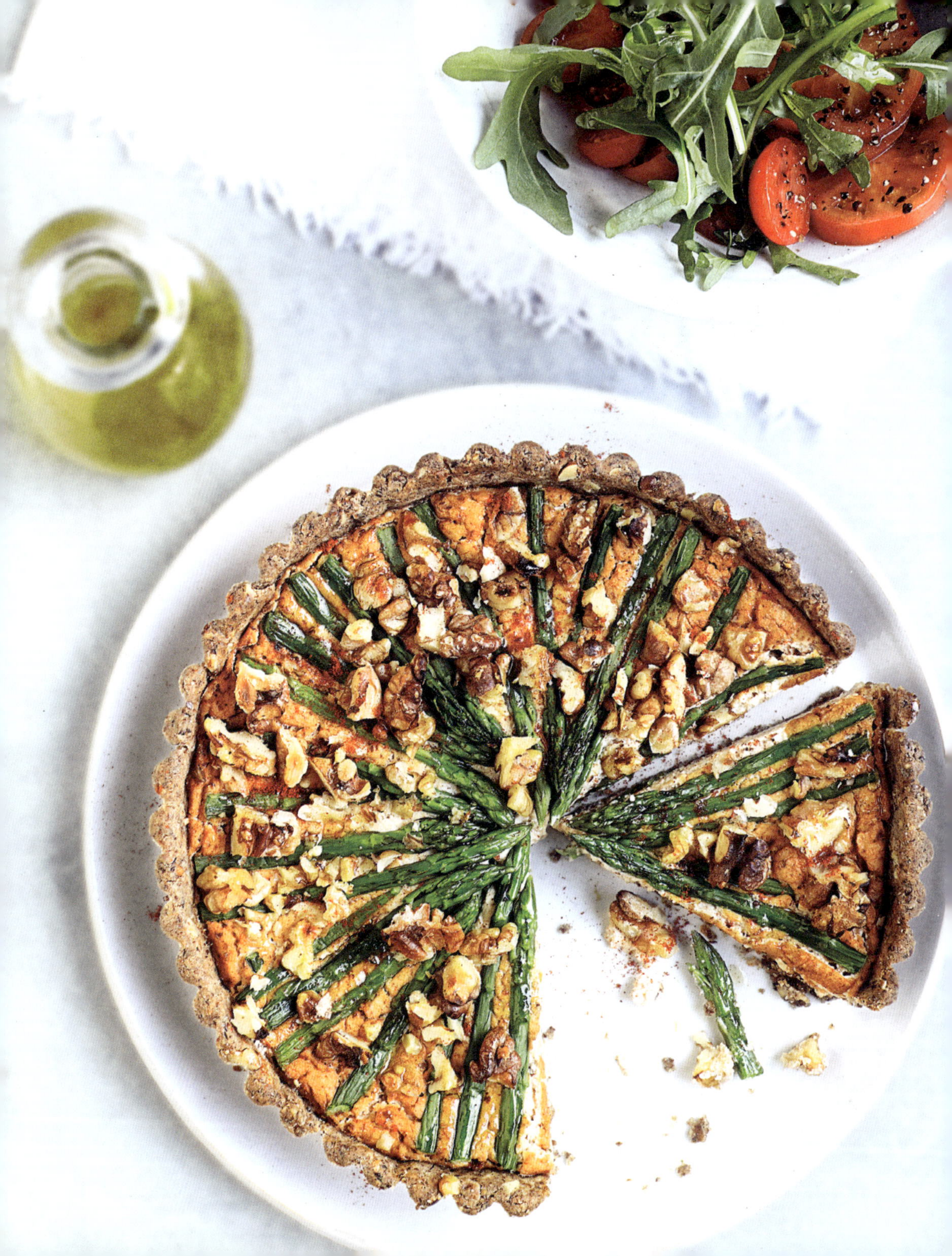

ASPARAGUS, TOFU & PAPRIKA TART

Nutritional yeast acts as a vegan cheese substitute in sauces and goes really well with paprika. Asparagus is prolific in spring, and full of vitamin K, so this is a great fresh and wholesome dish to welcome in the new season.

FOR THE PASTRY
2 tablespoons ground golden flaxseed
80 g/½ cup brown rice flour
60 g/⅓ cup buckwheat flour
pinch of sea salt
50 g/¼ cup vegan spread
30 g/¼ cup walnuts, toasted and roughly chopped

FOR THE FILLING
16 fine asparagus spears, trimmed
200 g/7 oz. smoked firm tofu, cubed
160 ml/⅔ cup unsweetened plant-based milk
1 teaspoon dried parsley
1 tablespoon freshly squeezed lemon juice
1 teaspoon paprika
1 tablespoon tapioca flour
2½ tablespoons nutritional yeast
2 tablespoons chopped walnuts
salt and freshly ground black pepper, to season

20-cm/8-in. loose-bottomed non-stick tart pan

pie weights/baking beans

SERVES 4

To make the pastry, mix the flaxseed with 6 tablespoons water and leave to stand for 10 minutes.

Mix the flours and salt together and add to a food processor with the vegan spread, flaxseed mixture and walnuts. Mix until a ball of dough is formed. Wrap the dough in plastic wrap and refrigerate for 1 hour.

Preheat the oven to 200°C/400°F/gas mark 6.

Roll out the pastry on a lightly floured surface and line the tart pan (the pastry doesn't need to be too thin – roll until it is just large enough to line the tart pan). Lay parchment paper and pie weights/baking beans on top to weigh down the pastry. Blind bake in the centre of the oven for 12–15 minutes. Remove the weights/beans and paper and bake for a further 5 minutes or until the pastry is golden brown. Remove from the oven.

Blanch the asparagus in boiling water for 2 minutes, drain, and set aside to cool. Place the tofu in a blender with half the milk and blend until combined (unlike other recipes in this book, there is no need to press the tofu before use). Add the tofu mixture to a small pan with the parsley, lemon juice, half the paprika, and the remaining milk. Stir and heat until almost at boiling point. Turn off the heat and whisk in the flour until a thick sauce forms. Leave to cool for a minute, then stir in the nutritional yeast and seasoning. Pour the sauce over the pastry base. Decorate with the asparagus tips, placing them in a circle with tips facing inward. Scatter the walnuts over the top. Bake in the oven for 15 minutes.

Remove the tart from the pan and sprinkle with the remaining paprika before serving.

TOFU SCRAMBLE

This is a particularly yummy way of using tofu, and former egg-lovers are especially keen on it since it looks and tastes very similar to scrambled eggs. Actually, way better than scrambled eggs! You can use many different types of vegetables, herbs and spices; this is just one suggestion for springtime, when asparagus (wild and cultivated) is abundant at farmers' markets. A big cast-iron wok is ideal to make this dish, but you can also use a heavy-bottomed frying pan/skillet.

150 g/2 cups fresh shiitake mushrooms
4 tablespoons olive oil
120 g/1 cup onions sliced into thin half-moons
½ teaspoon sea salt
80 g/1 cup trimmed asparagus, sliced diagonally at the bottom
2 tablespoons tamari
½ teaspoon ground turmeric
300 g/10 oz. tofu, mashed
4 tablespoons water, if necessary
1 teaspoon dark sesame oil
½ teaspoon dried basil or 2 tablespoons freshly chopped basil
freshly ground black pepper, to season

TO SERVE
slices of freshly toasted bread
mixed salad greens, to serve (optional)

SERVES 2–3

Cut the mushrooms in half lengthways, then cut into thinner wedges. Add the olive oil, onions and salt to a wok or frying pan/skillet and sauté over a medium heat briefly, stirring to prevent sticking.

Add the mushrooms, asparagus, tamari and turmeric and continue stirring with two wooden spoons. When the mushrooms have soaked up a bit of tamari, turn up the heat, add the tofu and stir for another 1–2 minutes. The scramble should be uniformly yellow in colour. At this point you can add the water to make the scramble juicy, and continue cooking for a couple more minutes. However, whether you need water or not depends on how soft your tofu was to begin with – softer types are moist and don't need any water at the end of cooking.

Mix in the dark sesame oil and basil, season with pepper and serve warm with a few slices of toasted bread and mixed salad greens, if you like.

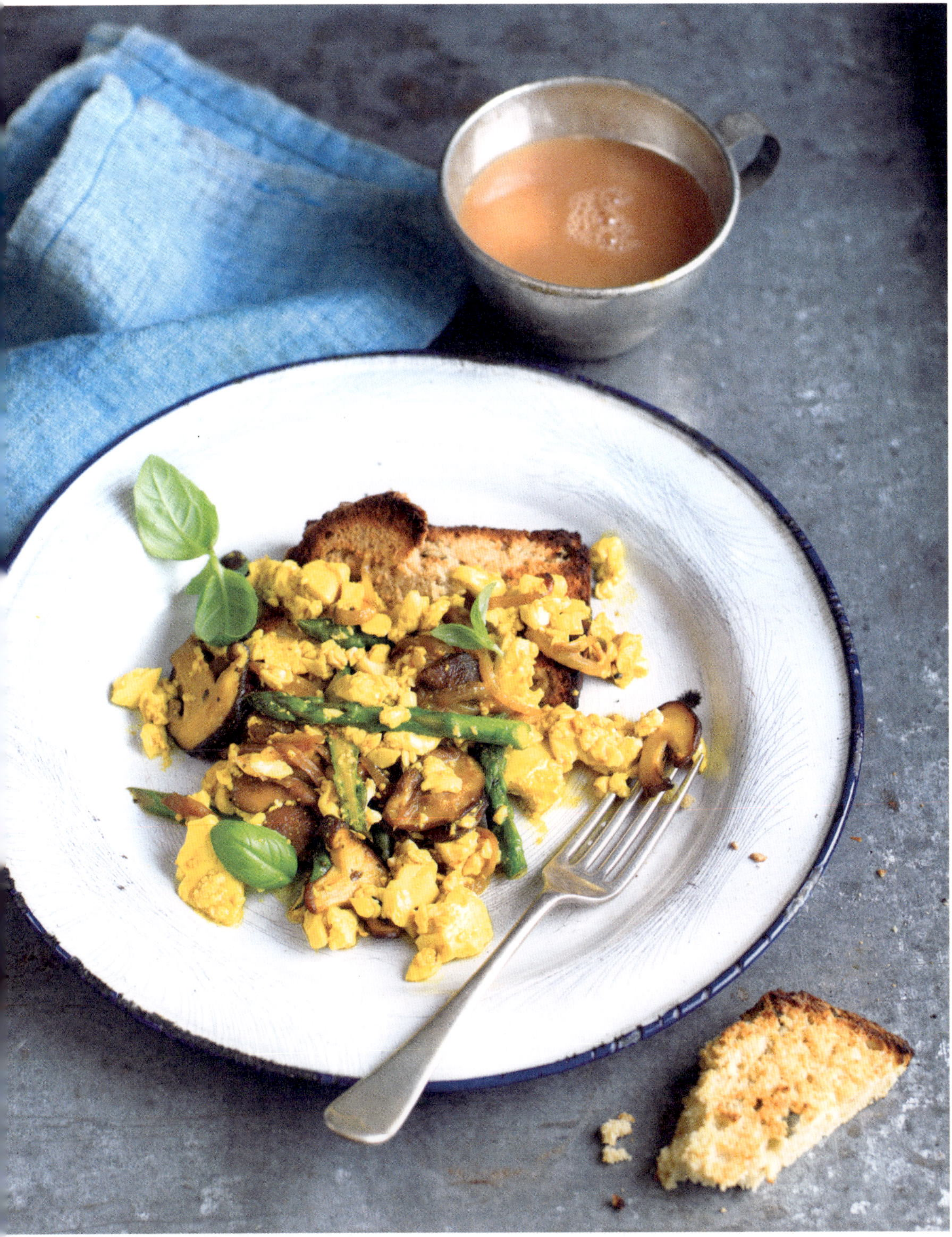

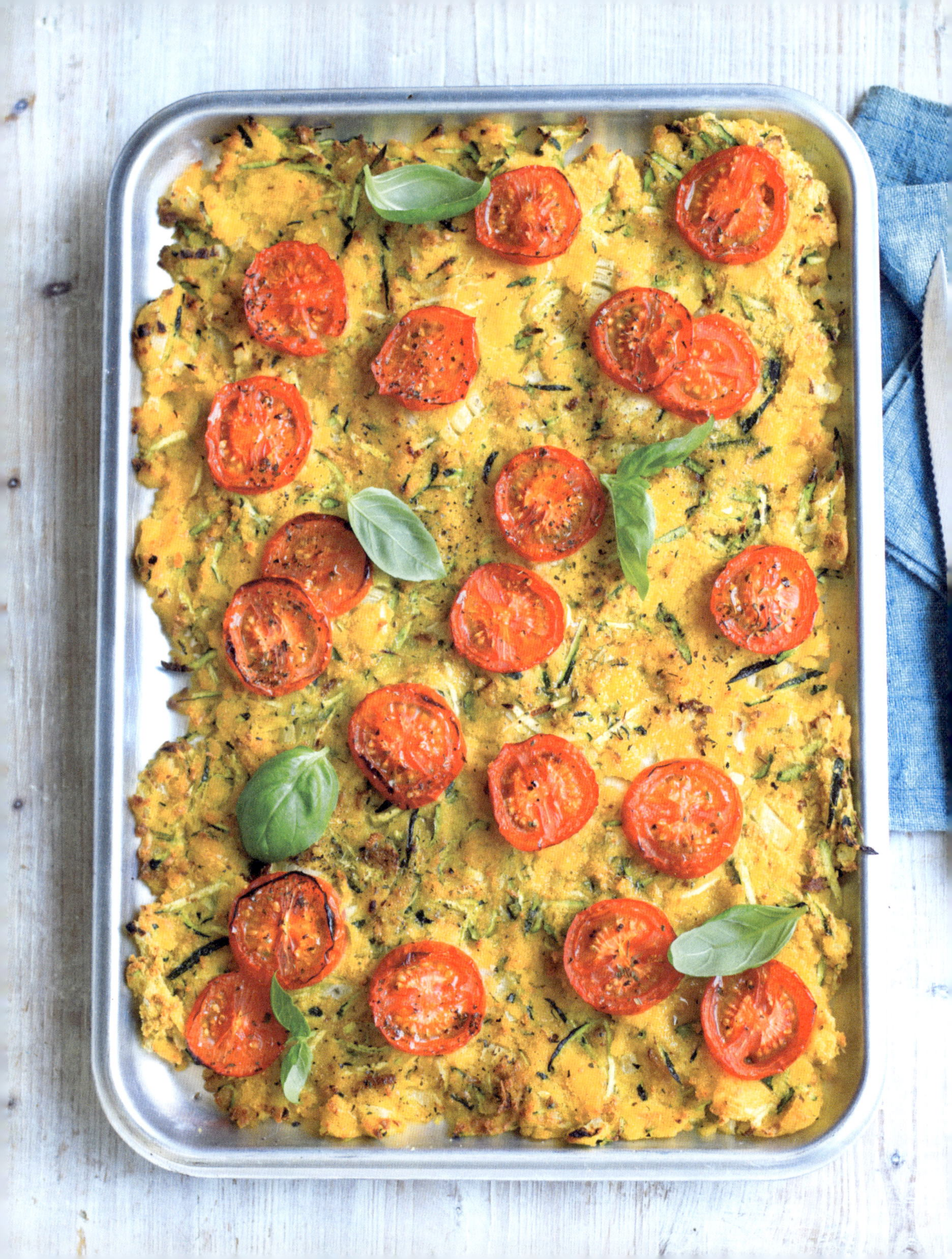

POLENTA TARTE FLAMBÉE

Not only is this dish visually appealing and a song for your taste buds, it is crispy and packed full of vibrant summer flavours. This is a gluten-free and vegan version that you are sure to enjoy sharing with friends on a warm summer's evening.

750 ml/3 cups water
160 g/1 cup polenta/cornmeal
100 g/1 cup grated courgette/zucchini
50 g/⅓ cup finely diced onion
70 g/½ cup finely grated smoked tofu
2–3 firm tomatoes
olive oil for drizzling and serving
½ teaspoon dried basil
½ teaspoon sea salt
salt freshly ground black pepper, to season
fresh basil leaves, to garnish

35 x 25-cm/14 x 10-in. casserole dish or baking pan, well-oiled

SERVES 2–3

Preheat the oven to 200°C/400°F/gas mark 6. Bring the water to a boil, add the sea salt and whisk in the polenta/cornmeal. Lower the heat, cover and let cook for 15 minutes. There's no need to stir. Lightly salt the grated courgette/zucchini, let sit for 5 minutes and then squeeze out as much of the water as you can. Add the onion, courgette/zucchini and grated smoked tofu to the cooked polenta/cornmeal and mix well. Add salt and pepper, to taste. Spoon the polenta/cornmeal mix into the oiled casserole dish or baking pan, evening the surface with a spatula or wet hands.

Slice the tomatoes into 5-mm/⅕-inch thick slices and discard any excess juice and seeds. Arrange the tomato slices in a single layer over the top and drizzle with olive oil, then sprinkle with dried basil and salt and black pepper, to taste. Bake for 20–25 minutes or until golden brown and until the tomatoes are well baked and sizzling. Let it cool a little, and then slice and serve with fresh basil leaves, a generous splash of olive oil and some tomato sauce to make this dish more juicy.

You can make variations on this recipe; topping the polenta/cornmeal with thin slices of courgette/zucchini, (bell) peppers or aubergine/eggplant instead of tomatoes.

CORN & TOFU PIE

A vegan version of Greek filo/phyllo pie, this dish makes an excellent lunch or dinner and is very filling. Corn kernels add a nice sweetness and texture to the smooth tofu layers, but using some blanched greens instead of corn is also a delicious variation worth trying. Serve with a big bowl of salad, or a cup of non-dairy yogurt if you're in a hurry.

500 g/1 lb. 2 oz./17 sheets of filo/phyllo pastry
100 g/½ cup olive oil

FOR THE FILLING
250 g/2 cups sweetcorn/corn kernels, fresh, canned, or frozen and thawed
500 g/1 lb. 2 oz. medium-soft tofu
2 tablespoons olive oil
2¼ teaspoons salt
460 ml/2 cups soya/soy milk
230 ml/1 cup hot water
130 g/1 cup fine cornmeal

20 x 30-cm/8 x 12-in. baking pan, well oiled

SERVES 6-8

First make the filling. If using canned sweetcorn/corn, wash it and drain well. In a big bowl, crumble the tofu with your fingers and add the sweetcorn/corn, oil, salt, milk and hot water and mix until well combined. Whisk in the cornmeal. The filling should be moderately smooth besides the sweetcorn/corn and small pieces of tofu.

Preheat the oven to 180°C/350°F/gas mark 4.

If the sheets of filo/phyllo are bigger than your baking pan, cut them to size. Don't worry if a sheet tears as you can easily patch up any damage – only the top 2 sheets need to stay undamaged.

Place a sheet of filo/phyllo in the baking pan. (Cover the remaining sheets with clingfilm/plastic wrap to prevent them from drying out.) Brush oil lightly over the sheet. Cover with another sheet and oil it. Repeat this process with 2 more sheets.

Spread one-fifth of the filling evenly over the top with a spatula.

Cover with one sheet, oil lightly and cover with a second sheet (this one doesn't need oiling). Spread one-fifth of the filling evenly over the top. Continue like this until you have used up all the filling, and you have 5 layers each of filling and filo/phyllo sheets.

To finish, brush a little oil over the remaining 5 sheets of filo/phyllo and lay them on top of the pie – the 2 best, undamaged sheets should be on the top. Tuck in any pastry or filling sticking out of the pan by pushing a spatula between the pie and the sides of the pan. Use a sharp knife to score 12 squares into the pastry.

Bake in the preheated oven for 45 minutes, or until the top turns golden brown and the pie isn't wobbly or soft to the touch.

Allow to cool completely (at least 5 hours, or overnight) in the pan before serving.

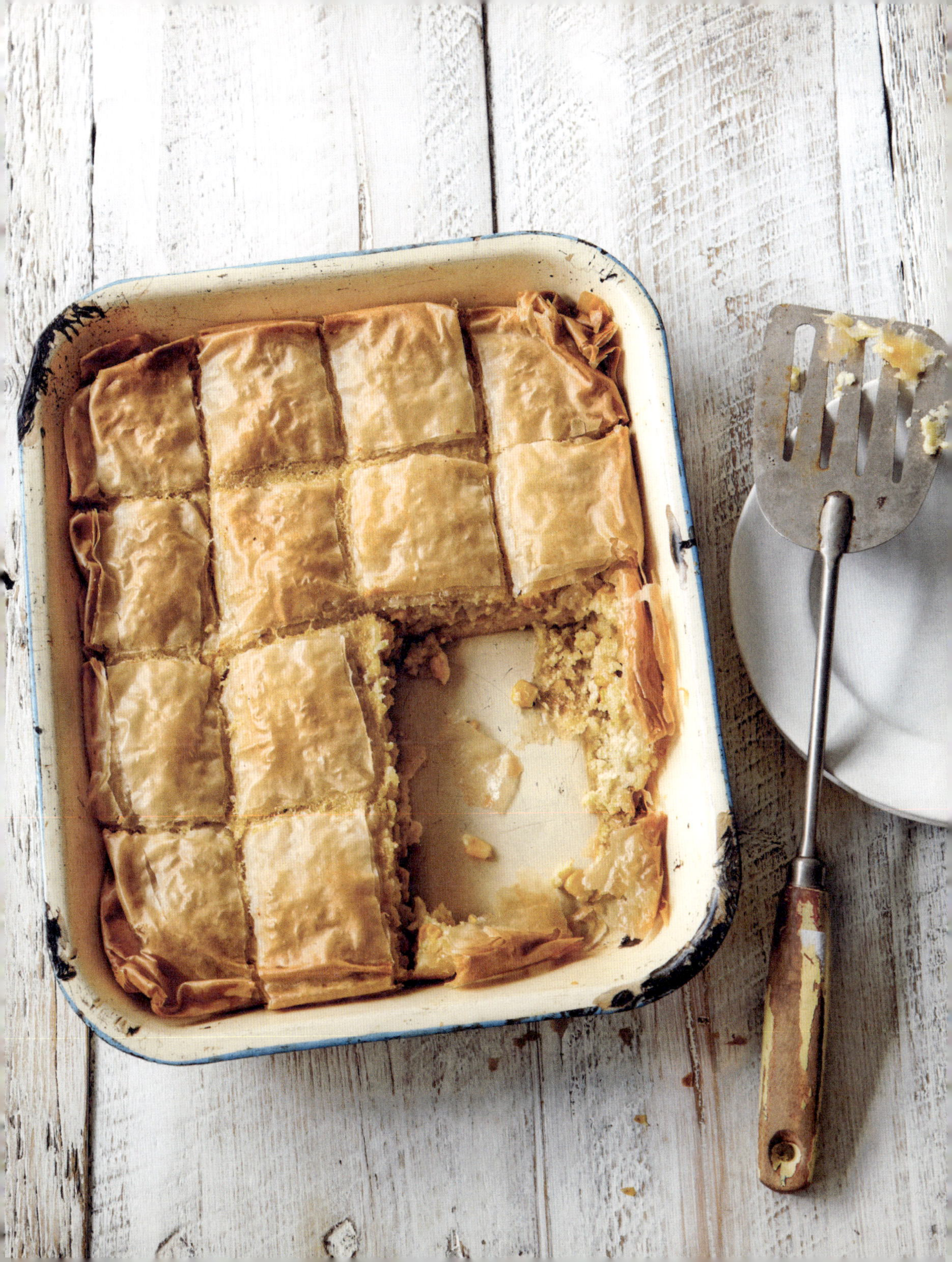

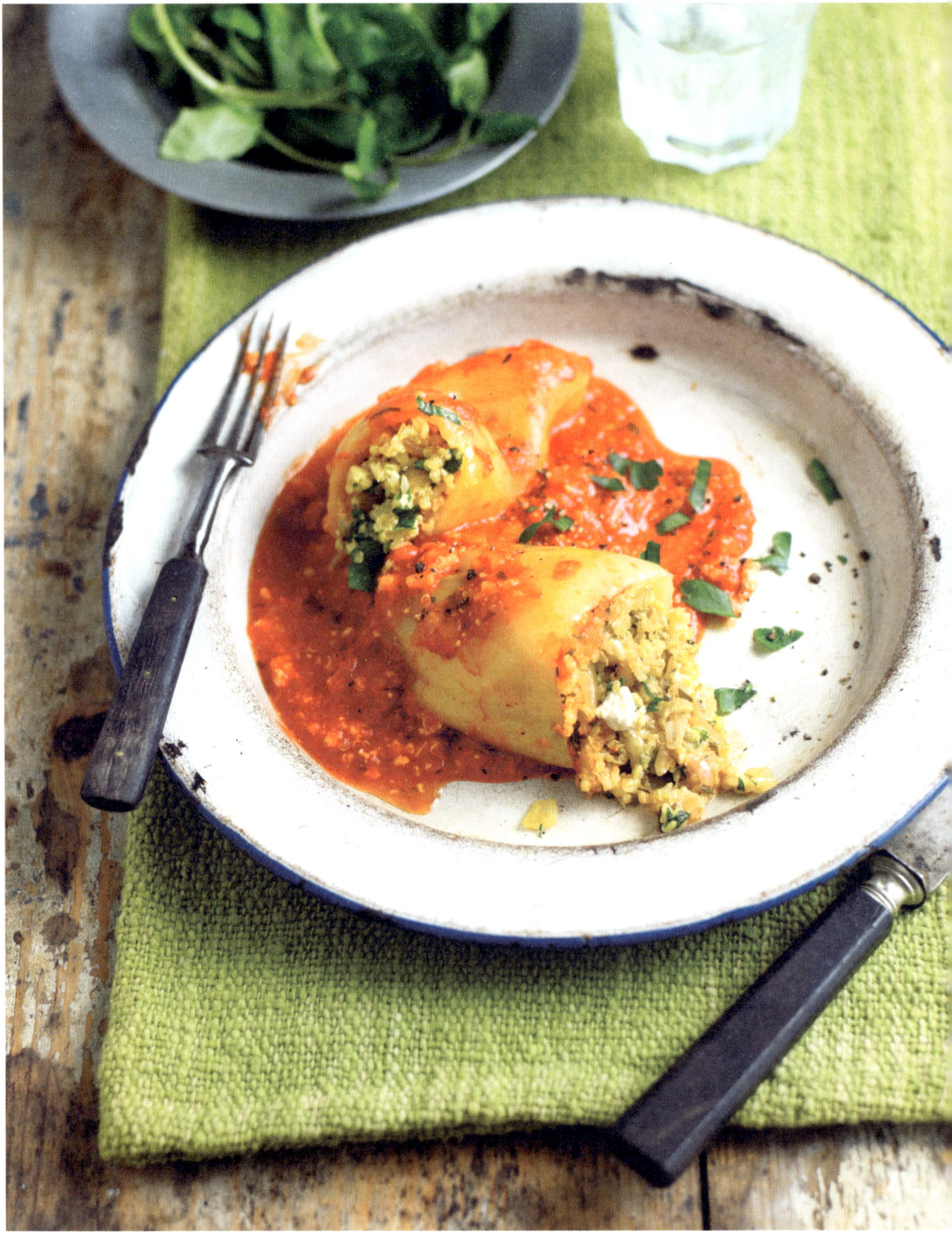

STUFFED BABURA PEPPERS WITH TOFU STUFFING

This dish is a perfect example of vegan comfort food. In some versions of this recipe the stuffed peppers are baked, but here you boil them in sauce, making them especially juicy and full of flavour. These tofu-stuffed peppers taste equally good and are actually much healthier than their non-vegan counterparts!

1 quantity Tofu Stuffing (see page 98)
7 Babura peppers (see Note)
230 ml/1 cup tomato passata/strained tomatoes
1 litre/4 cups water
2 bay leaves
1 teaspoon sea salt
1–2 tablespoons kuzu, arrowroot powder or cornflour/cornstarch (optional)
2 tablespoons freshly chopped parsley, to garnish

20-cm/8-in. diameter saucepan

SERVES 3–4

Prepare the stuffing and set aside. Gently cut off the caps of the peppers and deseed them. Fill each with about 100 g/^{2}/$_3$ cup of the stuffing. Arrange the cut side of the peppers so that they face upwards in saucepan (if the pan is narrower, the peppers will not fit; if it's wider, the peppers will flip to the side and the stuffing will fall out during cooking). Add the passata/strained tomatoes and just enough of the water to cover the peppers, followed by the bay leaves and salt. Cover with a lid and bring the pan to a slow boil; then turn the heat down to a simmer until the peppers are soft, which should be about 25 minutes.

Using a serving spoon, gently take out each pepper and serve them on plates, leaving the sauce in the pan over a medium heat, and slowly add the kuzu, arrowroot powder or cornflour/cornstarch, if required (diluted in cold water), whisking vigorously until your desired thickness is reached. You can leave the sauce runny, without thickening it, if you prefer.

Serve a ladleful of the sauce over each portion of peppers, and garnish with the chopped parsley.

Note In case you cannot find Babura peppers – the best kind for stuffing because their skin is thinner and they are smaller than regular (bell) peppers – you can use (bell) peppers of any colour. Just bear in mind that (bell) peppers are bigger, will take in more filling and need to cook for a bit longer. You'll also have to determine the size of pan to use to fit them tightly and prevent them from falling over.

TOFU STUFFING

It's fun to fill different types of vegetables, then bake or cook them for a quite impressive and really delicious result! The combination of protein, vegetables and grains makes this type of stuffing a complete meal. You can use it to stuff peppers (see page 97), tomatoes, courgettes/zucchini or aubergines/eggplants, as well as using it as a filling for cabbage rolls or spring rolls.

250 g/9 oz. tofu
50 g/⅓ cup finely diced onion
4 tablespoons sunflower or olive oil
pinch of chilli powder
½ teaspoon ground ginger
¼ teaspoon ground turmeric
1 teaspoon herbes de Provence
3 teaspoons soy sauce
300 g/10½ oz. whole grains, cooked (brown rice, millet, quinoa, etc.)
2 tablespoons rolled/old-fashioned oats or millet flakes
salt and freshly ground black pepper, to season

MAKES 1 QUANTITY

In a mixing bowl, mash the tofu with a fork. In a large frying pan/skillet over a low heat, sauté the onion until softened, then add the dry spices and herbs and cook for a minute more. Add the soy sauce and bring up the heat. After the soy sauce is well incorporated, add the cooked grains and rolled oats or millet flakes and mix everything well before seasoning with salt and pepper, to taste. When the stuffing looks like a thick risotto, it's ready for filling.

Remember that the mixture will expand a little bit during cooking, so don't overfill the vegetables.

You can always make the stuffing a day or two in advance, as well as freeze it, if you have leftovers.

MIXED VEGETABLE GRATIN WITH TOFU

This combination of vegetables offers a pleasing mix of colours, tastes and textures, but you could just as easily make this with a different combination or even a single vegetable. Cauliflower or broccoli are both especially nice, and they should be blanched beforehand like the greens in this recipe.

200 g/2 cups sliced greens, such as cabbage or spinach
1 leek, thinly sliced
1 large carrot, grated/shredded
1 sweet potato, finely chopped or coarsely grated/shredded
400 ml/1$^{2}/_{3}$ cups dairy, soya/soy or oat cream
100 g/4 oz. silken tofu
1 egg (optional)

3–4 tablespoons breadcrumbs
3–4 tablespoons finely grated vegetarian or vegan Parmesan-style cheese
cooked wholegrains or a mixed leaf salad, to serve

30 x 20-cm/12 x 8-in. baking dish, oiled

SERVES 6

Preheat the oven to 200°C/400°F/gas mark 6.

Bring a large saucepan of water to the boil. Add the greens and cook for 1–2 minutes, just to blanch. Drain. Combine the blanched greens, leek, carrot and sweet potato in the prepared baking dish. Season well and mix to blend.

Combine the cream, tofu and egg (if using) in a food processor and process until smooth. Pour over the vegetables. Sprinkle with the breadcrumbs and grated cheese.

Bake in the preheated oven for 30–40 minutes, until bubbling.

Serve immediately with your choice of side.

MAIN PLATES

WILD GARLIC MISO TOFU STIR-FRY

Wild garlic/ramps has a great affinity with Asian flavourings, such as ginger, soy sauce and Japanese miso paste. Cooked in just minutes and served simply with rice or noodles, this tofu dish makes a perfect midweek supper.

1 tablespoon sunflower or vegetable oil
1 cm/^{1}/$_2$-in. piece fresh ginger, peeled and finely chopped
400 g/14 oz. firm tofu, sliced into 1-cm/^{1}/$_2$-in. strips
1 tablespoon rice wine or Amontillado sherry
1 tablespoon dark soy sauce
1 tablespoon dark miso paste
40 g/1^1/$_2$ oz. wild garlic leaves/ramps, rinsed well and chopped into 2.5-cm/1-in. lengths

SERVES 4

Heat a wok until hot. Add the oil and heat through. Add the ginger and fry briefly, stirring, until fragrant.

Next, add the tofu and fry, stirring, until it takes on a little colour. Pour in the rice wine and allow to sizzle briefly. Add the soy sauce and miso paste and stir-fry for a further 2–3 minutes.

Finally, add the wild garlic/ramps and stir-fry until just wilted. Serve at once in bowls.

MAPO TOFU & AUBERGINE RICE BOWLS

This Chinese-inspired Japanese dish is soft tofu set in a spicy bean sauce and is traditionally made with minced/ground pork. It's a dish that goes particularly well with steamed rice – maybe that's why the Japanese love it so much! Sichuan spices can be very fiery to the point of numbing, so here is a milder, but still fragrant version, which also uses using aubergine/eggplant instead of meat. It's just as soft but much lighter… guilt-free seconds are a must!

400 g/14 oz. soft tofu
1 tablespoon toasted sesame oil
1 tablespoon vegetable oil
10 g/¼ oz. garlic, chopped
20 g/¾ oz. fresh ginger, peeled and finely chopped
½ leek, thinly sliced
1 aubergine/eggplant, diced into small cubes

FOR THE MAPO SAUCE
2 tablespoons sake
2 tablespoons red miso
1 tablespoon mirin
1 tablespoon soy sauce
2 teaspoons honey or maple syrup
1 teaspoon Sichuan broad/fava bean chilli/chili paste
½ tablespoon cornflour/cornstarch mixed with ½ tablespoon cold water
400 g/3 cups cooked white Japanese rice, to serve
1 spring onion/scallion, thinly sliced, to garnish

SERVES 2

Dice the tofu into small cubes, then wrap in two layers of paper towels to remove any excess water. Set aside. Meanwhile, to make the mapo sauce, combine the sake, red miso, mirin, soy sauce, honey or maple syrup and Sichuan broad/fava bean chilli/chili paste in a small bowl. Stir together and set aside.

Heat the toasted sesame oil and vegetable oil in a medium frying pan/skillet over a medium heat. Fry the garlic, ginger and leek for 1 minute to infuse the flavour into the oil, then add the aubergine/eggplant. Fry for 2 minutes until browned.

Add the mapo sauce and 80 ml/⅓ cup water to the pan with the vegetables, reduce the heat to low and simmer, uncovered, for 3 minutes.

Add the tofu cubes gently, then pour the cornflour/cornstarch and water mixture around the rim of the pan. Bring to the boil for about 1 minute to thicken the mixture slightly, then remove from the heat.

Divide the cooked rice between serving bowls and add the mapo tofu. Garnish the dishes with sliced spring onion/scallion.

TOFU KEBABS WITH NOODLES

The longer you marinate the tofu the more flavourful it becomes – overnight is best. You may want to make additional noodle sauce to offer for dipping, or just use plain soy or tamari. To increase the heat, sliced fresh red chillies and a splash of mirin can be added to the noodle sauce, as well as a sprinkling of toasted sesame seeds. You can simply serve the tofu as fingers or, after cooking, skewer onto wooden skewers.

FOR THE KEBABS/KABOBS
200 g/7 oz. firm tofu, cut into fingers
1 tablespoon maple syrup
1 tablespoon Dijon mustard
1 tablespoon soy sauce
45 g/1 cup fresh wholemeal/whole-wheat breadcrumbs
a large pinch of paprika
1 teaspoon fine sea salt
rapeseed oil, for cooking

FOR THE NOODLES
200 g/7 oz. any fine oriental noodles of your choice
1 tablespoon vegetable oil
1 tablespoon honey
60 ml/¼ cup orange juice or apple juice
3–4 tablespoons soy sauce or tamari
spring onions/scallions, to serve (optional)

SERVES 2–3

Arrange the tofu fingers in a dish which is just large enough to hold them in a single layer.

In a small bowl, combine the maple syrup, mustard and soy sauce and mix well. Pour over the tofu and coat the tofu on all sides. Cover with clingfilm/plastic wrap and refrigerate until needed – up to 24 hours and for at least 30 minutes.

When ready to cook the tofu, season the breadcrumbs with the paprika and salt.

Spread them over a plate. Remove the tofu from the marinade and pat dry lightly with paper towels. Transfer each finger to the breadcrumbs and turn to coat on all sides, pressing the crumbs into the tofu. Transfer to a clean plate.

Heat 2–3 tablespoons oil (enough to cover the bottom of the pan) in a non-stick frying pan/skillet. Add the tofu and cook for about 2 minutes, until just browned. Turn carefully with tongs and continue cooking about 2 minutes on each side, until browned all over. Transfer to a plate lined with paper towels, insert a skewer into each one and set aside.

Cook the noodles according to the package instructions. Drain, toss with the oil to prevent sticking. Combine the honey, orange juice and soy sauce in a large frying pan/skillet. Heat and stir to blend. Add the cooked noodles and toss to coat them in the sauce. Cook over low heat just until warmed through.

Serve the tofu kebabs/kabobs with the noodles and some green beans. Offer additional noodle sauce or soy sauce for dipping, as preferred, and serve with shredded spring onions/scallions, if liked.

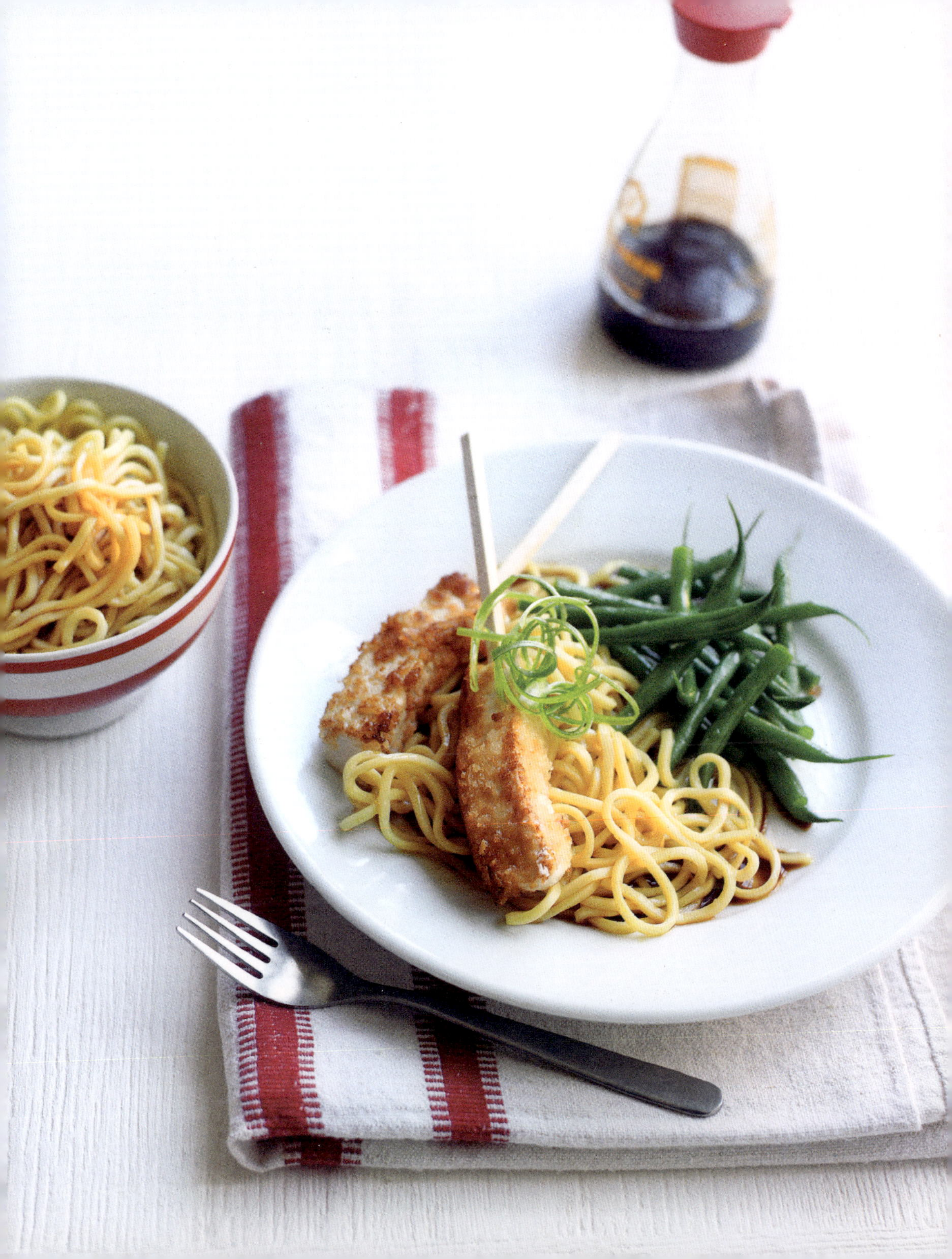

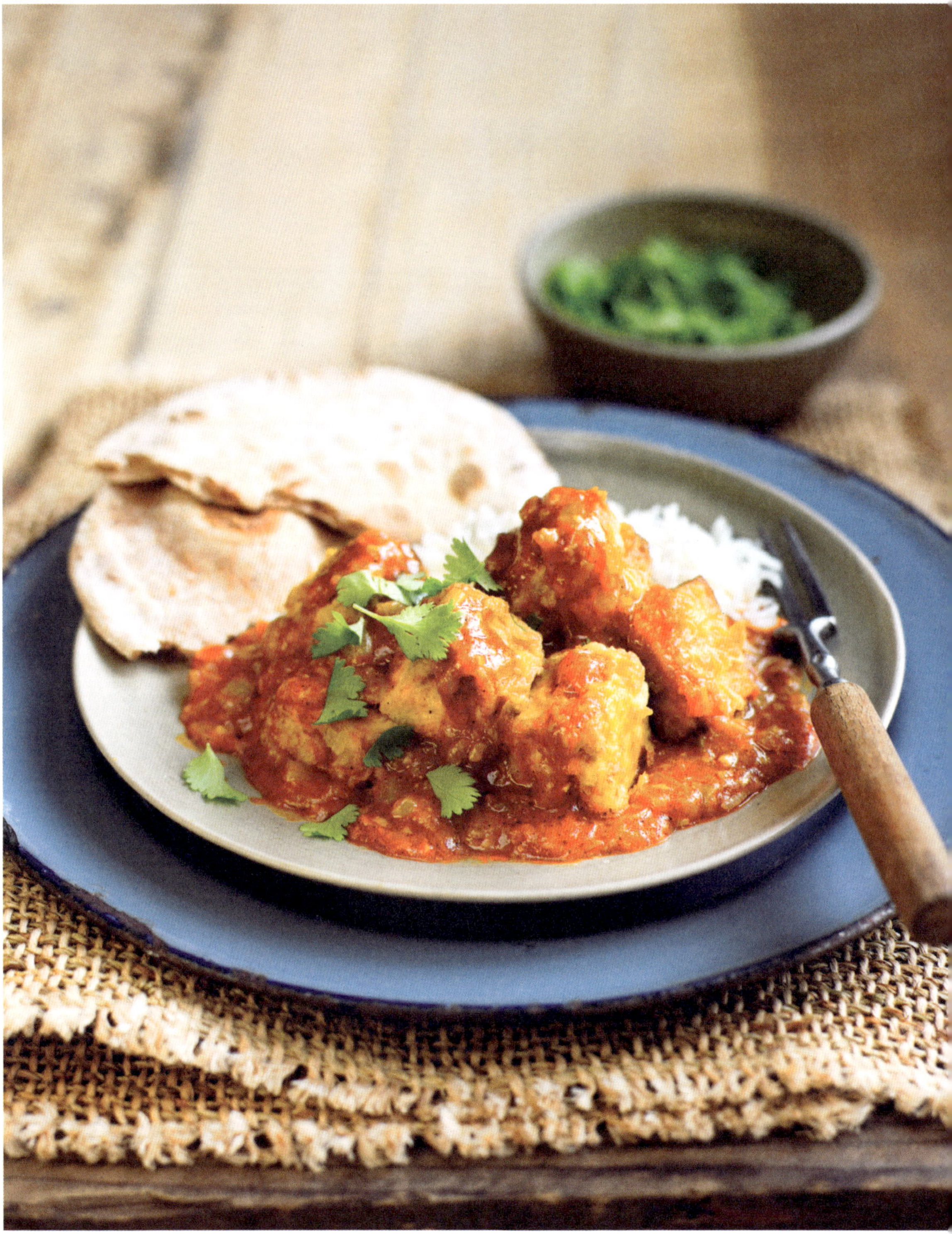

DELICIOUS TOFU CURRY

This delicious curry recipe is so good you'll almost always want to come back for more! Make sure you marinate and fry the tofu first – it makes a big difference to the taste and texture. Serve this to guests and make everybody fall in love with it.

FOR THE TOFU
290 g/10 oz. tofu, cut into 2-cm/3/4-in. cubes
1 teaspoon curry powder
1/2 teaspoon crushed coriander seeds
1/2 teaspoon ground cumin
5 tablespoons sunflower, coconut or olive oil, for frying

FOR THE CURRY
180 g/1 1/2 cups diced onions
2 tablespoons finely grated fresh ginger
4 garlic cloves, crushed
2 teaspoons curry powder (or curry paste)
1/4–1/2 teaspoon chilli/chili powder
1 teaspoon ground turmeric
1 tablespoon tomato purée/paste
1/2 teaspoon sea salt
300 ml/1 1/4 cups water
1 teaspoon kuzu, ground arrowroot or cornflour/cornstarch
2 tablespoons freshly chopped coriander/cilantro, chives or parsley, to garnish

TO SERVE
cooked basmati rice
chapatis

SERVES 2–3

To prepare the tofu, refer to the instructions on page 8, using the herbs and spices listed here. Marinate and fry the tofu as instructed.

Heat the oil in a large (lidded) frying pan/skillet and fry the onions, ginger and garlic over a medium heat until fragrant.

Add all the curry spices, the tomato purée/paste and salt and stir until slightly brown. Stir in the marinated fried tofu, then add the water and cover with the lid. Bring to the boil, stir again, lower the heat and cook for 5–10 minutes. You can add more water if you like your curry more stew-like. At the end, dilute the kuzu, arrowroot or cornflour/cornstarch in a little cold water and add it to the curry, stirring until it boils again. Garnish with your choice of herbs and serve with freshly cooked basmati rice and/or chapatis.

SWEET & SOUR TOFU

This simple dish is ideal if you are trying to introduce tofu into your diet; the sauce is fresh, tangy and surprisingly tasty. If you want to introduce more vegetables, switch out some of the tofu and replace with equal weight in steamed broccoli florets, mangetout/snow peas or green beans. Serve with rice and a green vegetable, if liked.

1 tablespoon vegetable oil
1 medium onion, cut in 2-cm/ ¾-in. pieces
1 red (bell) pepper, cut in 2-cm/ ¾-in. pieces
1 carrot, sliced into thin rounds
1 celery stick, cut in 2-cm/ ¾-in. pieces
1 teaspoon plain/all-purpose flour
225-g/8-oz. can pineapple chunks, drained and juice reserved
125 ml/½ cup apple juice
125 ml/½ cup tomato ketchup
1 tablespoon soy sauce
1–3 teaspoons cider vinegar
350-g/12 oz. tofu, cubed
cooked rice, to serve

SERVES 3–4

Combine the oil, onion and pepper in a frying pan/skillet with a lid and cook for about 3 minutes, until just beginning to soften.

Add the carrot and celery and continue cooking for 5–10 minutes more, stirring often, until just tender.

Stir in the flour and cook for 1 minute. Add the reserved pineapple juice, apple juice, ketchup, soy sauce and 1 teaspoon of the vinegar. Mix well, cover and let simmer for 5 minutes.

Gently stir in the pineapple chunks and the tofu. Cover and cook over low heat for 3–5 minutes, just to warm through. Time permitting, let stand, covered, for about 30 minutes to allow the tofu to absorb all the flavours and reheat gently before serving.

Alternatively, serve immediately with rice.

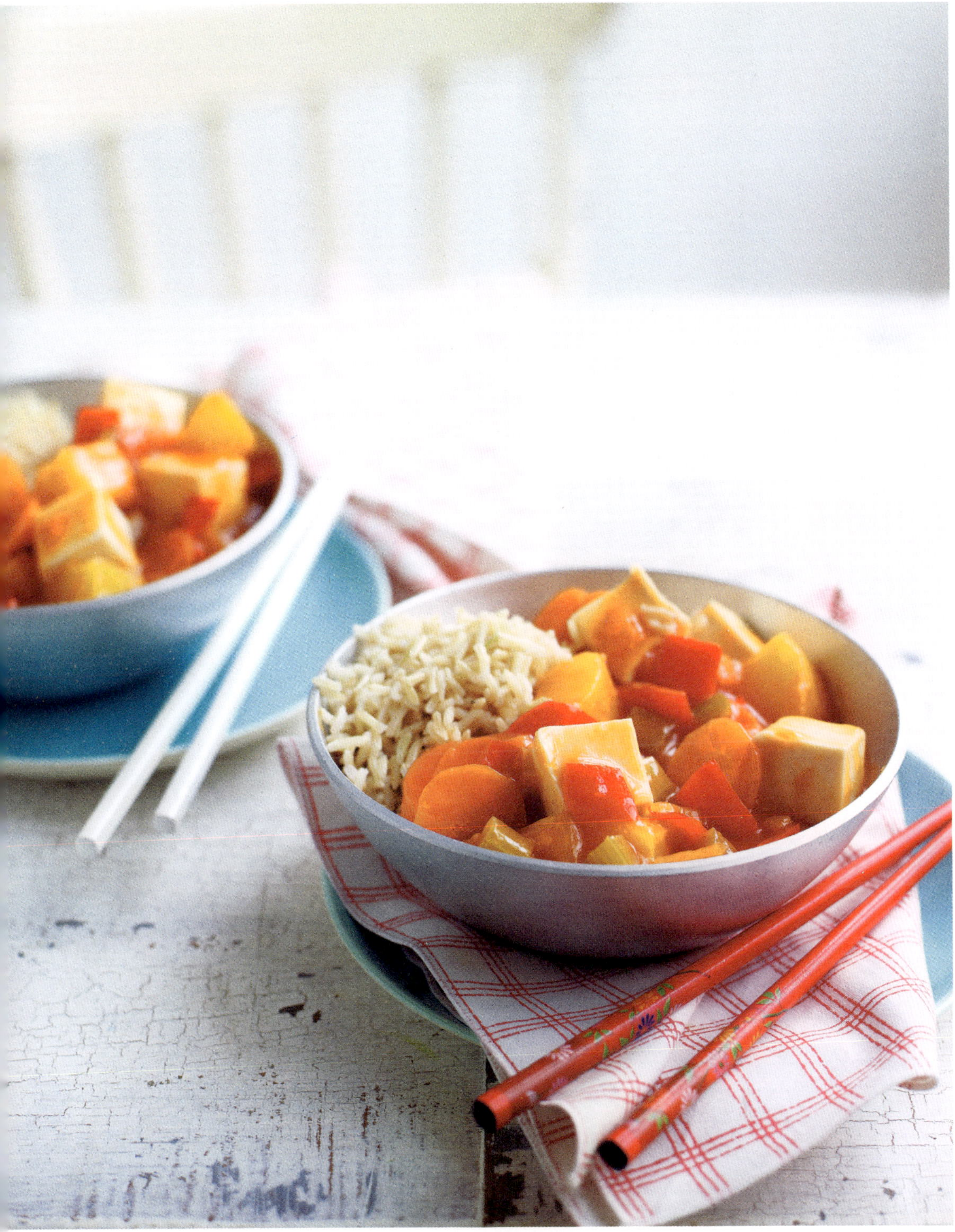

VERSATILE TOFU PIZZA

By using all kinds of toppings – such as olives, onion slices, mushrooms, (bell) peppers, or chillies/chiles – you will find yourself with a multitude of different pizzas fit for everybody's tastes. Sprinkle with dried oregano, then bake and enjoy amongst friends! Here is a recipe for a tangy tofu and rice mix that, by adding the right amount of spices, has a nice texture and the creamy taste of cream cheese.

1 quantity Basic Pizza Dough (see recipe on opposite page)
300 ml/2 cups passata/strained tomatoes
vegetables of your choice (olives, sliced onion, sliced mushrooms, etc.), for topping
1 tablespoon olive oil
1 teaspoon dried oregano

FOR THE TOFU CREAM CHEESE
150 g/¾ cup cooked brown rice
200 g/6½ oz. soft tofu
60 g/1½ cup finely diced onion
4 tablespoons olive oil
1 tablespoon umeboshi vinegar or 2 teaspoons umeboshi paste
sea salt, to taste

40 x 32-cm/16 x 12½-in. baking pan, well-oiled

MAKES ONE 27-CM/10½-IN. DIAMETER PIZZA

To make the tofu cream cheese, blend the rice, tofu, onion, oil and vinegar or paste in a food processor or blender until smooth. Depending on how soft your tofu is, you might need to add water little by little, to achieve a consistency of thick cream cheese. Add salt (umeboshi vinegar/paste is salty, so be careful not to add too much). This cheese is even better if left to rest in the fridge for 24 hours. Try adding dark sesame oil or tahini instead of olive oil, for a slightly different aroma.

Preheat the oven to 240°C/475°F/gas mark 9.

Place a piece of parchment paper on your work surface and use a rolling pin to gently flatten your risen basic pizza dough into a 29-cm/11½-inch circle. Transfer your pizza base to the baking pan, spread with passata/strained tomatoes, then top with spoonfuls of the tofu cream cheese and vegetables of your choosing, and sprinkle with olive oil and oregano. Lower the oven temperature to 220°C/425°F/gas mark 7 and bake on the bottom surface of the oven for 12–15 minutes.

Baking the pizza on the bottom surface of the oven is the best way to do it, since baking the pizza for too long in the middle of the oven makes the dough hard and overly crispy.

BASIC PIZZA DOUGH

FOR THE STARTER
40 g/¼ cup rye flour
55 ml/¼ cup lukewarm water
2 teaspoons active dry yeast

FOR THE DOUGH
200 g/1½ cups spelt flour, plus extra for kneading
30 g/¼ cup wholemeal/ whole wheat flour
½ teaspoon sea salt
110 ml /½ cup lukewarm water
1 tablespoon olive oil
1 tablespoon soya/soy milk

MAKES 1 QUANTITY

Mix together all the starter ingredients in a bowl, cover and allow it to rest for 30 minutes. For the dough, mix together the flours and salt in another bowl. In a jug/pitcher, mix together the water, oil and milk, then add the starter ingredients and mix well. Finally, add the contents of the jug/pitcher to your dry ingredients in the bowl and mix with a wooden spoon.

Place the dough on a lightly floured work surface and knead for a couple of minutes (adding flour as you do so) until it is soft and slightly sticky. Put the dough into a large oiled bowl and rub a little oil on the surface of the dough, too. Cover the bowl with a damp tea/dish towel and allow to rise for 2½ hours in a warm place. Punch the dough down and allow it to rise for another 45 minutes.

Continue with the recipe instructions on page 108.

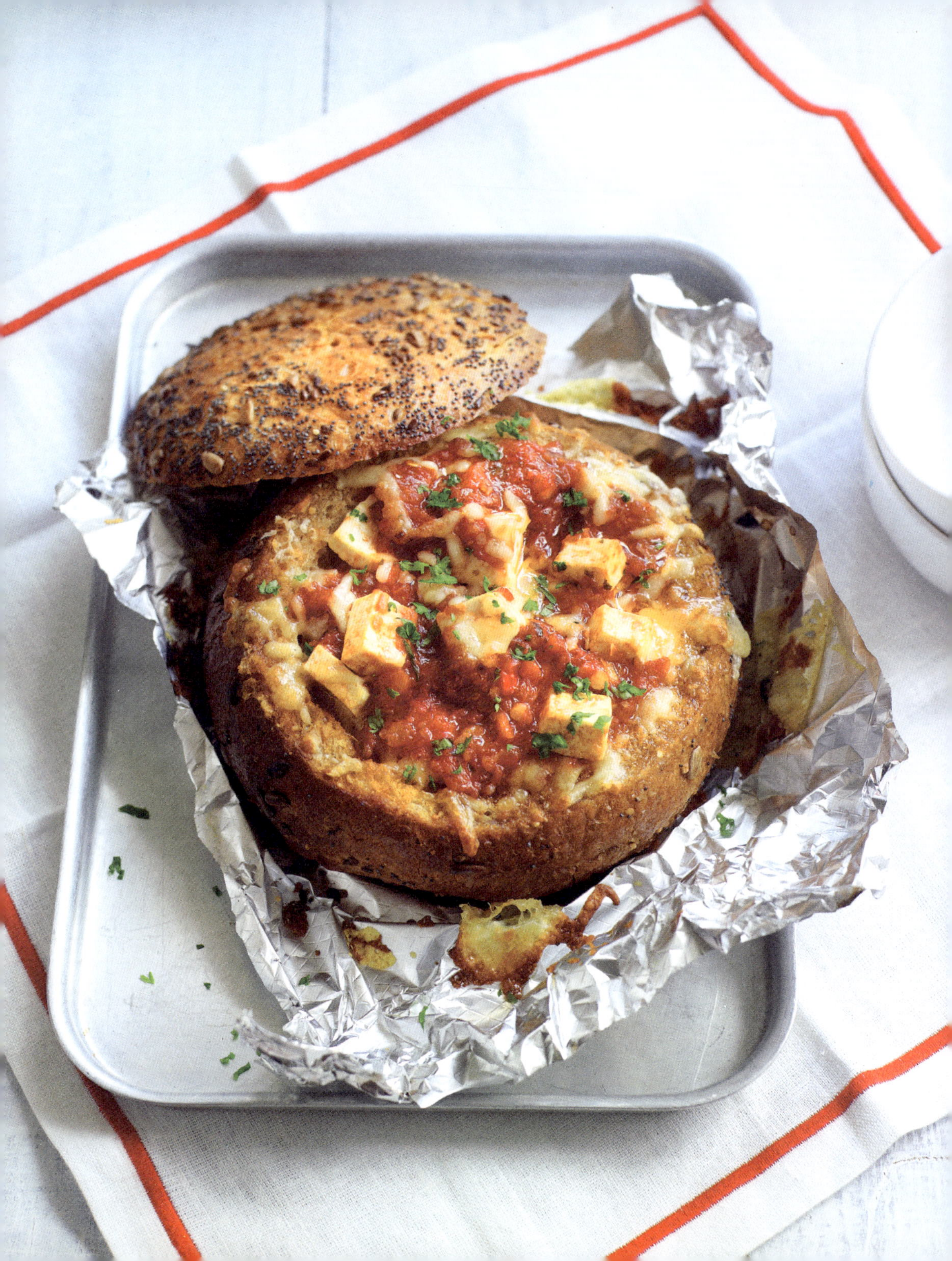

BREAD LOAF BBQ WITH TOFU SAUCE

Bread Loaf BBQ is a family favourite, and here you can create a fantastic vegan version that everyone is sure to tuck into!

1 onion, coarsely chopped

1 red (bell) pepper, coarsely chopped

1 celery stick, chopped

2 tablespoons extra virgin olive oil or vegetable oil

2 garlic cloves, crushed

400 ml/1⅔ cups passata/strained tomatoes

2 teaspoons vegetarian Worcester sauce

1 teaspoon dried oregano

1 teaspoon ground cumin

1 tablespoon ketchup

1 tablespoon cider vinegar

1 generous tablespoon dark brown sugar

2 tablespoons barbecue sauce

400 g/14 oz. firm tofu, crumbled

400-g/14-oz. bread loaf

grated vegetarian Cheddar cheese, to serve (optional)

salt and freshly ground black pepper, to season

MAKES 4–6 SERVINGS

Put the onion, red (bell) pepper and celery in a food processor and blend until minced. Alternatively, chop very finely.

Combine in a large frying pan/skillet with the oil and cook until soft, stirring often. Add the garlic and cook for 1 minute. Stir in the passata/strained tomatoes, Worcester sauce, oregano, cumin, ketchup, vinegar, sugar and barbecue sauce, and let simmer for 10 minutes. Taste and adjust the seasoning.

Squeeze the tofu of its moisture by wrapping it in paper towels and weighing down with a heavy item, then leave for 10 minutes to compress and squeeze out any excess water. Chop the tofu into bite-sized cubes and stir it into pan, and simmer, covered, for about 15–20 minutes more.

Meanwhile, slice the top off the loaf and set aside. Hollow out the loaf by pulling out the soft bread, shred and stir into the tofu mixture.

Preheat the oven to 200°C/400°F/gas mark 6.

Set the bread loaf on a piece of kitchen foil large enough to wrap around the bread. Fill the hollow loaf with the tofu mixture and replace the bread lid. Enclose with the foil and bake in the preheated oven for 20 minutes.

Remove from the oven and serve, with grated cheese, if liked.

For Tofu Sloppy Joes, omit the loaf and replace with bread rolls or hamburger buns. Do not hollow the bread, simply serve the tofu mixture piled on the halved rolls.

RAINBOW CHARD WITH SMOKED TOFU & CASHEWS

This is a simple, quick and effortless dish that is good for your whole body. It is perfect when you are in a hurry and want something satisfying yet light. Rainbow chard is always a pleasure on the plate – visually pleasing and full of vitamins.

200 g/7 oz. smoked firm tofu
large bunch of rainbow chard, chopped
60 g/½ cup raw cashews
1 teaspoon paprika
1 teaspoon ground cumin
2 teaspoons nigella seeds
1 tablespoon olive oil
freshly squeezed juice of ½ lemon
freshly ground black pepper, to season

SERVES 2

To prepare the tofu, wrap it in paper towels, weigh down with a heavy item, then leave for 10 minutes to compress and squeeze out any excess water.

Steam the chard for 2–3 minutes.

Slice the tofu and dry-roast with the cashews, paprika, cumin, and half the nigella seeds in a wok or skillet/frying pan over a low-medium heat for 4–5 minutes, turning regularly.

Add the steamed chard to a separate pan, toss in the olive oil, then stir-fry for 1 minute.

Serve on warmed plates and drizzle over the lemon juice. Garnish with the remaining nigella seeds and season with black pepper.

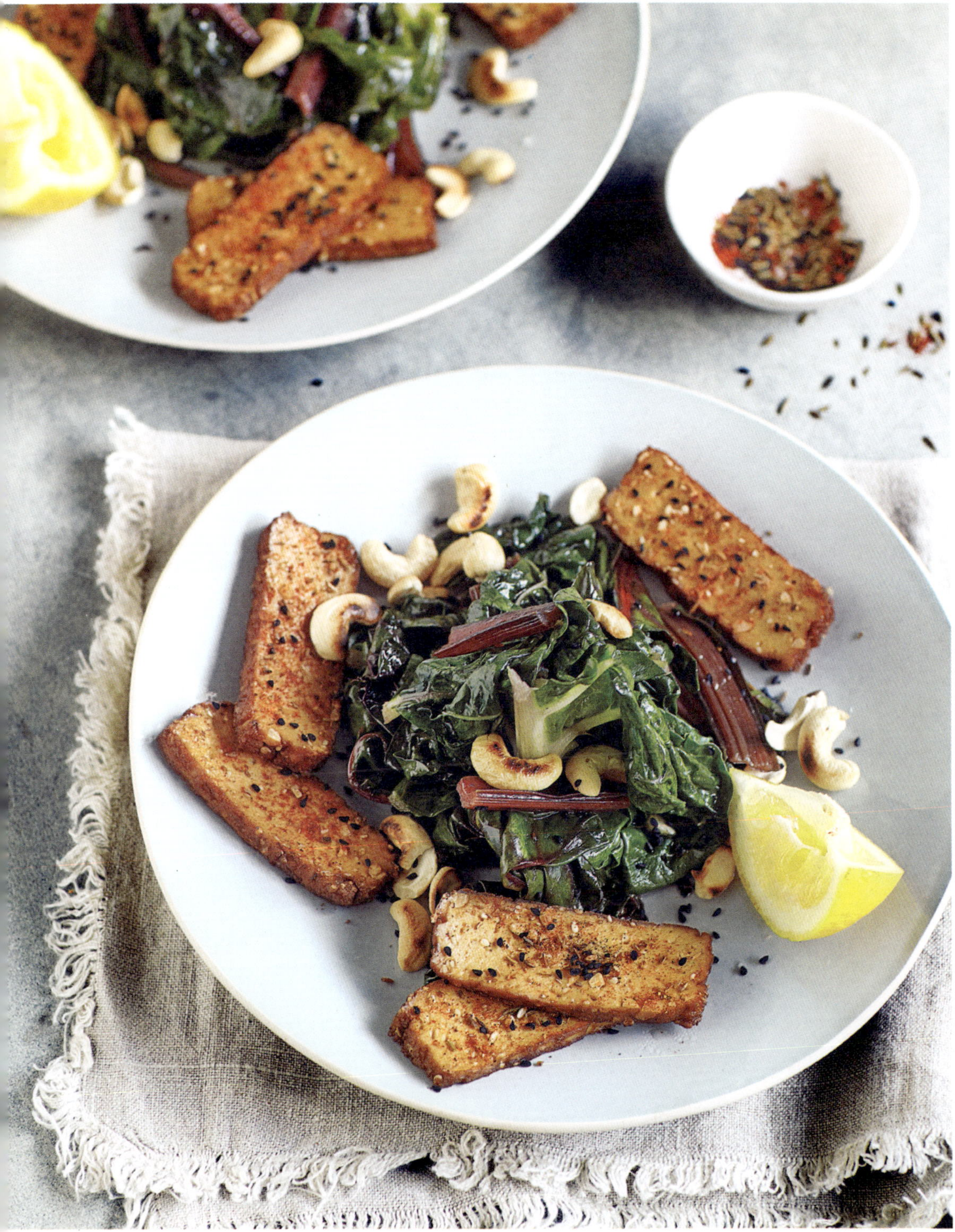

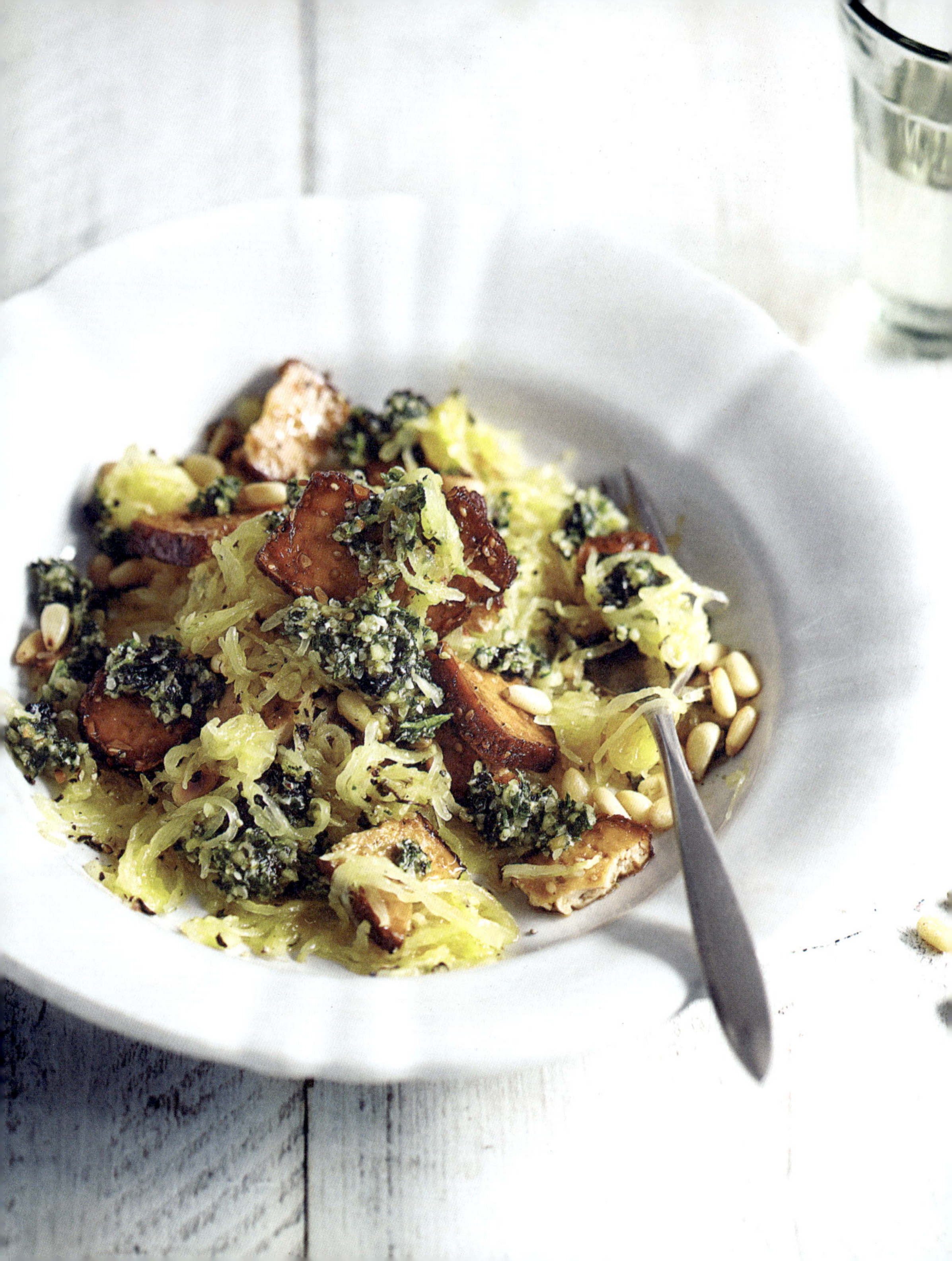

SPAGHETTI SQUASH WITH TOFU, NORI & KALE PESTO

An excellent lighter alternative to pasta, spaghetti squash is full of fibre and low in carbohydrates. The pesto is packed with delicious ingredients, including vitamin- and mineral-rich nori. This works well with the tofu to create a satisfying protein-based meal that supports your wellbeing… and tastes good!

1 large spaghetti squash
100 ml/½ cup olive oil, plus 2 extra tablespoons
½ teaspoon sea salt
1 teaspoon dried Italian herbs (such as a mixture of thyme, oregano, marjoram and rosemary)
400 g/14 oz. smoked or herb-marinated tofu
35 g/¼ cup pine nuts, plus extra toasted to garnish
35 g/1¼ oz. kale
10 g/⅓ oz. dried green nori (sheets or sprinkles)
35 g/1¼ oz. fresh basil
freshly squeezed juice of ½ lemon
2 garlic cloves
2 tablespoons shelled hemp seeds
freshly ground black pepper, to season

SERVES 4

Preheat the oven to 220°C/425°F/gas mark 7.

Prepare the squash by slicing in half lengthwise. Scoop out the seeds and the central flesh. Place both halves on a baking sheet, hollow side up, and drizzle over 2 tablespoons of olive oil, plus salt and pepper, to taste. Scatter the dried herbs over the squash (if you prefer to use fresh herbs, chop finely before adding). Roast in the preheated oven for 35 minutes.

Meanwhile, prepare the tofu by draining it, then wrapping in paper towels. Place between two chopping boards, weigh it down with a heavy item and leave for 10 minutes until pressed firm.

Dry-roast the pine nuts in a pan over a medium heat, tossing until brown on all sides. Place in a food processor with the kale, nori (tear into smaller pieces if using the sheets), basil, lemon juice, garlic cloves, hemp seeds, and the remaining olive oil and process until the pesto reaches a coarse consistency.

Slice the tofu 5 mm/¼ inch thick, place on a non-stick baking sheet, and roast in the oven for 8–10 minutes.

Use a fork to scrape the flesh of the squash into spaghetti strands, toss with the pesto and tofu, and serve on warmed plates. Season to taste with black pepper and garnish with extra toasted pine nuts.

MAIN PLATES

SPICY MAPLE-BAKED TOFU WITH BUCKWHEAT NOODLES

The slight sweetness of the maple syrup combines well with the earthiness of the spice, then topped with a breath of the ocean with nori seaweed. Serve the tofu warm or chilled – either way it's heaven in a bowl.

450 g/1 lb. firm tofu
70 ml/⅓ cup maple syrup
1 tablespoon olive oil
2 teaspoons smoked pimentón
1 teaspoon freshly cracked black pepper
pinch of sea salt
270 g/9½ oz. buckwheat soba noodles
tamari or soy sauce, to drizzle
1 sheet of nori seaweed, crumbled or finely sliced

SERVES 4

Preheat the oven to 200°C/400°F/gas mark 6.

Slice the tofu into pieces 1 cm/½ inch thick and arrange in a single layer in a ceramic baking dish.

In a medium bowl whisk together the maple syrup, olive oil, smoked pimentón, pepper, and sea salt. Pour over the tofu to coat, then bake in the preheated oven for 30 minutes.

Bring a large pan of water to a boil over a high heat and add the noodles. Cook for 4 minutes, then drain, rinse under cold water, and set aside.

To serve, divide the noodles between four bowls and drizzle with a touch of tamari or soy sauce. Top with a couple of pieces of tofu and sprinkle with a little of the seaweed.

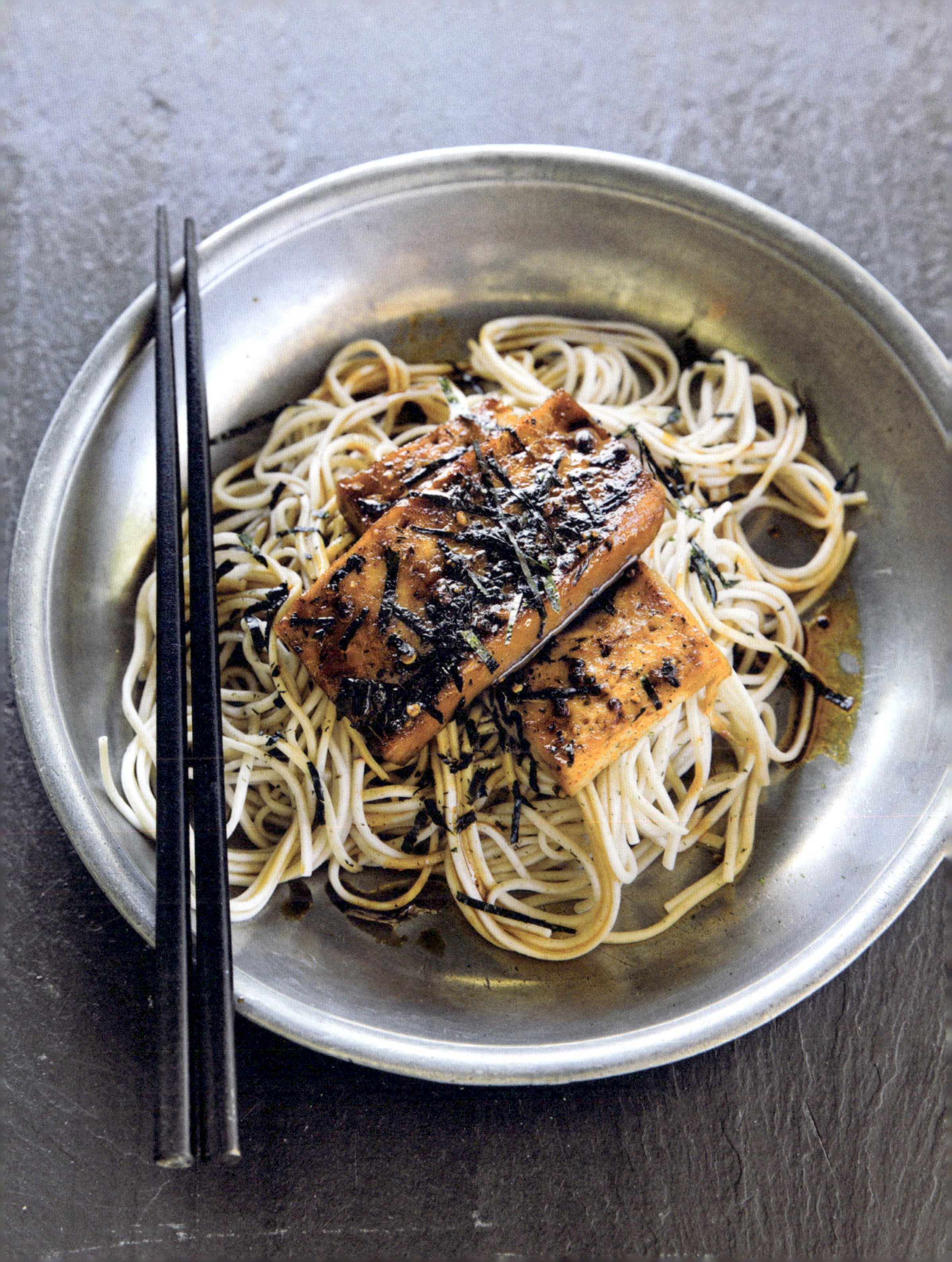

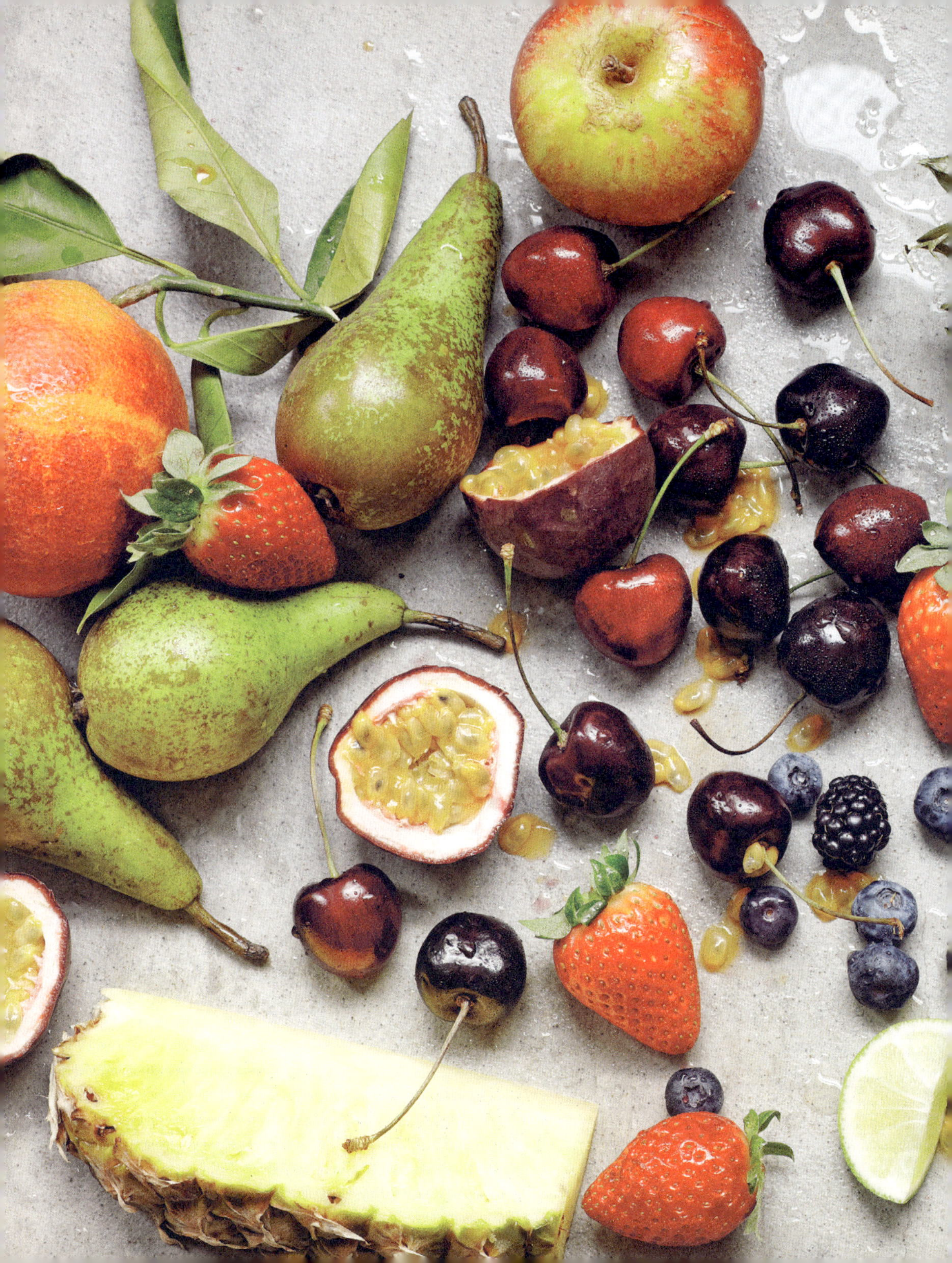

Sweet
THINGS & DRINKS

APRICOT & TOFU CHEESECAKE

Cheesecakes come in many guises. You can find unbaked or baked, chocolate or even fruit flavoured. This vegan version is baked, apricot flavoured, has a pie crust... and looks beautiful!

FOR THE SWEET PIE DOUGH
400 g/3 cups plain/all-purpose flour
150 g/1 cup fine cornmeal
3 teaspoons baking powder
½ teaspoon salt
240 g/2 cups margarine, chilled
130 g/½ cup agave syrup
grated zest of 1 lemon

FOR THE TOFU CREAM
500 g/1 lb. 2 oz. medium-soft tofu
100 g/scant ½ cup vanilla soy custard
1½ tablespoons margarine
85 g/⅓ cup agave syrup
freshly squeezed juice of
   1½ lemons
grated zest of 2 lemons
1 tablespoon plain/all-purpose
   flour
4–5 ripe firm apricots, pitted/
   stoned and sliced

FOR THE APRICOT JELLY
1 teaspoon agar powder or
   2 teaspoons agar flakes
110 ml/½ cup apple concentrate
135 g/½ cup apricot jam/jelly

40 x 28-cm/16 x 11-in. (for a thin crust) or 23 x 30 cm/9 x 12-in. (for a thick crust) baking pan

28-cm/11-in. springform cake pan or loose-based tart pan

SERVES 6–8

First, make the sweet pie dough. Put the flour, cornmeal, salt and baking powder in a food processor and pulse. Add the margarine and pulse 6–8 times until the mixture resembles coarse breadcrumbs. Add the syrup and lemon zest and pulse again a couple of times.

Add ice-cold water one tablespoon at a time (up to 110 ml/½ cup) pulsing until the mixture just begins to clump together. Place the dough on a lightly floured work surface. Knead it just enough to form a ball but do not over-knead it. Shape it into a disc, wrap it in clingfilm/plastic wrap and refrigerate it for at least 1 hour.

Preheat the oven to 180°C/350°F/gas mark 4.

For the tofu cream, blanch the tofu in boiling water for 2 minutes. Put it in a food processor with the custard, margarine, syrup, lemon juice and zest, and flour. Blend until smooth.

Take the dough out of the fridge 10 minutes before rolling out. Place it between 2 sheets of parchment paper and roll the dough out to a circle 31 cm/13 inches in diameter. Loosely roll the dough around the rolling pin and unroll it over the tart pan. Neatly line the pan with the dough and trim off any excess from the edges. Prick the base all over with a fork and bake in the preheated oven for 8–10 minutes. Remove the pan from the oven and pour the tofu cream into the tart crust, spreading it level. Put back in the oven and bake for 20 minutes, or until the tofu cream starts turning very lightly golden. Allow to cool completely in the pan. Arrange the apricot slices over the cooled tofu cream, if using.

For the apricot jelly, put the agar, apple concentrate, jam/jelly and 285 ml/1¼ cups water in a saucepan. Bring to the boil, whisking/beating occasionally. Lower the heat and cook for 2 minutes if you are using agar powder, or 8 minutes if you are using flakes.

Gently ladle the hot jelly over the cooled cheesecake but if you think it will leak over the edges, only ladle some of it in, then wait for 3–4 minutes for it to firm slightly before adding the rest. Allow to cool completely. This is best done in the fridge. Cut into slices with a sharp knife dipped in hot water, and serve.

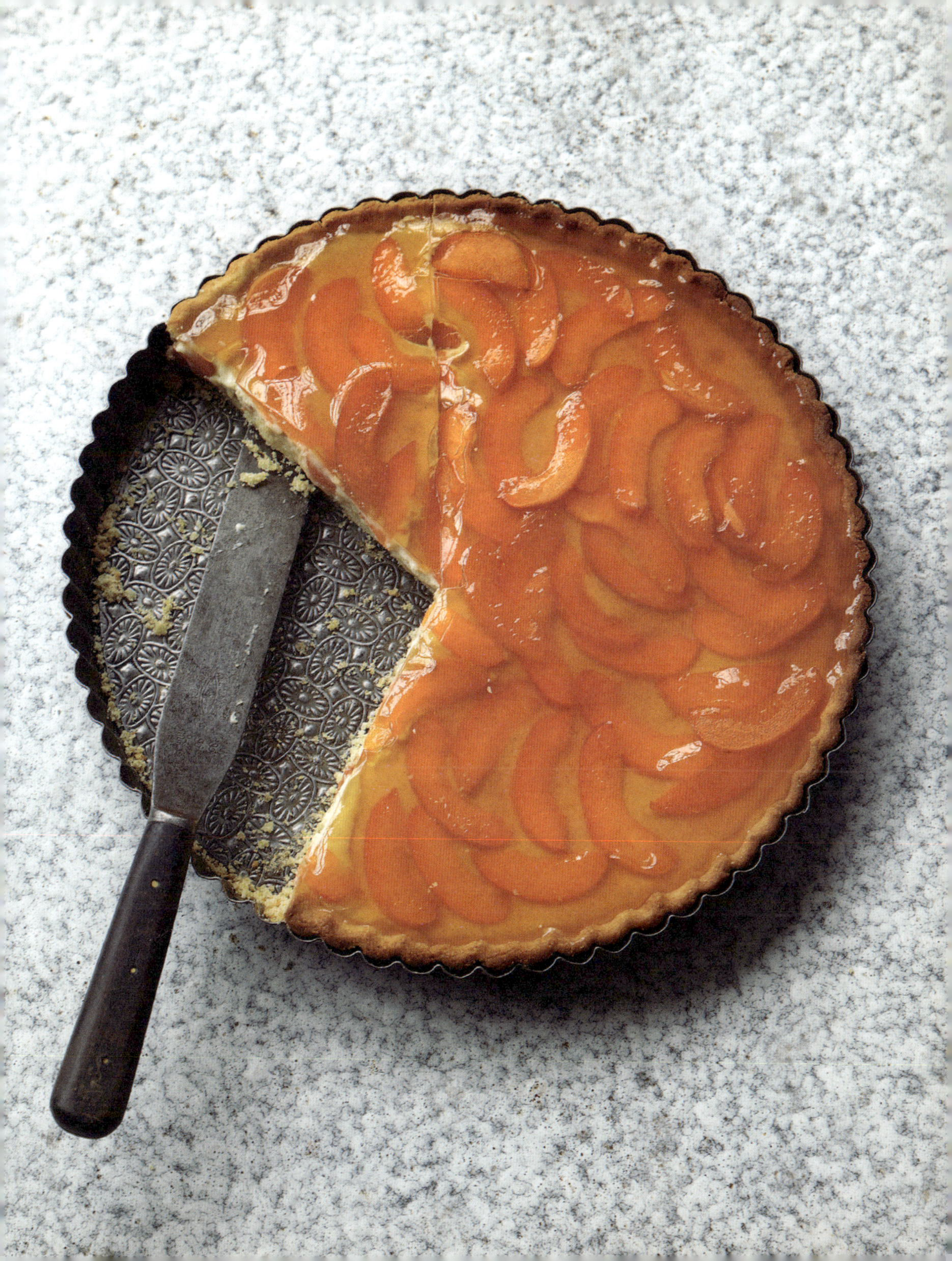

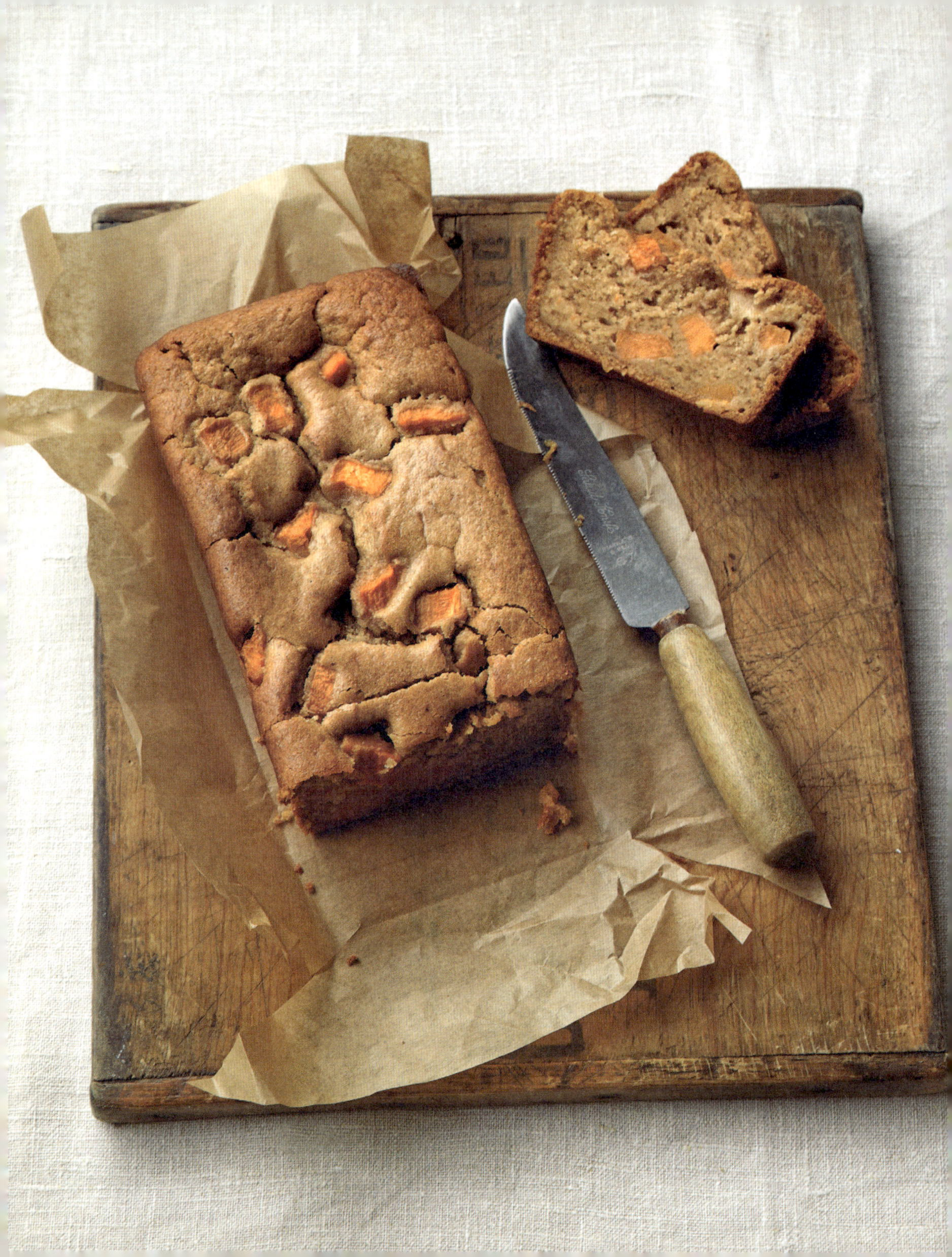

SWEET POTATO & TOFU POUND CAKE

Made with cubed sweet potatoes and silky soft tofu, this pound cake is interesting both texturally and visually. You can also use pumpkin or rhubarb in the same way, when sweet potatoes aren't available.

125 g/1 full cup peeled and cubed sweet potato
130 g/1 cup plain/all-purpose flour
65 g/½ cup plain wholemeal/whole-wheat flour
1 teaspoon bicarbonate of/baking soda
1 teaspoon baking powder
¼ teaspoon salt
100 g/½ cup raw/unrefined brown sugar
110 ml/½ cup sparkling mineral water
3 tablespoons apple concentrate (see method for an alternative)
65 g/⅓ cup sunflower oil
100 g/⅔ cup soft tofu
100 ml/½ cup oat or soy/soya cream

1-kg/2-lb. loaf pan, lined with baking parchment

SERVES 8–10

Preheat the oven to 180°C/350°F/gas mark 4.

Steam the cubes of sweet potato for 10 minutes or until they are soft, but they should not fall apart when you prick them. Sift together the flours, bicarbonate of/baking soda, baking powder and salt in a bowl and mix well.

Mix together the sparkling water and apple concentrate. You can use apple juice instead, but the sparkling water works well with bicarbonate of/baking soda and baking powder and makes this cake moist and spongy.

In a separate bowl, mix together the apple juice, oil, tofu and cream until smooth.

Combine the dry and liquid ingredients and mix until smooth.

Fold in the steamed cubes of potato, reserving a couple of pieces for decoration.

Pour the mixture into the prepared loaf pan and spread level with a spatula. Sprinkle the reserved potatoes over the top and press them in lightly.

Bake the cake in the preheated oven for 25 minutes or until a skewer inserted in the middle comes out clean. Allow to cool in the pan for 10 minutes, then remove it, peel off the paper and allow to cool completely on a wire rack. The best way to keep the cake moist is wrapped in a clean kitchen towel. Slice to serve.

SWEET THINGS & DRINKS

APPLE, POPPY-SEED & WALNUT PIE

This is a vegan version of the dessert 'gibanica', from the border between Croatia and Slovenia.

500 g/1 lb. 2 oz./12 sheets of filo/phyllo pastry
100 g/½ cup sunflower oil

FOR THE POPPY-SEED LAYER
400 ml/1¾ cups non-dairy milk
200 g/2⅓ cups ground poppy seeds
5 tablespoons brown rice syrup
40 g/3 tablespoons raisins
¼ teaspoon vanilla powder
1 tablespoon rum
grated zest of 1 lemon

FOR THE TOFU LAYER
400 g/14 oz. medium-soft tofu
2 tablespoons cornflour/cornstarch
110 ml/½ cup non-dairy milk
55 ml/⅓ cup freshly squeezed lemon juice
3 tablespoons brown rice syrup

FOR THE WALNUT LAYER
200 g/1¼ cups walnuts
30 g/⅓ cup fine breadcrumbs
5 tablespoons brown rice syrup
230 ml/1 cup non-dairy milk

FOR THE APPLE LAYER
500 g/1 lb. 2 oz. tart apples
40 g/3 tablespoons raisins
¼ teaspoon ground cinnamon
2 tablespoons brown rice syrup
freshly squeezed juice of ½ lemon

20 x 30-cm/8 x 12-in. baking pan, well oiled

MAKES 12 SQUARES

For the poppy-seed layer, bring the milk to a boil and pour it over the remaining ingredients. Mix well and cover until ready to use.

For the tofu layer, crumble the tofu with your fingers. Dilute the arrowroot in a little milk, then whisk/beat together the ingredients.

For the walnut layer, finely grind the walnuts in a spice mill. Mix with the breadcrumbs and syrup. Boil the milk and pour it over the walnut mixture. Cover until ready to use.

For the apple layer, peel and grate the apples with a grater, or core them and use a food processor to grate them. Combine with the remaining ingredients.

Preheat the oven to 180°C/350°F/gas mark 4.

If the sheets of filo/phyllo are bigger than your baking pan, cut them to size. Don't worry if a sheet tears as you can easily patch up any damage – only the top 3 sheets need to stay undamaged.

Place a sheet of filo/phyllo in the baking pan. Cover the remaining sheets with clingfilm/plastic wrap to prevent them from drying out. Brush oil lightly over the sheet. Cover with another sheet and oil it. Cover with a third sheet (this one doesn't need oiling).

Spread the poppy-seed layer evenly over the top with a spatula. Cover with one sheet, oil lightly and cover with a second sheet. Spread the tofu layer on top. Cover with one sheet, oil lightly and cover with a second sheet. Spread the walnut layer on top (but if the mixture has soaked up all the milk, just sprinkle it). Cover with one sheet, oil lightly and cover with a second sheet. Spread the apple layer on top. Brush a little oil over the remaining 3 undamaged sheets and lay them on top of the pie. Brush a little more oil on the top sheet.

Tuck in any pastry or filling sticking out of the pan by pushing a spatula between the pie and the sides of the pan. Use a sharp knife to score 12 squares into the pastry. Bake in the preheated oven for 45–50 minutes, or until the top turns golden brown and the pie isn't wobbly or soft to the touch.

Remove from the oven and allow to cool completely in the pan before serving. It tastes much better when left to soak up the juices.

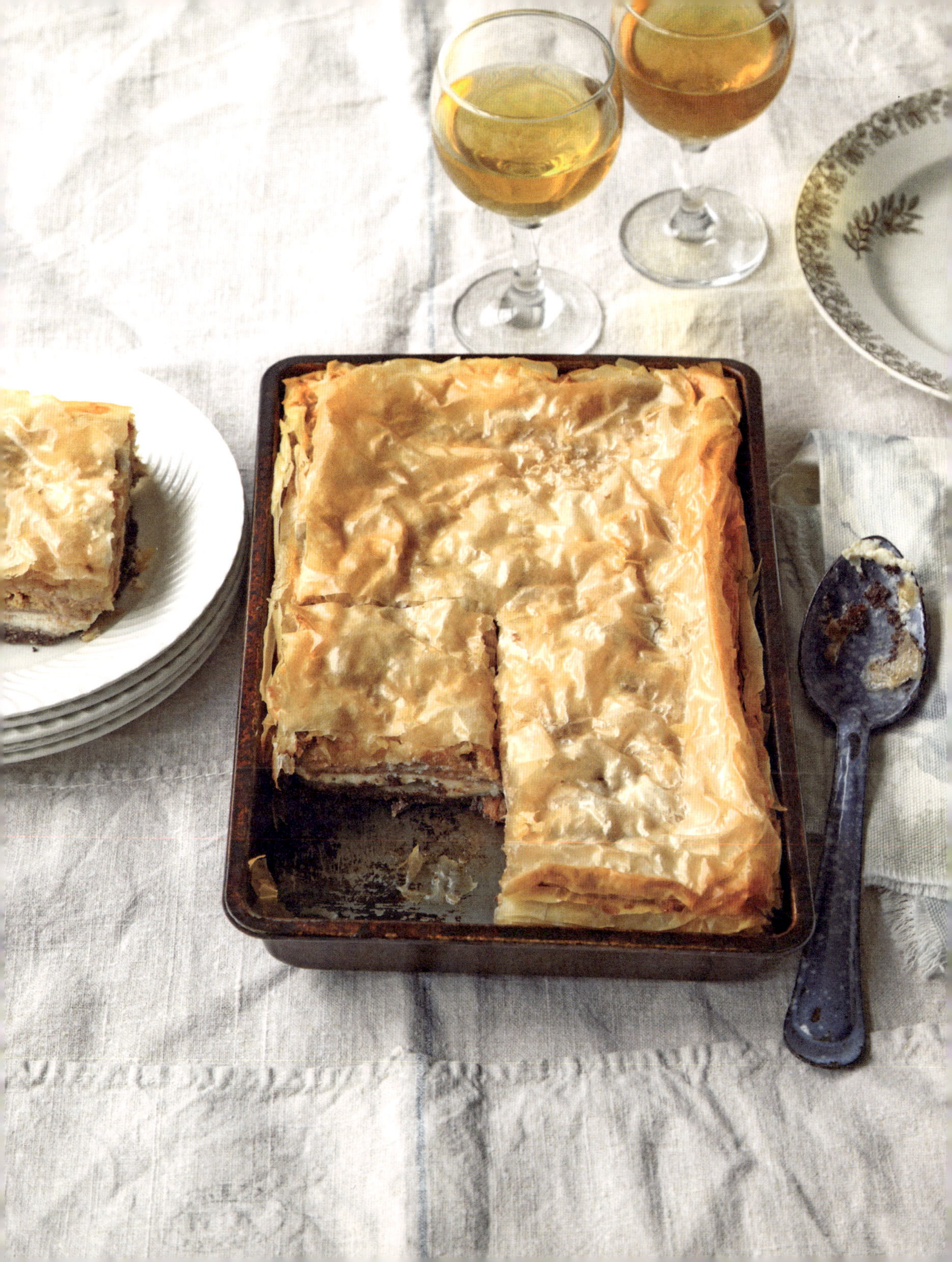

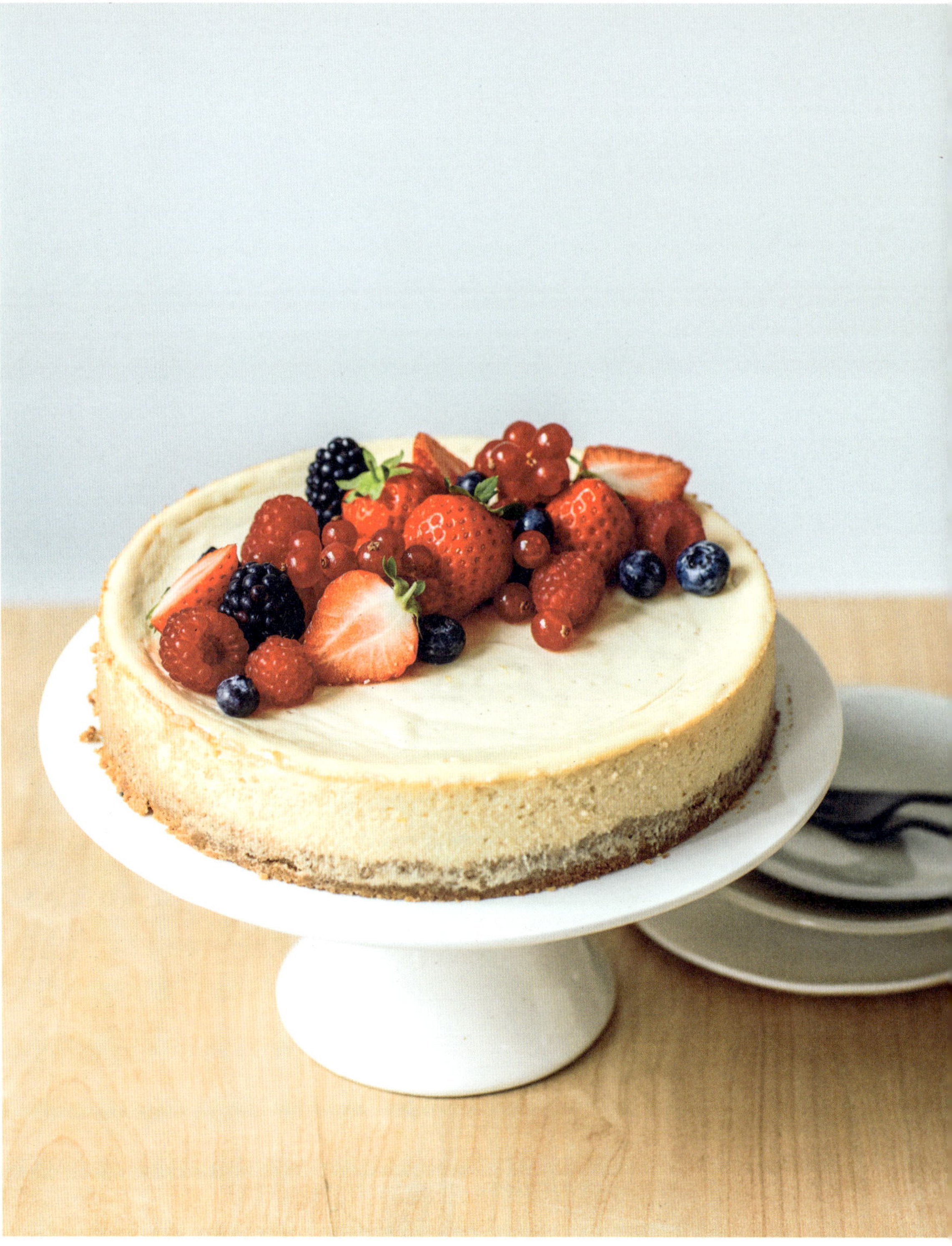

BAKED TOFU CHEESECAKE

Combining tofu and cream cheese to make this baked cheesecake recipe keeps it light and moist – each mouthful almost melts in the mouth. The touch of cinnamon and addition of lemon zest makes it the perfect dessert to comfort you when the colder days arrive. Perfect for eating while curled up in a cosy armchair with a hot cup of tea!

FOR THE BASE
160 g/5¾ oz. digestive biscuits/graham crackers
60 g/½ stick butter, melted
1 teaspoon ground cinnamon

FOR THE CHEESECAKE
350 g/12 oz. firm tofu
500 g/2¼ cups soft cheese
175 g/¼ cup plus 2 tablespoons caster/granulated sugar
2 UK large/US extra-large eggs
finely grated zest of 1 lemon
seeds scraped from 1 vanilla pod/bean
200 g/7 oz. mixed fresh berries

20-cm/8-inch round loose-based cake pan

SERVES 6–8

For the cheesecake, wrap the tofu in plenty of paper towels and compress under a heavy kitchen utensil for 30 minutes to remove excess water.

Preheat the oven to 180°C/350°F/gas mark 4.

For the cheesecake base, crush the biscuits/crackers to fine crumbs in a food processor or by putting them into a resealable bag and bashing them with a rolling pin. Transfer the crumbs to a mixing bowl and stir in the melted butter and cinnamon until well combined. Spread the biscuit/cracker mixture evenly over the bottom of the cake pan and press down to flatten.

Combine the tofu and soft cheese in the rinsed-out food processor, and blend to combine. Transfer to a bowl and add the sugar, eggs, lemon zest and vanilla seeds. Mix well until all the ingredients are evenly combined. Pour the mixture over the top of the biscuit/cracker base. Bake in the preheated oven for 10 minutes, then reduce the oven temperature to 160°C/325°F/gas mark 3 and bake for a further 45–50 minutes.

Turn the oven off and allow the cheesecake to cool completely for 2–3 hours in the oven. This should help stop cracks from forming.

Remove from the oven and leave at room temperature for a few hours before transferring to the refrigerator and chilling overnight.

The next day, remove the cheesecake from its pan, transfer to a serving plate and scatter fresh berries on top to serve.

YUZU & TOFU NO-BAKE CHEESECAKES

These no-bake cheesecakes are super creamy and almost velvety thanks to the combination of both soft cheese and soft tofu. Refreshing and fragrant yuzu is a small Japanese citrus fruit used in so many dishes, both savoury and sweet. You can now find yuzu juice in big supermarkets in the Asian section, but if you can't find yuzu jam/jelly, marmalade works just as well. Make this dessert in separate individual glasses or jars for a beautiful presentation!

FOR THE BASE
90 g/3¼ oz. digestive biscuits/graham crackers
30 g/2 tablespoons butter, melted

FOR THE CHEESECAKE
2 teaspoons agar agar powder
40 ml/2¾ tablespoons yuzu juice
175 g/6 oz. soft tofu
150 g/⅔ cup cream cheese
100 ml/scant ½ cup double/heavy cream
50 g/¼ cup caster/granulated sugar
30 g/1 oz. yuzu jam/jelly (or orange marmalade), plus extra to serve
seeds scraped from ½ vanilla pod/bean

5 serving glasses or glass jars (approx. 180 ml/¾ cup)

MAKES 5 INDIVIDUAL CHEESECAKES

For the cheesecake bases, crush the biscuits/crackers to fine crumbs in a food processor or by putting them into a resealable bag and bashing them with a rolling pin. Transfer the crumbs to a mixing bowl and stir in the melted butter until well combined. Divide the biscuit/cracker mixture evenly between the five glasses or jars and press down firmly to flatten.

To make the cheesecake, add the agar-agar powder to the yuzu juice and stir together over a low heat until just melted and combined. Allow to cool.

Combine the tofu, soft cheese, double/heavy cream, sugar, yuzu jam/jelly (or orange marmalade), vanilla seeds and cooled yuzu mixture in a food processor and blend until smooth. Alternatively, you can simply mash the tofu until smooth, then whisk/beat in the rest of the ingredients by hand in a bowl until smooth and thick.

Spoon the cheesecake mixture into the glasses or jars over the biscuit/cracker bases. Remove any air from the containers by tapping them lightly on the work surface. Refrigerate for 2 hours to set.

Top with extra yuzu jam/jelly or marmalade to serve. The cheesecakes will keep for 5 days refrigerated.

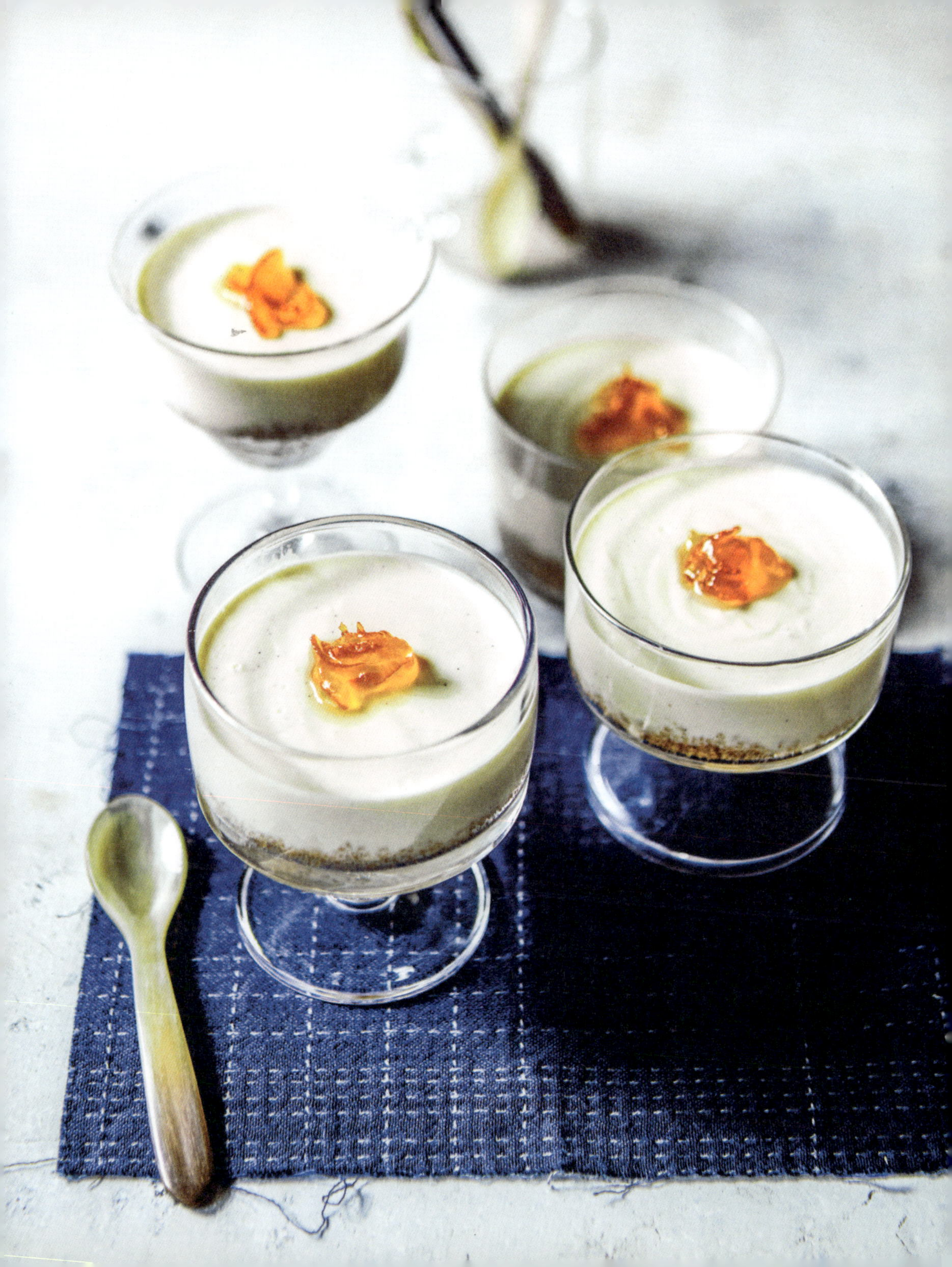

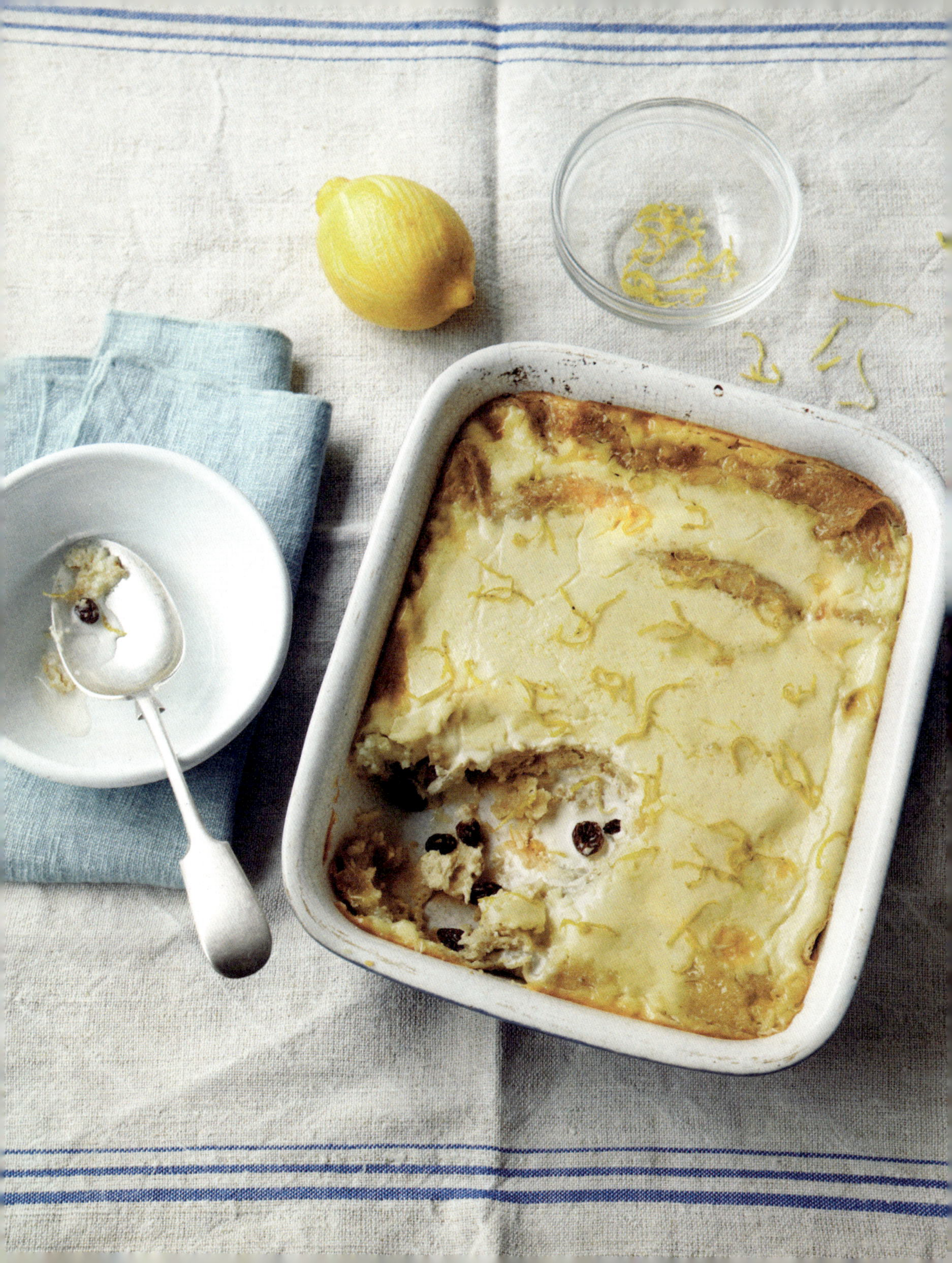

BAKED, LEMON-SCENTED PANCAKES

Sweet, baked pancakes are a childhood favourite for many. Here you can transform the recipe into a vegan version by replacing the eggs and fresh cheese with tofu and non-dairy cream, and it tastes the same, if not better! It's a light dessert but you can even eat it instead of lunch – a feast for anyone who prefers sweet food to savoury!

FOR THE PANCAKES
340 ml/1½ cups plain soy/soya milk
¼ teaspoon salt
¼ teaspoon baking powder
grated zest of 1 lemon
215 g/1⅔ cups plain/all-purpose flour
coconut or sunflower oil, for frying

FOR THE FILLING
340 g/2 cups firm tofu
685 ml/3 cups thick soy/soya or oat cream
pinch of salt
freshly squeezed juice of 2 lemons
grated zest of 3 lemons, plus extra to garnish
brown rice or agave syrup, to taste
30–60 g/¼–½ cup raisins (optional)

23 x 30-cm/9 x 12-in. baking pan or ovenproof dish, oiled

SERVES 4–6

For the pancakes, mix the milk and 225 ml/1 cup water in a bowl. Stir in the salt, baking powder and lemon zest. Gradually add the flour, whisking/beating vigorously until smooth. The batter should be thicker than conventional, egg-based pancake batter. Allow to rest for at least 15 minutes.

Heat a heavy-based frying pan and brush a little oil over it.

When hot, pour a small ladle of batter into the pan and tilt the pan to spread the batter evenly over the surface. Once the edges start turning golden brown, flip the pancake over and cook until golden on the reverse. Transfer to a plate, re-oil the pan and keep making pancakes in this way until all the batter is used up. Try to make the pancakes quite thin and that should give you 10 pancakes in total.

Preheat the oven to 180°C (350°F) gas mark 4.

For the filling, put the tofu, 225 ml/1 cup of the cream, the salt, lemon juice and zest and syrup, to taste, in a food processor and blend until smooth. Mix in the raisins: they give a lovely tangy flavour to this dish, but you can omit them and add a little more syrup, if you wish.

Divide the filling between the pancakes, spreading it over each one. Roll the pancakes up tightly and arrange in the prepared baking pan. Pour the remaining cream evenly over the pancakes and garnish with some lemon zest.

Bake in the preheated oven for 15–20 minutes, until golden. Remove from the oven and serve warm or cold.

SWEET THINGS & DRINKS

DARK CHOCOLATE TOFU TART

In conventional recipes, a dark chocolate ganache is made from cream, but you can use soft tofu instead, and the result is a smooth and rich ganache.

100 g/3½ oz. mixed fresh or warmed berries, to serve (optional)

FOR THE CRUST
200 g/1½ cups plain/all-purpose flour
75 g/½ cup fine cornflour/cornstarch
1 teaspoon baking powder
¼ teaspoon sea salt
120 g/½ cup margarine, chilled
60 g/scant ¼ cup brown rice syrup or agave syrup
zest of 1 organic lemon

FOR THE CHOCOLATE GANACHE
600 g/20 oz. medium-soft tofu
400 g/14 oz. vegan dark/bittersweet chocolate (60–70% cocoa), in pieces
1 tablespoon lemon juice concentrate
zest of 2 organic lemons
brown rice syrup, or other sweetener, to taste (optional)
dash of non-dairy milk or cream, if necessary

28-cm/11-in. springform cake pan or 28-cm/11-in. tart pan

SERVES 12

To make the crust, combine the flours, baking powder and salt in a food processor and use the pulse setting to mix. Add the margarine and pulse 6–8 times until the mixture resembles coarse meal, with pea-sized pieces of margarine. Add the syrup and lemon zest and pulse again a couple of times. If you pinch some of the crumbly dough and it holds together, it's ready. If the dough doesn't hold together, add a little water and pulse again. Be careful not to add too much water, as it will make the crust tough. Place the dough in a mound on a clean work surface. Work the dough just enough to form a ball – do not over-knead. Form a disc, wrap in clingfilm/plastic wrap and refrigerate for at least 3 hours, but it's best to leave it overnight. Let the dough sit at room temperature for 5–10 minutes before rolling.

Preheat the oven to 180°C/350°F/gas mark 4.

For the ganache, blanch the tofu in a pan for 10 minutes and then drain it. In a double boiler, melt the chocolate. Blend the tofu with the chocolate, lemon juice and zest in a blender until very smooth. If it's too bitter, blend in the syrup. If it's too thick, add non-dairy milk or cream while blending.

Take the dough out of the fridge and roll it between two sheets of parchment paper into a circle 31 cm/12¼ inches in diameter. With the help of a rolling pin, line the cake/tart pan with the dough. Trim the edges using a pastry wheel, if using a springform pan, or remove the excess dough by pressing it outwards with your fingers, if using a tart pan. Patch up any holes with leftover dough. Prick the base all over with a fork and bake in the preheated oven for 8–10 minutes.

Remove from the oven and spoon the ganache over the crust and even it with a spatula. Return to the oven and bake until the edges turn lightly golden, around 15 minutes. Take it out of the oven and allow to cool before serving with mixed berries, if liked.

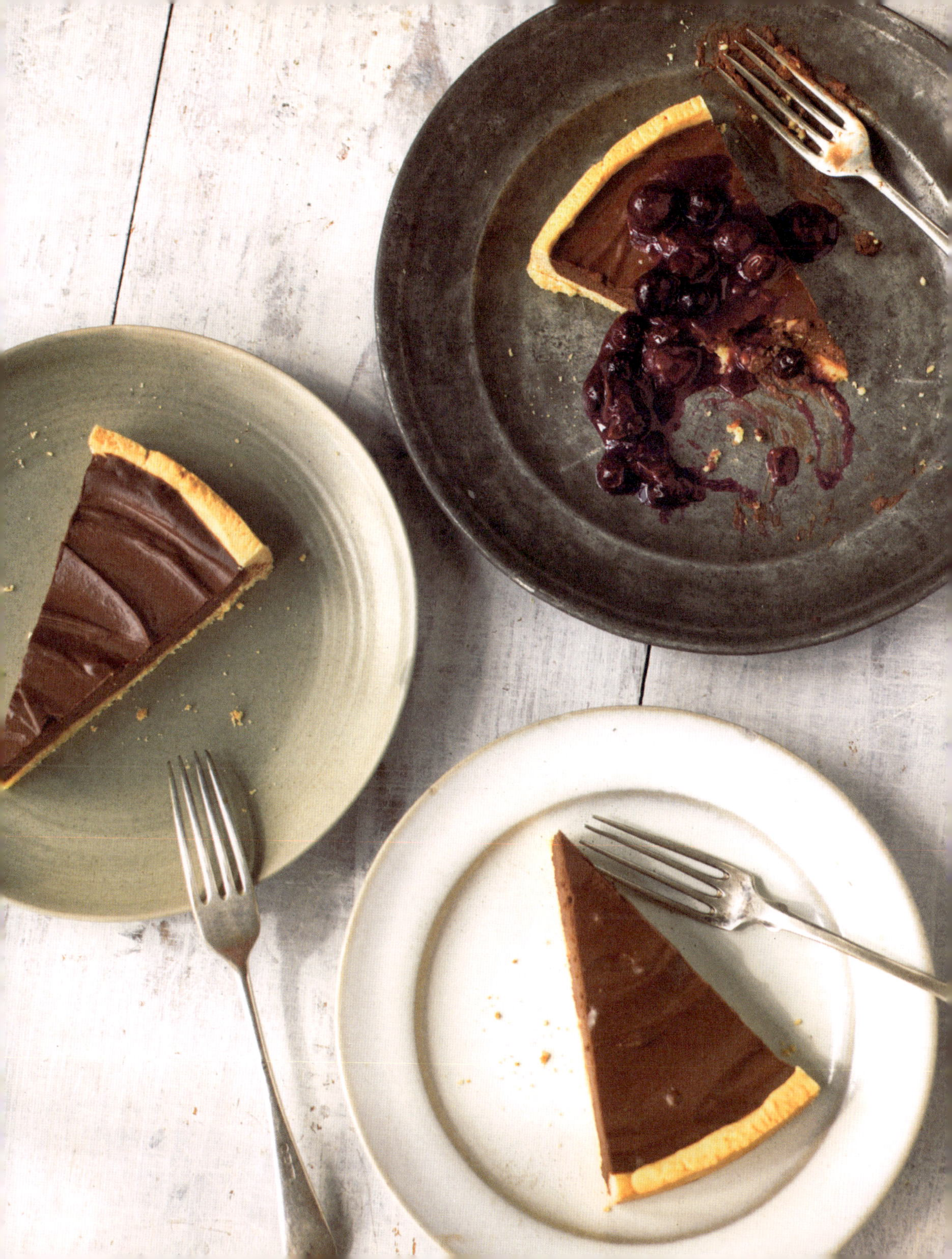

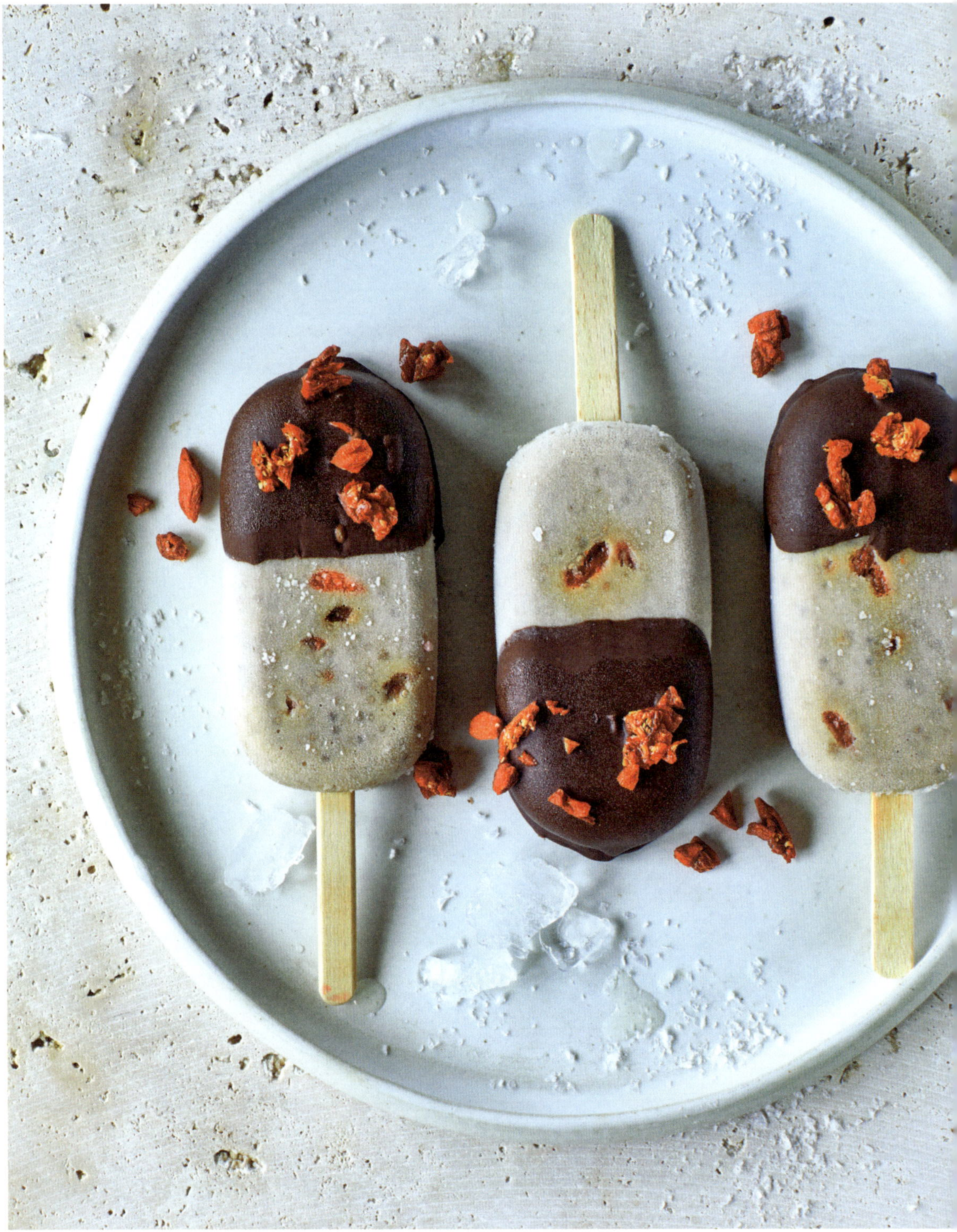

TOFU POPSICLES

For all of the gym junkies and fitness fanatics out there, these popsicles are guilt-free and will give you an energy boost before – or nourishment after – a workout.

1 banana
250 g/9 oz. soft tofu
250 ml/1 cup plus 1 tablespoon soya milk
60 ml/¼ cup coconut flower syrup (or date syrup)
2 tablespoons chia seeds
25 g/1 oz. goji berries, chopped, plus extra to serve
100 g/3½ oz. vegan dark/bittersweet chocolate, melted

6 popsicle moulds and sticks

small baking sheet, lined with baking parchment

MAKES 6 POPSICLES

Peel and chop the banana and place in a blender with the tofu, soya milk and coconut flower syrup (or date syrup). Blend until smooth. Transfer to a bowl, then stir in the chia seeds. Refrigerate for 2 hours or until the seeds have swelled and softened.

Fold in the goji berries, then divide the mixture between the six popsicle moulds.

Add the sticks in an upright position at this stage, or freeze first for a while until the mixture is firm enough to hold the sticks straight. Freeze for 4–6 hours until frozen. 20 minutes before you are ready to serve, put the prepared baking sheet into the freezer.

After 10 minutes, dip the moulds into hot water for a second or two, then gently pull out the popsicles. Dip the ends of the popsicles into the melted chocolate. Place on the prepared chilled baking sheet and immediately scatter over the extra goji berries. Return to the freezer for a further 10 minutes to set.

SWEET THINGS & DRINKS

STRAWBERRY TOFU 'YOGURT'

People definitely don't consume sweet strawberries as often as they should, so this is one of the ways to use them in (or out of) season. You can substitute with other milder-tasting berries like blueberries or raspberries, or even mix different berries in one batch.

160 ml/²/₃ cup agave syrup
2 teaspoons agar agar powder or 10 g/3½ tablespoons agar flakes
500 g/3 cups organic strawberries, fresh or frozen
330 g/1½ cups soft tofu
2 tablespoons white tahini
handful of fresh strawberries, sliced or some strawberry jam/preserves, to decorate (optional)
edible flowers, to decorate (optional)

4 ramekins or serving glasses

SERVES 4

In a small saucepan, whisk/beat together the agave syrup and agar agar powder/flakes with 100 ml/⅓ cup plus 1 tablespoon water. Bring to the boil, whisking/beating occasionally. If using agar flakes, simmer for about 5 minutes until the flakes have dissolved.

While the liquid is still hot, blend together the strawberries, silken tofu, tahini and cooked agar liquid.

Pour into four serving cups or ramekins and chill well in the fridge before serving. If you wish, decorate with fresh strawberries or a tiny dollop of strawberry jam/preserves, and edible flowers.

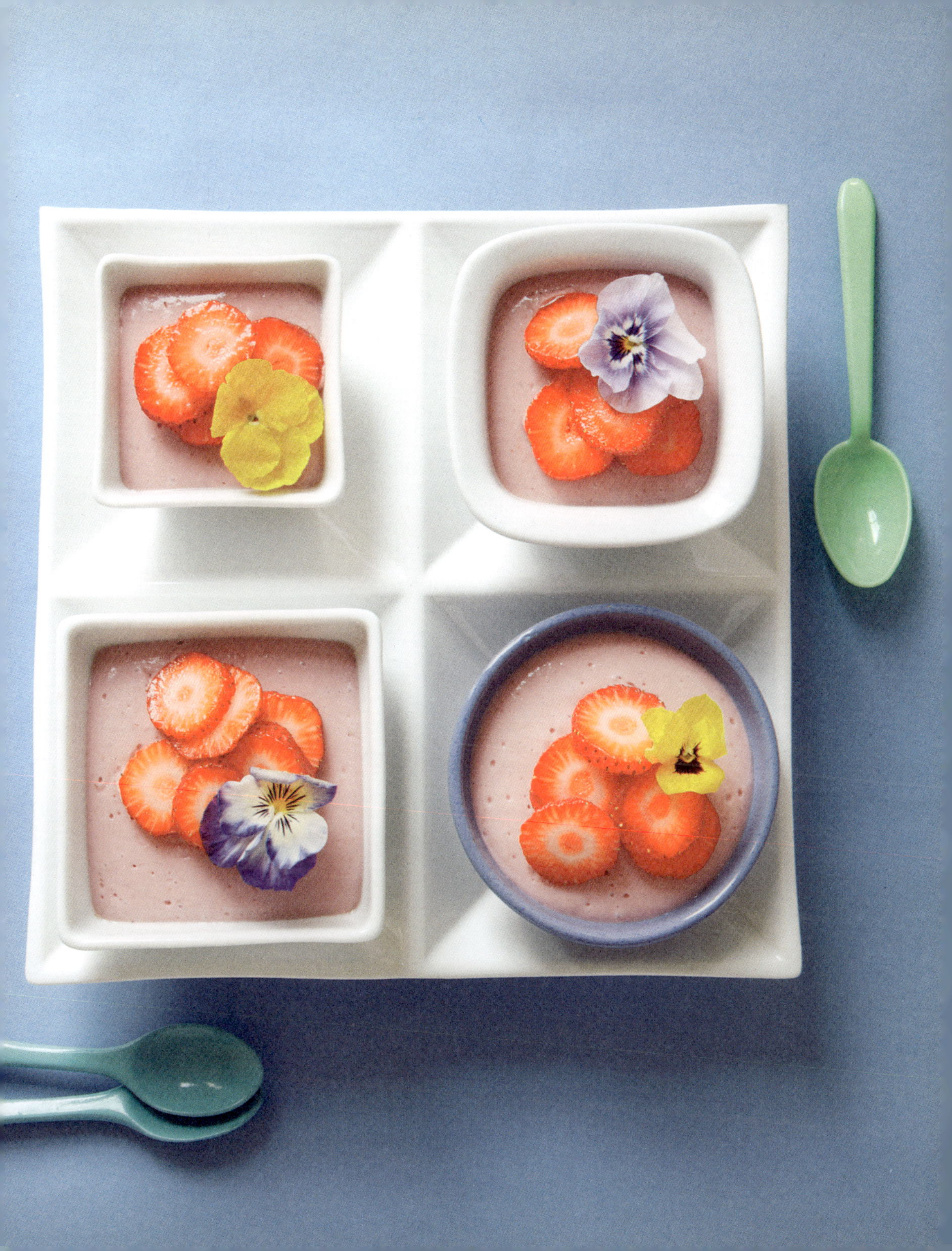

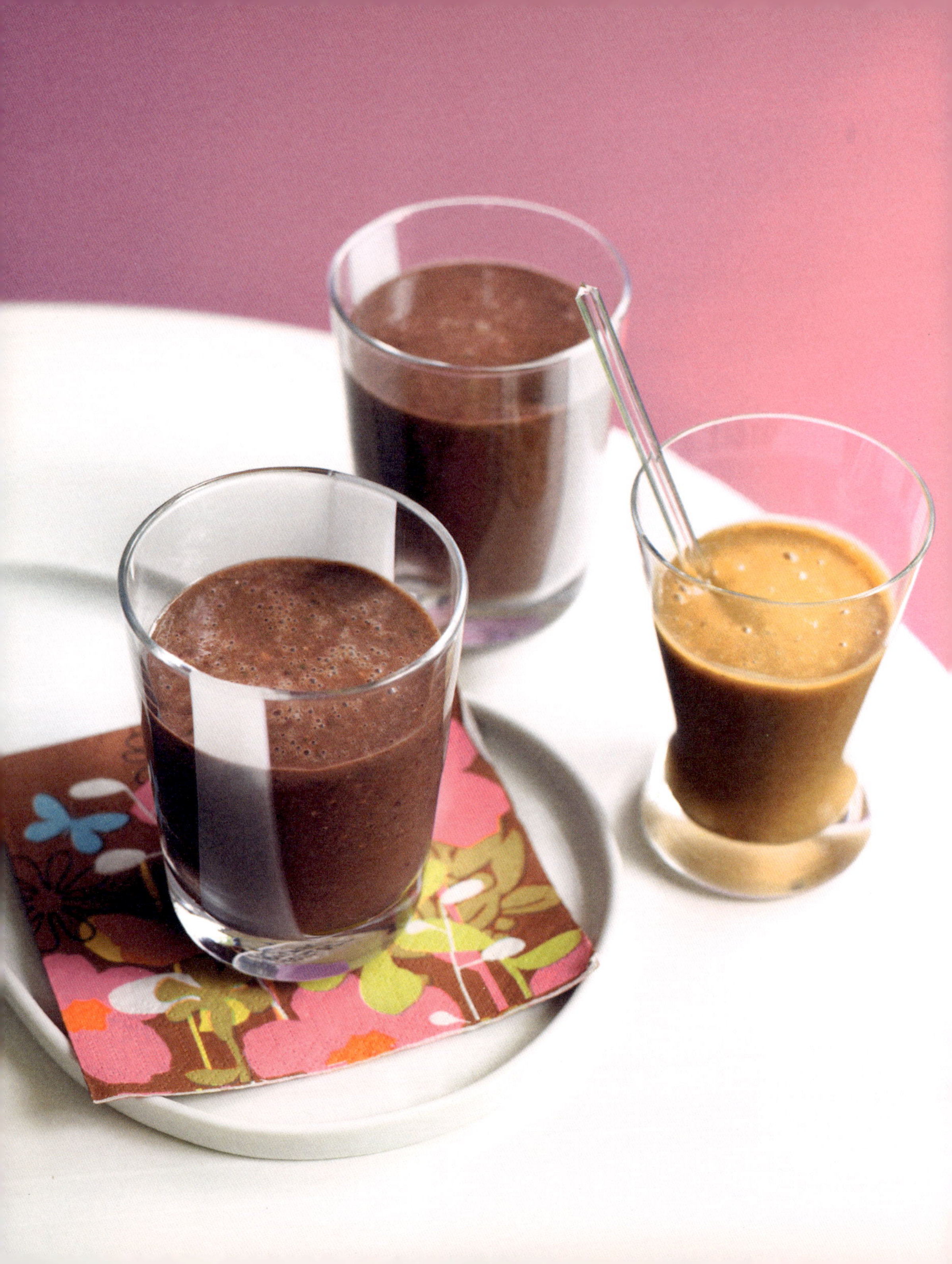

AVOCADO BABY

This green smoothie definitely tastes a lot better than it looks, but don't be put off as you don't want to miss its fruity, chocolatey taste and thick, creamy consistency. What's more, it will help give your energy levels a real boost!

½ medium avocado, peeled and sliced
1 small mango, peeled, pitted/stoned and chopped
freshly squeezed juice of 3 oranges
2 teaspoons silken tofu
½ teaspoon ground nutmeg
1–2 teaspoons barleygrass powder
2 teaspoons raw cacao powder

SERVES 2

Put the avocado, mango, orange juice, tofu, nutmeg, barleygrass and raw cacao powder in a blender and blend until smooth.

ROSY CHEEKS SMOOTHIE

You can use frozen raspberries here, rather than buy fresh fruit when it's not in season. In fact, it's a good idea to keep a ready supply of frozen fruit for smoothies or juices. There's no need to defrost the fruit, just throw a handful into the blender straight from the freezer.

2 large handfuls of fresh or frozen raspberries
2 pears, peeled, cored and chopped
150 ml/⅔ cup fresh apple juice or 2 small apples, juiced
125 ml/⅔ cup natural/plain dairy or soya/soy yogurt
1 tablespoon silken tofu
2 teaspoons camu camu powder
¼ teaspoon freshly grated nutmeg, plus extra to serve

SERVES 2

Put the raspberries, pears, apple juice, yogurt, tofu, camu camu powder and grated nutmeg in a blender and blend until smooth. Serve sprinkled with a little extra nutmeg.

SWEET THINGS & DRINKS

BLACKBERRY CRUMBLE

This smoothie is reminiscent the traditional British crumble dessert, but served in a glass! Great for breakfast when time is against you and you're looking for nutritious sustenance for the day ahead, or why not serve it as a healthy dessert?

2 handfuls fresh or frozen blackberries
2 ripe pears, peeled, cored and roughly chopped
100 ml/1/3 cup natural/plain dairy or soya/soy yogurt
100 ml/1/3 cup milk of your choice
1 tablespoon silken tofu
1 teaspoon lacuma powder
1 teaspoon baobab powder
1/2 teaspoon ground cinnamon
granola, for sprinkling

SERVES 2

Put the blackberries, pears, yogurt, milk, tofu, lacuma, baobab and cinnamon in a blender and blend until smooth. Pour into glasses and spoon the granola on top. Eat with a spoon!

BREAKFAST IN A GLASS

Providing a beneficial combination of complex carbohydrates, protein, fibre and essential fatty acids, this makes a sustaining, filling breakfast smoothie. Pears with their sweet, almost creamy texture are surprisingly low in calories, which makes them great value when you are craving something sweet to start your day.

2 small bananas, peeled and frozen
2 ripe pears, peeled, cored and chopped
200 ml/generous 3/4 cup coconut milk
1 tablespoon silken tofu
seeds from 4 cardamom pods, ground
1 teaspoon ground flaxseeds

SERVES 2

Put the bananas, pears, coconut drinking milk, tofu, cardamom seeds and half the flaxseeds in a blender and blend until smooth. Serve sprinkled with the remaining flaxseeds.

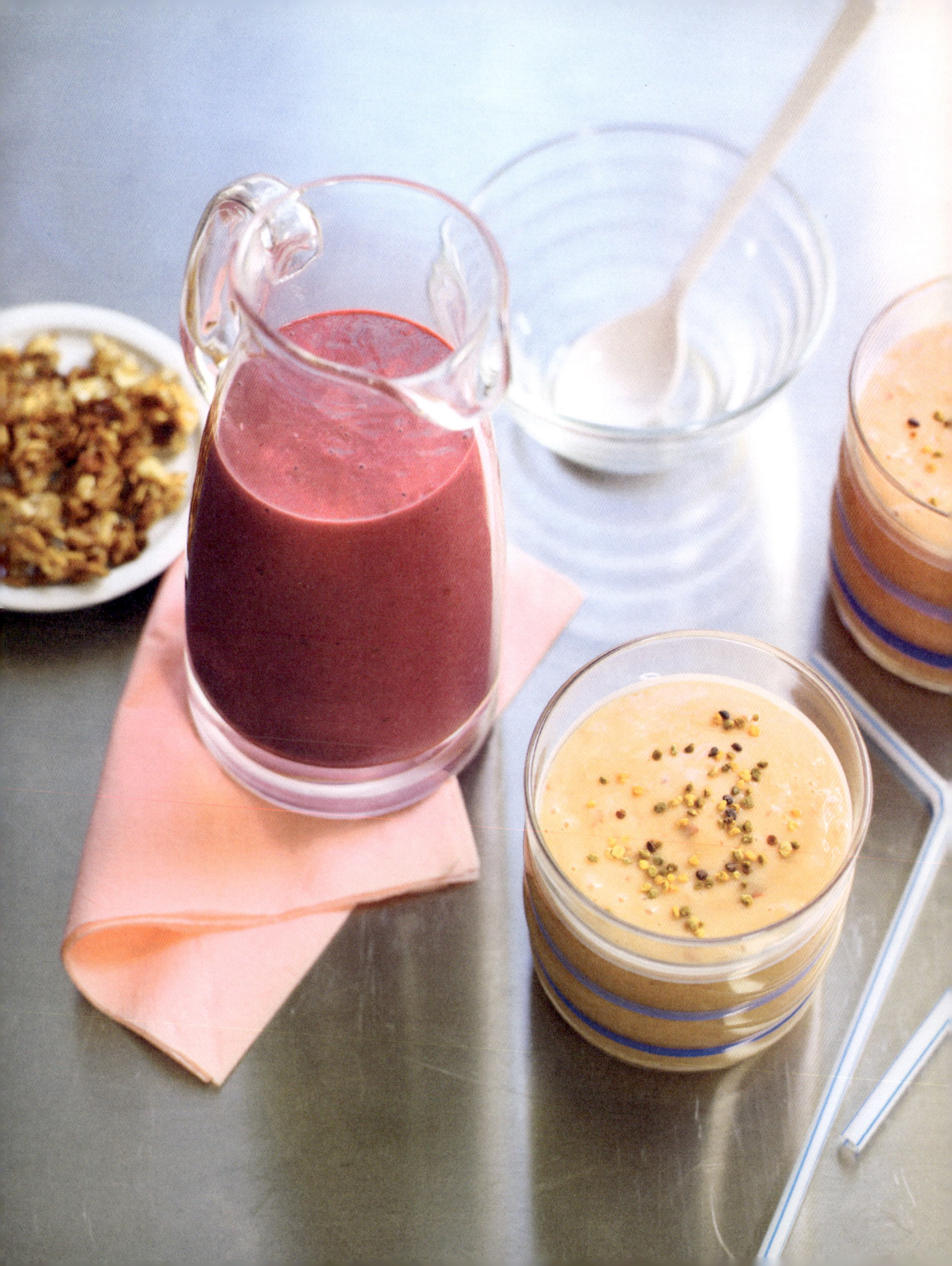

INDEX

apple, poppy-seed & walnut pie 124
apricot & tofu cheesecake 120
asparagus, tofu & paprika tart 89
aubergines (eggplants): Mapo tofu & aubergine rice bowls 101
avocados: avocado baby 139
  whipped tofu, avocado & herb dip 15

bananas: breakfast in a glass 140
beans: aduki bean salad 50
  bean pâté 39
  easy bean & tofu dip 15
  tofu yota 82
berries: baked tofu cheesecake 127
  dark chocolate tofu tart 132
blackberry crumble 140
bread: bread loaf BBQ with tofu sauce 111
  fried tofu sandwiches 20
broccoli: sesame-full tofu quiche 86

cabbage: egg noodle, black cloud ear fungus & tofu salad 62
  rice noodle & smoked tofu salad 57
  Vietnamese spring rolls 24
cake, sweet potato & tofu pound 123
canapés, smoked tofu 39
carrots: brown rice & smoked tofu faux-lafel 19
  salad Olivier with tofu mayonnaise 52
  tofu 'cheese' nachos 23
cashews, rainbow chard with smoked tofu & 112
cheesecakes: apricot & tofu cheesecake 120
  baked tofu cheesecake 127
  yuzu & tofu no-bake cheesecakes 128
chillies: tofu, ginger & chilli balls 35
chocolate: avocado baby 139
  dark chocolate tofu tart 132
  tofu popsicles 135
corn & tofu pie 94
courgettes (zucchini): creamy courgette & tofu soup 68

polenta tarte flambée 93
cream cheese: tofu cream cheese 108
  yuzu & tofu no-bake cheesecakes 128
curry: delicious tofu curry 105
  warm curried lentil & mango salad 54

dashi: deep-fried tofu in tsuyu broth 81
  Japanese Buddhist vegetable & tofu soup 77
  magical miso soup 69
  spicy miso soba noodle soup with ginger teriyaki tofu 74
dips: dipping sauces 28, 30, 32
  easy bean & tofu dip 15
  Japanese tofu dip with vegetables 14
  whipped tofu, avocado & herb dip 15
dressings: rich miso-tofu dressing 11
  sesame-miso dressing 45
  spiced dressing 54
drinks: avocado baby 139
  blackberry crumble 140
  breakfast in a glass 140
  rosy cheeks smoothie 139
dumplings: pumpkin & leek dumplings 27
  tofu & vegetable gyoza 30
  tofu, sun-dried tomato & olive dumplings 28

falafels: brown rice & smoked tofu faux-lafel 19
  crunchy tofu faux-lafel 16
filo (phyllo) pastry: apple, poppy-seed & walnut pie 124
corn & tofu pie 94

ginger: spicy miso soba noodle soup with ginger teriyaki tofu 74
  tofu, ginger & chilli balls 35
  tofu, ginger & lime spoons 31
goulash, tofu & mushroom 80
gratin, mixed vegetable 99
greens: Thai soup with tahini & tofu 66
gyoza, tofu & vegetable 30

herbs: rice noodle salad with tofu & herbs 53

whipped tofu, avocado & herb dip 15
hotpot, Chinese-style tofu & mushroom 78
hummus, tofu & rice 36

kale: Asian tofu & raw kale salad 46
  spaghetti squash with tofu, nori & kale pesto 115
kebabs: tofu kebabs with noodles 102

leeks: pumpkin & leek dumplings 27
lemon-scented pancakes 131
lentils: warm curried lentil & mango salad with tofu & spiced dressing 54
limes: tofu, ginger & lime spoons 31

mangetout (snow peas): Asian-style hot & sour salad with marinated tofu 49
  udon noodle soup with crispy tofu 73
maple syrup: spicy maple-baked tofu with buckwheat noodles 116
mapo sauce 101
mayonnaise, tofu 11
  salad Olivier with 52
miso: magical miso soup 69
  rich miso-tofu dressing 11
  sesame-miso dressing 45
  spicy miso soba noodle soup with ginger teriyaki tofu 74
  wild garlic miso tofu stir-fry 100
mushrooms: Chinese-style tofu & mushroom hotpot 78
  egg noodle, black cloud ear fungus & tofu salad 62
  tofu & mushroom goulash 80
  tofu scramble 90
  Vietnamese spring rolls 24

nachos, tofu 'cheese' 23
noodles: egg noodle, black cloud ear fungus & tofu salad 62
  rice noodle & smoked tofu salad 57
  rice noodle salad with tofu & herbs 53
  spicy maple-baked tofu with buckwheat noodles 116

spicy miso soba noodle soup with ginger teriyaki tofu 74
Thai soup with tahini & tofu 66
tofu kebabs with noodles 102
udon noodle soup with crispy tofu 73
Vietnamese spring rolls 24
warm noodle & tofu salad 58
nori: spaghetti squash with tofu, nori & kale pesto 115

olives: crunchy tofu faux-lafel 16
tofu, sun-dried tomato & olive dumplings 28
vegan Greek salad with tofu feta 42

pancakes, baked lemon-scented 131
pâté, bean 39
pea shoots: sesame-coated tofu with aduki bean salad 50
peanuts: Thai soup with tahini & tofu 66
pears: blackberry crumble 140
breakfast in a glass 140
rosy cheeks smoothie 139
peppers: bread loaf BBQ with tofu sauce 111
stuffed babura peppers with tofu stuffing 97
sweet & sour tofu 106
Thai soup with tahini & tofu 66
tofu tacos with fresh tomato salsa 22
vegan Greek salad with tofu feta 42
pesto, spaghetti squash with tofu, nori & kale 115
pies: apple, poppy-seed & walnut pie 124
corn & tofu pie 94
pineapple: sweet & sour tofu 106
pizza: basic yeast dough 109
versatile tofu pizza 108
polenta: polenta tarte flambée 93
poppy-seeds: apple, poppy-seed & walnut pie 124
popsicles, tofu 135
potatoes: salad Olivier with tofu mayonnaise 52
tofu yota 82
warm noodle & tofu salad 58
pumpkin & leek dumplings 27

quiche, sesame-full tofu 86

radishes: deep-fried tofu in tsuyu broth 81
rainbow chard with smoked tofu & cashews 112
raspberries: rosy cheeks smoothie 139
rice: brown rice & smoked tofu faux-lafel 19
Mapo tofu & aubergine rice bowls 101
tofu & rice hummus 36
tofu cream cheese 108

salads 40–63
aduki bean salad 50
Asian-style hot & sour salad with marinated tofu 49
Asian tofu & raw kale salad 46
egg noodle, black cloud ear fungus & tofu salad 62
rice noodle & smoked tofu salad 57
rice noodle salad with tofu & herbs 53
salad Olivier with tofu mayonnaise 52
shredded vegetable & tofu salad with sesame-miso dressing 45
Thai-style salad with tofu & cashews 61
vegan Greek salad with tofu feta 42
warm curried lentil & mango salad with tofu & spiced dressing 54
warm noodle & tofu salad 58
salsa, fresh tomato 22
sandwiches, fried tofu 20
satay: spicy tofu satay with soy dipping sauce 32
sauerkraut: tofu yota 82
sesame seeds: sesame-coated tofu with aduki bean salad 50
sesame-full tofu quiche 86
sesame-miso dressing 45
soups: creamy courgette & tofu soup 68
healing soup with tofu 70
Japanese Buddhist vegetable & tofu soup 77
magical miso soup 69
spicy miso soba noodle soup with ginger teriyaki tofu 74
Thai soup with tahini & tofu 66
udon noodle soup with crispy tofu 73
spaghetti squash with tofu, nori & kale pesto 115
spring rolls, Vietnamese 24
squash: spaghetti squash with tofu, nori & kale pesto 115
stew: tofu yota 82
stir-fry, wild garlic miso tofu 100
strawberry tofu 'yogurt' 136
stuffing, tofu 98
sweet potato & tofu pound cake 123
sweetcorn: corn & tofu pie 94

tacos, tofu 22
tahini: bean pâté 39
Thai soup with tahini & tofu 66
tarts: asparagus, tofu & paprika tart 89
dark chocolate tofu tart 132
polenta tarte flambée 93
teriyaki: ginger teriyaki tofu 74
tomatoes: fresh tomato salsa 22
polenta tarte flambée 93
stuffed babura peppers with tofu stuffing 97
tofu, sun-dried tomato & olive dumplings 28
vegan Greek salad with tofu feta 42
versatile tofu pizza 108
tortilla chips: tofu 'cheese' nachos 23
tortillas: tofu tacos with fresh tomato salsa 22

vegetables: Japanese Buddhist vegetable & tofu soup 77
mixed vegetable gratin with tofu 99
shredded vegetable & tofu salad 45
Japanese tofu dip with vegetables 14
tofu & vegetable gyoza 30
see also individual types of vegetable
Vietnamese spring rolls 24

walnuts: apple, poppy-seed & walnut pie 124
wild garlic miso tofu stir-fry 100

'**y**ogurt', strawberry tofu 136
yuzu & tofu no-bake cheesecakes 128

CREDITS

RECIPES

Valerie Aikman-Smith
Spicy maple-baked tofu with buckwheat noodles

Caroline Artiss
Asian tofu & raw kale salad
Magical miso soup

Ghillie Basan
Spicy tofu satay with soy dipping sauce

Jordan Bourke
Rice noodle salad with herbs
Teriyaki tofu with shiitake mushrooms & soba noodles
Udon noodle soup with crispy tofu

Julia Charles
Whipped tofu, avocado & herb dip

Chloe Coker & Jane Montgomery
Asian-style hot & sour salad with marinated tofu
Warm curried lentil salad with tofu & spiced dressing

Amy Ruth Finegold
Shredded vegetable & tofu salad with sesame-miso dressing

Mat Follas
Thai-style salad with tofu & cashews

Ben Fordham & Felipe Fuentes Cruz
Tofu tacos with fresh tomato salsa

Nicola Graimes
Avocado baby
Blackberry crumble
Breakfast in a glass
Japanese rice balls
Rice noodle & smoked tofu salad
Rosie cheeks smoothie
Sesame-coated tofu with aduki bean salad
Tofu, ginger & chilli balls

Dunja Gulin
Apple poppyseed & walnut pie
Apricot & tofu cheesecake
Baked lemon-scented pancakes
Corn & tofu pie
Crunchy tofu faux-lafel
Dark chocolate tofu tart
Delicious tofu curry
Fried tofu sandwiches
Healing soup with tofu
Marinating & frying tofu
Smoked tofu canapés with bean pâté
Polenta tarte flambée
Rich miso-tofu dressing
Salad Olivier with tofu mayonnaise
Sesame-full quiche
Strawberry tofu 'yogurt'
Stuffed babura peppers
Sweet potato & tofu pound cake
Thai soup with tahini & tofu
Tofu 'cheese' nachos
Tofu & mushroom goulash
Tofu & rice hummus
Tofu mayonnaise
Tofu scramble
Tofu stuffing
Vegan Greek salad with tofu feta
Versatile vegan pizzas
Tofu yota

Carole Hilker
Vietnamese spring rolls

Atsuko Ikeda
Deep-fried tofu in tsuyo broth
Baked tofu cheesecake
Buddhist vegetable tofu soup
Japanese tofu dip with vegetables
Mapo tofu & aubergine rice bowls
Spicy miso soba noodle soup with ginger teriyaki tofu
Tofu & vegetable gyoza
Tofu steaks with sesame & soy dressing
Yuzo & tofu no-bake cheesecakes

Jenny Linford
Chinese-style tofu & mushroom hotpot
Wild garlic miso tofu stir-fry with rice

Loretta Liu
Pumpkin & leek dumplings
Tofu, sun-dried tomato & olive dumplings

Louise Pickford
Egg noodle, black cloud ear fungus & tofu salad
Tofu popsicles
Warm noodle & puffed tofu salad

Milli Taylor
Tofu, ginger & lime spoons

Laura Washburn Hutton
Easy bean & tofu dip
Bread loaf BBQ
Creamy courgette & tofu soup
Mixed vegetable gratin with tofu
Sweet & sour tofu with rice
Tofu kebabs with noodles

Sarah Wilkinson
Asparagus & paprika tart
Rainbow chard with smoked tofu & cashews
Spaghetti squash with tofu, nori & kale pesto

PICTURES

Ed Anderson 47
Tim Atkins 17, 18
Peter Cassidy 25
Tara Fisher 72
Louise Hagger 26, 29
Richard Jung 33
Mowie Kay 37
Erin Kunkel 117
Adrian Lawrence 88, 113, 114
Steve Painter 60
William Reavell 9, 10, 21, 48, 55, 91, 92, 98, 104, 133
Matt Russell 12–13 40–41, 51, 56
Toby Scott 2–3, 43, 64–65, 71, 83, 84–85
Yuki Sugiura 1, 7, 71, 75, 126, 129
Ian Wallace 59, 63, 134
Kate Whitaker 103, 107, 110, 138, 141
Claire Winfield 34, 38, 44, 67, 79, 87, 95, 118–119, 121, 123, 125, 130, 137